CW01044222

Sentimentalism, Ethics and the Culture of Feeling

Also by Michael Bell

CONTEXT OF ENGLISH LITERATURE, 1900–1930

D. H. LAWRENCE: Language and Being

F. R. LEAVIS

GABRIEL GARCÍA MÁRQUEZ: Solitude and Solidarity

LITERATURE, MODERNISM AND MYTH: Belief and Responsibility in the Twentieth Century

PRIMITIVISM

THE SENTIMENT OF REALITY: Truth of Feeling in the European Novel

Sentimentalism, Ethics and the Culture of Feeling

Michael Bell
Professor of English and Comparative Literary Studies
University of Warwick
Coventry

First published 2000 by
PALGRAVE
Houndmills, Basingstoke, Hampshire RG21 6XS and
175 Fifth Avenue, New York, N.Y. 10010
Companies and representatives throughout the world

PALGRAVE is the new global academic imprint of
St. Martin's Press LLC Scholarly and Reference Division and
Palgrave Publishers Ltd (formerly Macmillan Press Ltd).

ISBN 0–333–72110–1 hardback

This book is printed on paper suitable for recycling and
made from fully managed and sustained forest sources.

A catalogue record for this book is available
from the British Library.

Library of Congress Cataloging-in-Publication Data
Bell, Michael, 1941–
    Sentimentalism, ethics, and the culture of feeling / Michael Bell.
        p. cm.
    Includes bibliographical references and index.
    ISBN 0–333–72110–1
    1. Sentimentalism in literature. 2. Literature, Modern—History and
criticism. I. Title.

PN56.S475 B45 2000
809'.93353—dc21
                                                            00–033327

10   9   8   7   6   5   4   3   2   1
09 08 07 06 05 04 03 02 01 00

Printed and bound in Great Britain by
Antony Rowe Ltd, Chippenham, Wiltshire

I thank Anne Janowitz, Kay Kondo and Martin Warner for generously reading drafts of this study

Contents

List of Abbreviations   ix

Introduction: the Transformations of Sentiment   1

1 'Affective Individualism' and the Cult of Sentiment   11

2 Feeling and/as Fiction: Illusion, Absorption and
   Emotional Quixotry   57

3 Friedrich Schiller and the Aestheticizing of Sentiment   74

4 Wordsworth: the Man of Feeling, Recollected Emotion
   and the 'Sentiment of Being'   92

5 Victorian Sentimentality: the Dialectic of Sentiment and
   Truth *of* Feeling   118

6 Feeling as Illusion: Rousseau to Proust   150

7 Modernism and the Attack on Sentiment   160

8 Henry James and D. H. Lawrence: 'Felt Life' and
   Truth *to* Feeling   170

Conclusion: Literature, Criticism and the Culture of Feeling   205

Notes   208

Select Bibliography   219

Index   227

List of Abbreviations

AEM	Friedrich Schiller, *On the Aesthetic Education of Man in a Series of Letters*
CJ	Immanuel Kant, *Critique of Judgement*
CPR	Immanuel Kant, *Critique of Pure Reason*
GB	Henry James, *The Golden Bowl*
NSD	Friedrich Schiller, *Über Naiv und Sentimentalische Dichtung*
NSL	Friedrich Schiller, *On the Naive and Sentimental in Literature*, trans. Helen Watanabe-O'Kelly
PII	*Phoenix II: Uncollected, Unpublished and Other Prose Works of D. H. Lawrence*
SCAL	D. H. Lawrence, *Studies in Classic American Literature*
TMS	Adam Smith, *The Theory of Moral Sentiments*
VRM	Mary Wollstonecraft, *A Vindication of the Rights of Man*
VRW	Mary Wollstonecraft, *A Vindication of the Rights of Woman*

Ariel	... if you now beheld them, your affections
	Would become tender.
Prospero	Dost thou think so spirit?
Ariel	Mine would, sir, were I human.
Prospero	And mine shall.
	Hast thou, which art but air, a touch, a feeling,
	Of their afflictions, and shall not myself,
	One of their kind, that relish all as sharply
	Passion as they, be kindlier mov'd than thou art?

(William Shakespeare, *The Tempest*, v, i, 18–24)

Bitter and earnest writing must not hastily be condemned; for men cannot contend coldly, and without affection, about things which they hold dear and precious. A politic man may write from his brain, without touch or sense of his heart; as in a speculation that apperraineth not unto him; – but a feeling Christian will express, in his words, a character of zeal or love. Lord Bacon.

(Epigraph to William Wordsworth's *Convention of Cintra*)

The development of man's capacity for feeling is, therefore, the more urgent need of our age, not merely because it can be a means of making better insights effective for living, but precisely because it provides the impulse for bettering our insights.

(Friedrich Schiller, *On the Aesthetic Education of Man*)

... a man who is *emotionally* educated is as rare as phoenix.

(D. H. Lawrence on John Galsworthy)

Introduction: the Transformations of Sentiment

We have no language for the feelings.[1]

There is a pervasive confusion about the value of emotion in modern Anglophone culture, perhaps especially in Britain. Personal relations and moral behaviour implicitly rely on feeling while the prevailing discourse distrusts it. During the all-Ireland referendum in 1998, which sought a lasting settlement for that country's historical divisions, politicians seeking a 'yes' vote exhorted the people to put their feelings on one side and vote rationally. The motive is unimpeachable but why not ask them to put bitterness, hate and vengefulness aside and vote with generosity? And how does rationality as such enter the sphere of the ethical if there is no feeling to motivate it? In a sense it is inconsequential. Everyone understands what is meant: as David Hume observed, what we call 'reason' is frequently a particular calm state of feeling.[2] Yet the political context confirms that feeling is a troubling element, and habitual distrust of it helps to keep it so.

At the same time, even as 'feeling' is distrusted in favour of 'rationality', common usage reflects the opposite recognition: that most important thinking is imbued with feeling. The word 'feel', as a near synonym for 'think', suggests, half subliminally, the mixture of the affective and the conceptual in what we call 'thought'. Feeling seems an obscure antecedent to, and therefore perhaps a necessary part of, conceptualization; as if thought has an affective component, or feeling is a form of understanding. Yet at a more conscious and evaluative level comes the familiar, dismissive charge that someone is arguing 'emotionally'. It ought to be a more damaging criticism, where the matter is worth arguing about, *not* to argue emotionally. When someone is said to have argued powerfully the emotional factor, a force of personal conviction, is usually

1

being acknowledged. Again, the charge of emotivism has a legitimate force, but the distrust, or snobbery, towards feeling affects the quality of thought. It is as if we both know and don't know something at the same time, as if the dualistic discourse represses a partly functional, rather than conscious, knowledge. The reliance on feeling, that is to say, is like Wittgenstein's 'form of life', or the 'implicit dimension' variously argued by Michael Polanyi and Charles Taylor.[3] Much of our knowledge is manifest in the process of living, and probably could never be brought fully into consciousness even if that were thought desirable.

The slippage between implicit knowledge and conscious discourse with regard to feeling has a historical derivation. There lingers into modernity both the classical fear of the power of passion and the Christian emphasis on its sinfulness. But the modern phase of this confusion dates from the upward evaluation of emotion in the eighteenth century known as the cult of sentiment, or more precisely from the reactions against this. Eighteenth-century sentimentalism was part of an Enlightenment celebration of humane feeling which attempted to base the moral life itself on feeling. In many ways, this was so simplistic and overblown as to come into discredit even at the time and the subsequent reaction has cast into modernity the long shadow of disapproval reflected in the modern use of the word 'sentimental'. But to an important extent this has been an overreaction, at the level of discourse, which has thrown the baby of feeling out with the bathwater of sentimentality while disguising the more crucial impact of the 'affective turn' on modern culture. That impact is so pervasive and internalized as to be invisible. We are too thoroughly constituted by it to see it clearly.

The history of the term 'sentimental' between the mid eighteenth and early twentieth centuries encapsulates the dual legacy of sentiment. From being one of the most honorific terms in Enlightenment vocabulary, it dwindled to a term of near abuse referring to mawkish self-indulgent and actively pernicious modes of feeling. But while we usually assume that the declining value of a word represents a downgrading of its object, in the case of 'sentimental' this assumption, while partly correct, would be highly misleading. For the decline in this term, far from being a rejection of feeling, or of the underlying impulse of eighteenth-century sentiment-alism, is the development of an implicit criterion of true feeling on which the modern pejorative sense rests. 'Sentimental' has become the crucial term for discriminating *within* the realm of feeling and its new use rather indicates how important the realm of feeling, and the consequent need to discriminate within it, has become. It is not merely a historical accident, therefore, that our principal term for discriminating truth or authenticity of feeling should be a negative one, only invoking the positive by implication. The *history* of the term is a paradigm of its *meaning*. The fact that we have no single word to signify true or authentic feeling reflects the hard-won psychological recognition that truth, in this domain, can only be approached by indirection. In a critically self-conscious life of feeling, even the most confident emotional affirmation stands against the lurking threats of insincerity, self-interest and self-indulgence. It is only experienced in the light of these potentialities. Yet that does not mean we cannot trust feeling. It is rather that truth of feeling is inescapably noumenal and inferential. While the feeling itself may be direct and apodictic, the worth of the feeling is not directly knowable. In the emotional sphere, truth is in a vital dialectic with falsehood.

If the history of the word 'sentimental' represents such a double process of affirmation through negation, then the second important moment when the slippage between discourse and feeling has led to a permanent confusion was the early twentieth century. Just as the Enlightenment provided an ambivalent legacy in developing and theorizing the affective turn, so the modernist literary generation, in apparently bringing the era of sentiment to a close, rather enshrined the historical confusion lurking in the term. And the modern critical academy, which largely emerged from those writers, is still affected by that formation. The justified attack on sentimentalism by modern writers often led, at least on the discursive plane, to a damaging suspicion of feeling itself which has affected the subsequent practice of criticism. The German scholar, Jochen Barkhausen, taking a comparative view of sentimentalism, identifies here a long-standing, specifically Anglo-American, academic tradition.[4]

Irving Babbitt's *Rousseau and Romanticism* (1919), published at the time of the modernist reaction, is a classic critique of Enlightenment sentiment and its aftermath. In the latter half of the century, the two most substantial and synoptic treatments of this theme are Lionel Trilling's *Sincerity and Authenticity* (1972) and A. D. Nuttall's *A Common Sky* (1974). Both were written in the wake of the 1960s as if these were a resurfacing of the sentimental 1760s. Although these are substantial and subtle readings, something slips past them because of their very virtues. While making use of literary texts for their evidence, they understand the topic through a discourse of philosophical analysis and generality which is better at exposing the abstract contradictions than recognizing the positive cultural work of sentiment. More recently again, Alasdair MacIntyre's admirable *After Virtue* (1981), although it is explicitly written to expose the inadequacy of the analytic tradition in philosophy with respect to the sphere of ethics, and appeals to narrative as its exemplary alternative, suffers from a significant blankness with regard to feelings. In speaking dismissively of 'emotivism', a term taken from analytic philosophy, he startlingly reveals the extent to which he is still affected by the limitations of that tradition.[5]

In the domain of feeling, much hinges on the weight given to non-philosophical means, such as imaginative literature, as in itself a substantive mode of creative thought rather than as the mere reflection of ideas. Despite their sophistication of argument, and their detailed use of literary texts, all these critics use literature in this essentially reflective spirit. An opposite procedure underlies R. F. Brissenden's *Virtue in Distress: Studies in the Novel of Sentiment from Richardson to Sade* (1974), my own earlier study, *The Sentiment of Reality: Truth of Feeling in the European Novel* (1983), and Jerome McGann's *The Poetics of Sensibility* (1996). From the analytic point of view, the very appeal to literature as a substantive mode of understanding, rather than as merely reflecting a philosophical conception, is likely to be dismissed as sentimental. Indeed, in the proper historical sense of the word, it is so, which is why this study is devoted to the understanding of that proper historical sense.

If the impact of sentimentalism remained largely submerged, or eluded conceptual focus, it is not surprising that, up to the mid 1980s, it was constantly rediscovered in a series of lone studies. Since the mid 1980s, however, the social-historical significance of sentiment, and especially the feminist recognition that it is gendered female, has led to a flood of Anglophone studies with the interconnections not just of a debate but of a common cause. These have mainly concentrated on particular themes or periods covering the topic from the early eighteenth century to modernity. The most thorough study to date of the original period of sentiment is J. G. Barker-Benfield's *The Culture of Sensibility* (1996). Janet Todd's *Sensibility: An Introduction* (1986) emphasizes the gendered significance of sensibility within the same period while John Mullan's *Sentiment and Sociability* (1988) criticizes its damaging subjectivity. Chris Jones's *Radical Sensibility: Literature and Ideas in the 1790s* (1993) concentrates on the ideological division, or ambivalence, of the movement of sensibility after the French revolution. Mary Wollstonecraft is a pivotal, and divided, figure here as she is for Barker-Benfield and for Syndy Macmillen Conger in *Mary Wollstonecraft and the Language of Sensibility,* (1994). Jones also stresses the positive link between sensibility and the canonical romantic poets, a theme taken up by Jerome McGann, in *The Poetics of Sensibility* (1996), who carries its implications through into modernity. Fred Kaplan's *Sacred Tears* (1987) defends Victorian sentimentality, an area which is handled with a more sophisticated argument by

Wolfgang Herrlinger in *Sentimentalismus und Anti-Sentimentalismus: Studien zum Englischen Roman bis zur Mitte des 19–Jahrhundert* (1987). Philip Fisher's *Hard Facts* (1985), a study of nineteenth-century American sentimental fiction, argued a revaluation akin to Jane Tompkins's *Sensational Designs* (1985) which persuasively rereads the cultural significance of sentimental classics such as *Uncle Tom's Cabin*. Suzanne Clarke's *Sentimental Modernism* (1993) suggests a female canon against the values of the male-defined, anti-sentimental values of modernism. Finally, in this far from exhaustive list, Janice Radway's *Reading the Romance* (1991) studies the actual meaning of popular romance in the lives of representative female readers in the late twentieth century.

While these studies have helpfully brought out the positive significance of sentiment, I wish to argue a more analytic case about the nature of feeling and its place in modern culture. Despite its historical trajectory, the present study is analytic in purpose. More specifically, I wish to develop hints within the literature of sentiment suggesting that the nature of feeling is importantly focused through responses to fiction. The moral weight placed on sentiment in the eighteenth century increasingly revealed its imaginative character as against the literalism that initially underlay its assumed psychology and modes of representation. Hence the development of fictional form over the same period is essential to the story of sentiment. The feeling aroused by fiction is both liminal and subliminal. Existing in a twilight realm between the worlds of the reader and of the fiction, it constantly confounds these conceptually clear categories. In the moment of reading, the same feeling floods both realms which may be why such liminal porousness almost has to occur in a largely subliminal way. The categorial elusiveness of this emotion allows it constantly to slip from view or to be reductively defined. In discursive accounts of artistic meaning emotional response is so obvious as to be overlooked, or so embarrassing as to be repressed. Likewise, the recent debate about our feelings for fictional objects partly generated by Kendall Walton does not get at what is in question here: that fiction provides an intuitive appreciation of the ontology of feeling.[6]

Feeling and fiction

Fiction is more than an adventitious vehicle for the dramatization of feeling since whatever becomes an object of feeling, whether in the world or in a text, has to partake of an internal and imaginative dynamic. Feeling and fiction are so interwoven that the one can hardly be understood without the other. Although the modern forms of this interrelation are most pertinently to be traced from the eighteenth century, it has an extensive history in classical and medieval thought and it is useful to begin with a *locus classicus*, Augustine's *Confessions*, in which the interrelations of emotion and narrative are at once crucial and yet relatively unselfconscious. It shows why the liminal is so often subliminal.

Augustine is one of the most remarkable intellects in European tradition but in the process of his conversion emotion plays just as significant a role. In so far as he models his story on the parable of the prodigal son he seems at first to provide an exemplary instance of Alasdair MacIntyre's suggestive use of narrative to indicate the holism of the moral life which the analytic tradition in philosophy cannot adequately capture. But MacIntyre's general emphasis on narrative allows him to elide the more specific question of feeling within the response to narrative. Some of those influenced by MacIntyre have invested narrative with a grounding significance for the moral life which it cannot really bear and an emphasis on the role of feeling helps to show why this is so.[7] Narrative is not in itself a motivating category apart from the individual's investment of feeling in it. In this respect, Augustine's use of emotional subnarratives in the story of his conversion creates a revealing tension between his explicit disapproval of the emotions aroused by poetic fictions and his own dependence on an imaginative arousal of feeling.

Early in the text, Augustine deprecates his youthful enjoyment of pagan poetry, such as Virgil, and later offers a still classic meditation on the paradox of fictional compassion: that we are moved by painful events we know to be fictional, and have positive enjoyment in being so moved.[8] He detects self-indulgence in this and it becomes part of his general strategy of identifying the elements of illusion in temporal existence at large. Fiction is the emblem of this radical illusoriness yet, when we come to the moment of conversion in Book viii, it seems to have depended precisely on the emotional power of narrative. It is placed at the centre of an almost absurdly multiple nesting of subnarratives, one inside the other, as if to emphasize, without overtly acknowledging, their constitutive function at this crucial moment. These narratives are very different from the pagan literary ones rejected earlier, yet in terms of their emotional function the distinction is not so clear and Augustine himself blurs the distinction by stressing the common emotional dynamic of temporality in fiction and life. Narrative exploits the nature of temporal existence in which emotion is more strongly invested, for example, in what we fear to lose, or believe we have lost. The classic instance of this is the parable of the Prodigal Son which proves to be the underlying structure of the *Confessions* but 'everyday life is full of instances' and there is 'no pleasure in eating or drinking unless they are preceded by the unpleasant sensation of hunger and thirst' (*Confessions*, 137–8). It is as if God invented time to teach human beings to appreciate the value of things. Temporality is his way of bringing things home to us, and thereby bringing us home to him.

By the beginning of Book viii, Augustine has established this sense of divine Providence at work in the apparent processes of chance and is to that extent rather the narrator than the author of his *Confessions*. Also, by this time, he has gone through the intellectual process of understanding the Christian truth and was now 'attracted to the way, the Saviour himself, but was still reluctant to go along its narrow paths' (ibid. 133). His friend Simplicianus then tells him the story of the rhetorician Victorinus who was suddenly moved to confess his Christian faith, after which we hear how Augustine and his friend Alypius received 'a surprise visit ... from a man named Ponticianus' who '[b]y chance ... noticed a book on top of a gaming table' (ibid. 142). Ponticianus, recognizing the writings of the Apostle Paul and being himself now a believer, assumes Augustine to be likewise. When Augustine demurs, Ponticianus tells them the story of two of his friends who were so moved by reading the story of St Antony that they gave up their secular careers for the religious life. Ponticianus and another friend did not attempt to dissuade the converts, and indeed they wept, not for the converts, but for themselves. Their relation to the converts is one of moral and emotional empathy, rather as a reader might relate to a moving, or improving, fiction. And as Augustine in turn listens to Ponticianus, he finds that, while no apparent pressure is being put on him, the God to whom his *Confessions* are addressed has caused Ponticianus's story to make him think of himself: 'If I tried to avert my gaze from myself, his story continued relentlessly, and you once again placed me in front of myself...' (ibid. 144–5). Augustine catches here a recurrent feature of emotional response to all narrative, including fiction: because it is about someone else it allows a forgetfulness of the reader's self even as the feeling is being imagined within the reader's own emotional resources. A moving narrative requires the surrogate womb of the reader's feelings so that the emotional process, as opposed to the content, is most truly the reader's. It is not surprising, therefore, that reading should often prove to be a more intense experience of self through freedom from self while real persons require an imaginative sympathy.

The story occasions Augustine's famous remark, pithily encapsulating the enigma of identity in time: 'O Lord, grant me chastity and continence, but not yet' (ibid. 145). Intellectually he was ready to turn to God, but he remained as if caught between two separate wills, as in his Manichean phase, and could not make the emotional step. Yet he seemed increasingly to have seen it *as* a step that was to be taken, as if seeing at the time the teleology enshrined in his later narrative: 'Once more I made the attempt and came only a little short of my goal' (ibid. 150). Eventually, as the tension became unbearable, and Augustine threw himself 'under a certain figtree, and let [his] tears flow freely' (ibid. 152), a child's voice from a nearby house chanted over and over 'Pick up and read'. He interprets this as a 'divine command' and, on the remembered example of St Antony, he finds the text which finally precipitates his conversion.

What inference is to be drawn from the extraordinary nesting of narratives for which this is the culmination? On the face of it, the episode seems a godsend, not just to Augustine, but to the view of narrative as the primordial creator of significance. But therein lies the problem, that it is precisely a Godsend. Augustine's view of Divine Providence allows him to see the whole narrative of his life, including its repeated emphasis on 'chance', in the light of a transcendentally directed meaning and, if we translate this into a secular implication, it rather suggests how narrative is dependent on a worldview which it cannot ground out of itself. Narrative as such will not bear that kind of philosophical weight. Yet if one removes the grander claim for narrative significance as grounding, the episode emerges as truly exemplary in its treatment of the psychology of emotional response to narrative. Augustine already knew everything he needed for intellectual persuasion but required an emotional step which seemed to depend on the vicarious arousal of his own feelings by the series of stories. At one level, they are simply a series of good examples but to take them purely in that light is to leave them on the plane of intellectual reflection. It is the emotional impact which is crucial. Since it is Ponticianus's story of his friends' conversion which precipitates the crisis, we might conduct a thought experiment. Part of the emotional force of these stories for Augustine, in contrast to the pagan poetic fictions, is that they are true events concerning known individuals. Yet as far as Augustine is concerned, Ponticianus could have made up the tale and, if he should later reveal that he had done so, neither we nor Augustine would presumably feel this invalidated the conversion experience which the story had partly caused. Its emotional efficacy arises from what it has in common with fiction. The sharp contrast between the poetic fictions and the Christian stories begins to blur when the focus is put on the emotional response.

In this respect, the episode is emblematic of a continuing ambiguity of narrative emotion. One of the most formidable intellectuals of the European tradition tells the highly emotional story of his conversion in which narrative organization and feeling, as well as rigorous intellectual argument, combine to form the moments of moral significance or motivation. Based on the story of the Prodigal Son, its outcome explicitly transcends what can be expected in terms purely of rationality and justice and, in so far as we would now wish to secularize the understanding of Grace and Providence, this means a sudden overflow of feeling. The secular, or mythic, meaning of the story is of feeling interfusing rational considerations which were not adequate in themselves. As Augustine himself sees the story, however, the feeling is not the cause but the effect. He weeps for good reason and the aspect of feeling in the episode of the conversion, although it is constitutive and of the essence, remains merely an aspect and his distrust of the emotional power of poetic fiction remains in place without his needing to question how much his conversion involves a similar means. The relation of the rational and the nonrational elements, therefore, is highly ambiguous and circular. Feeling can be explained in terms of its object although the object was notoriously unable to exert its power until invested with feeling. Augustine distrusts the emotional power of fiction while actually using that same power under another sign. Feeling is distrusted except when it is justified as, or by, something else and that proves to be typical throughout the subsequent tradition of thought on this matter: consciously to distrust feeling while implicitly depending on it. Even the recent academic turn to 'narrative' as a way of explaining emotionally laden significances is a further example of this. It evades a direct engagement with the question of feeling and I wish, therefore, to explore the question frankly from the other side, the side of feeling. To touch the heart of the matter you must engage the matter of the heart.

Of course, to argue for the constitutive role and positive importance of feeling in the ethical life is not to deny that there are good reasons for distrusting it. On the contrary, the most significant outcome of the historical transformations of moral sentiment has been to create a means of internal discrimination within the realm of feeling. To understand this it will be necessary constantly to revisit two common distinctions in which a clear conceptual opposition masks an empirical continuity. The first is the dualistic conception of feeling as defined in contradistinction to some other faculty such as 'reason' or 'thought'. The second is the contrast of fact and fiction when considered as objects of feeling. For the object of feeling, in so far as it depends on imagination, is always a kind of internal fiction. But this is to present both questions at an unhelpfully generalized level. Conceptions of both fiction and feeling have changed over the formative period of modernity covered by this study, and the complex history of their interrelations requires a literary/philosophical excursus returning to the eighteenth-century origins of sentiment.

1
'Affective Individualism' and the Cult of Sentiment

Eighteenth-century sentiment must be understood through its longer-term origins and effects. Far from having the specifically eighteenth-century origins which used to be claimed, sentimentalism is a phase in a much larger process: the creation of what Lawrence Stone has called modern 'affective individuality'.[1] The eighteenth-century's massive investment of feeling in subjectivity was the moment when this became peculiarly self-conscious, and therefore problematic to itself. Seen in this light, the Enlightenment debate takes on a different meaning and becomes more symptomatic than substantive. Such a long-term rather than local purview also enforces the difficulty of finding a critical standpoint in modernity which is truly outside the process. Even now we are so thoroughly constituted by the affective turn as to make some of its major effects invisible. The impact of sentiment lives on as a cultural unconscious so that even those who nominally reject it are no less its products and only by appreciating the underlying cultural work it represents can its positive continuation in the present be understood.

Stone's highly influential thesis should not be taken for granted as if it were fact rather than an interpretation.[2] Earlier in the century, T. S. Eliot's meditation on English poetry produced a different analysis of the same period when he adopted Remy de Gourmont's phrase 'dissociation of sensibility' to suggest a coming apart of 'thought' and 'feeling' over the seventeenth and eighteenth centuries. But like the 'creation of sub-jectivity', this proved to be a moveable feast and Eliot gradually shifted the moment of supposedly unified sensibility back to Dante while also dissociating himself from the whole idea as being more mischievous than helpful.[3] Nonetheless, Eliot's use of the word 'sensibility' suggests a significant link with the era of sentiment and his emphasis on the *dissociation* of the subject along with Stone's on the *creation* of affective subjectivity, although they may at first seem opposed, are a useful combination for understanding the inner dynamic of sentiment. These theses point to something significant and some literary examples will indicate both the change that is in question and its fictional representation. Two historical benchmarks spanning the whole period are Thomas Nashe and Henry James. Between 1600 and 1900 there is a complete inversion by which the world depicted in the fiction is emotionally internalized.

At the beginning of Nashe's *The Unfortunate Traveller* (1594), the narrator, Jack Wilton, observes, with casual self-evidence, that 'the eye that sees round about itself sees not into itself'.[4] Given Wilton's scapegrace personality, the remark may be an unwitting reflection on the narrator himself, but the subsequent narrative bears out his disclaiming of introspection in a way that gives it a general force. Towards the end, Wilton describes the public torture and execution of a villain, Cutwolfe:

> The executioner needed no exhortation . . ., for he was a hackster good enough . . . At the first chop of his wood-knife would he fish for a man's heart and fetch it out as easily as a plum from the bottom of a porridge pot. He would crack necks as fast as a cook cracks eggs. . . Bravely did he drum on this Cutwolfe's bones, not breaking them outright but, like a saddler knocking in of tacks, jarring on them quaveringly with his hammer a great while together. No joint about him but with a hatchet he had for the nonce he disjointed half, and then soldered up the wounds from bleeding . . . Venomous stinging worms he thrust into his ears to keep his head ravingly occupied . . . In this horror they left him on the wheel as in hell, where, yet living, he might behold his flesh legacied amongst the fowls of the air.
>
> (*Unfortunate Traveller*, p. 369)

The linguistic exuberance of this passage is at once vividly concrete and emotionally distanced. If it communicates an enjoyment without seeming merely sadistic this is perhaps because the event is being staged for a purpose, and Wilton gets its message. He now finally reforms his own life and thereby vindicates the point of the spectacle, for the torture is a foretaste of Hell as well as a demonstration of the power of law. But for most modern readers it is shocking that his narrative does not internalize the experience as pity for, or identification with, the victim. On the contrary his, and apparently Nashe's, enjoyment provides an insight into the possible response to such public spectacles before the Enlightenment, including its emphasis on sentiment, began to put an end to them. For, given the size and participation of the crowd, it seems that a lack of internalization which would now be considered psychopathic was normal for Nashe's age, and of course sadism, as a personal condition, acquired articulate form only at the end of the Enlightenment.

The lack of internalization, moreover, works both ways. The victim, although we know his villainy, seems to be accorded little more personal depth than the actor who might represent a meaning on stage. Yet there is a curious wholeness in the complete externality of the sensibility which is revealed. Even while recognizing its rhetorical vigour, we cannot separate the rhetoric from the subjectivity of the narrator. This is all the subjectivity he has. By contrast with Nashe, Henry James's Prefaces to his own works repeatedly emphasize the opposite founding principle: that there can be no significant account of the outside world without an arena of sensitive consciousness in which to register it. The Jamesian 'eye/I' can only truly see the world when it looks into itself. Hence, when James conceived the crude situation for his novella, *The Spoils of Poynton* (1897), he had to invent a new character, Fleda Vetch, a young woman of refined sensibility, through whom it could be internalized.[5] James's world, however, is just as seamlessly whole, in its own way, as Nashe's although Eliot was right to note in the intervening period, and especially in the eighteenth century, a significant coming apart of thought and feeling. In the broader context this represents not so much a falling apart as a problematic self-consciousness within a process of change. In other words, in so far as a dissociation of 'thought' and 'feeling' can be seen in the period it is partly at the level of discourse and has something of the value for us now of an analytic separation of elements.

Taken in that spirit, a further aspect of the dualistic separation is suggested in the jump from Nashe to James. The switch from a male to a female central consciousness reflects a conventional gendering of feeling as female. Hence two novels at the midpoint between Nashe and James offer significant heroines of sensibility: Samuel Richardson's *Clarissa* (1748) and John Cleland's *Fanny Hill* (1749). Despite their evident contrast, as reflected in the names of the eponymous heroines, these novels have epochal features in common. They are transitional both culturally and in their modes of fiction.

If the violence in Nashe is a testing extreme for emotional subjectivity, the treatment of sexuality is another. David Foxon has traced a rise in pornographic publication from the mid-seventeenth century associated with materialist and libertine thought.[6] 'Libertine' is an objective category but pornography is in the eye of the beholder and writing about sex, as in

Rochester's poetry, may be celebratory rather than prurient. What characterizes pornography is not its erotic content but its masturbatory privacy. *Fanny Hill* belongs partly to the tradition of libertine, shameless and humorous eroticism and, as in the Nashe passage, its language is full of verbal enjoyment, notably in the naming of sexual parts and activities. *Fanny Hill* expresses the world of Richardson's libertine seducer, Lovelace, in a way that *Clarissa* itself could not, and would not. At the same time, even as it plays ironically on contemporary moralistic forms of fiction, such as the religious conversion narrative already adapted by Defoe's *Moll Flanders* (1722), *Fanny Hill* is suffused with affective values which turn the erotic into the pornographic.

The overt 'moral' is that sex is most pleasurable where there is true love, as Fanny finally discovers when, still only 19 years old, she marries the young man, Charles, to whom she had freely given her virginity and who had continued to love her despite their enforced separation. Fanny's reunion with Charles leads to her concluding description of their sexual encounter but before narrating this episode to the female friend for whom she is writing the originally private letters that constitute her memoir, she reveals a new note of embarrassment which stands, even for her, in odd contrast to her preceding frankness.

> And here, decency forgive me! if once more I violate thy laws and, keeping the curtains undrawn, sacrifice thee for the last time to that confidence, without reserve, with which I engaged to recount ... the most striking circumstances of my youthful disorders.[7]

This episode is crucial to the putative point of the narrative since the experience has to be distinguished as superior to the pleasures of what she now looks back on as her 'youthful disorders'. Of course, the reference to decency is titillating, just as the first stage of her initiation involved watching, along with the reader, sexual acts through a chink in a door but her subsequent initiation with a band of consciously libertine gallants is into an 'open public enjoyment' (ibid., 150) and it is therefore the more suggestive that, now she is to describe a sexual encounter with the man who has become her husband, and whose children she has borne, she invokes a deified decency and feels the need for privacy, of drawing the 'curtains', since this is precisely what the imminent end of the whole narrative in fact represents. The literal gesture of closure with which she anticipates the closure of her narrative is historically emblematic. The pre-marital and marital phases of her life suggest in microcosm the process of domestication, the creation of a private realm of feeling, between the sixteenth and nineteenth centuries. Whatever overall judgement we make of the book, its peculiar mixture reflects a new sensibility and shows how the privatization of feeling creates the conditions for pornography. At the same time, Fanny, in her own way, is a heroine of sensibility and, in her literal openness to sensory 'impressions' (ibid., 113, 161), a true daughter of John Locke.

The novel's Lockean psychology invites a different kind of rhetorical self-consciousness from Nashe's and provides a connection between sexuality, sensibility and the response to both language and fiction. For in Locke's sensationalist psychology, although there is a material base in sense impressions, we organize these into meaning at the level of ideas and imagination which, for him, should be closely disciplined by reality. Fanny likewise, despite her hedonistic commitment to sensation, is not a pure materialist and her reunion with Charles involves 'the combination of two distinct ideas': she was in touch physically 'with the instrument of pleasure' and emotionally with 'the great-seal of love', (ibid., 219). Meanwhile, throughout their separation, whenever she excites herself, as well as the reader, by watching sexual encounters, she always recognizes the power of imagination in this, so that the imaginative effect which is being exercised on the reader is simultaneously thematized within the text. Yet given the trade she practises, she is remarkably hostile to mere deception. When she has to deceive a client who wishes to believe she is a virgin, it is only after reluctantly acquiescing in Mrs Coles's argument that he fully deserves it, while Fanny herself continues to find the whole aspect of deception as distasteful as his need for this fantasy (ibid., 166–74).

For Fanny, then, sexual desire is largely in the imagination, whether for the characters or for the reader, yet is sharply distinguished from deceiving. She observes of a group of experienced gallants: 'These professors of pleasure knew too well to stale the impressions of it, or evaporate the imagination in words, before the time of action' (ibid., 150). Elsewhere she remarks on the intensifying effect of imagination which '. . . wound up to the height, could suffer no delay' (ibid., 189). The doubleness of imaginative and verbal play *within* a respect for reality is reflected in the metaphorical exuberance of her sexual descriptions to which she herself draws attention. Her apology for a language which she fears is excessively 'figurative' arises from the thought that the physical acts themselves do 'not admit of much variation' and would otherwise be monotonously repetitive in the telling. But the narrative effect, as she goes on to suggest, is to make explicit the imaginative appreciation which prevents the experience from being purely 'physical' even at the time. Indeed, it is 'properly the province of poetry, nay! is poetry itself, pregnant with every flower of imagination and loving metaphors...' (ibid., 207) *Fanny Hill*, hovering between a self-legitimizing exercise of erotic imagination and a critique of pornographic illusion, reflects an ambivalence about the emotional, the imaginative and the fictive which runs throughout the period but comes especially to the fore in any fiction, such as the literature of sentiment, which has a manifest intention of emotionally arousing the reader. In respect of the ontology of feeling, pornography is an extreme case of the sentimental.

A comparable problematizing of response runs through Samuel Richardson's *Clarissa*. Although Clarissa is a very different heroine of sensibility, the problems she encounters in maintaining her personal independence as a beautiful, and sexual, young woman are related to Fanny's if only because her would-be seducer, Lovelace, seeks to prove a view of human, and specifically female, nature derived from the same libertine tradition. Without being itself voyeuristic or sadistic, the novel enforces the value of privacy by its painful violation, including the abused privacy of Clarissa's correspondence. The moral feelings aroused by the narrative are constantly dramatized in the characters' own responses which are often, in the first instance, responses to letters, to words rather than things. Hence, even as the novel seeks to move its reader, it probes the ambiguity of emotional responses as induced by a rhetorical effect or by a real-life distress. But to appreciate the specifically period significance of this ambiguity it is necessary to look more closely at the underlying structure of contemporary sentiment.

The problem of origins

Early studies of sentiment tended to focus on the question of 'origins' as scholars argued the rival claims of various philosophical, social, religious and scientific influences. The principal intellectual context is the sensationalist psychology of John Locke, particularly as this came to be supported by physiological theories, although sentimentalism is in many respects an attempt to overcome the mechanistic limitations of Lockean psychology from inside its sensationalist premises. This revisionary impulse came most notably from Locke's one-time pupil, Anthony Ashley Cooper, the Third Earl of Shaftesbury, whose Deistic arguments had a pervasive impact on eighteenth-century European thought. In the essays collected as *Characteristics of Men, Manners, Opinions and Times* (1711) he argued, against Hobbes and Mandeville, that far from being motivated merely by selfish appetite, human beings have a natural instinct for virtue, sociability and benevolence. His own social and religious formation allowed him to see things, as it were naturally, in this light and sentimentalism continued to reflect contemporary transformations of religious feeling and outlook. Shaftesbury's first publication was an edition of Whichcote's sermons and the Latitudinarian movement within the Anglican church, following the upheavals of the Civil War and Restoration, sought to emphasize the virtues of charity and tolerance rather than the points of faith which had divided people. This spirit is evident in Fielding, just as the puritan tradition of close examination of conscience was manifest in Richardson's heroines. Over the course of the eighteenth century, the evangelical movement developed a more popular and affective style of worship reflected in the hymns of Isaac Watts and Charles Wesley. The journalism of Addison and Steele, most notably in *The Spectator* (1711–14), was a conscious attempt to create, through a realistically imagined model, an exemplary social community, including an Anglican parson, in which different economic and ideological interests, mercantile and landed, urban and rural, could live tolerantly and fruitfully together. Above all, it was the humorously tolerant sympathy of the Spectator himself which held the community together in the mind. The *Spectator* papers had a wide influence, both directly and through their many imitations, throughout Europe over the course of the century. Meanwhile medical theory continued to offer a materialist base somewhat counteracting these spiritual and social sublimations of sentiment and by the latter decades of the century the shift from moral sentiment to physiological sensibility gave renewed weight to the nervous and bodily constitution.

While these social and intellectual developments are clearly an important part of the story, their very multiplicity suggests the inappropriateness of looking among them for a single or major cause. The misleading focus on intellectual causes is emphasized here because the central problems of sentimentalism concerned precisely the sources of the ethical. Although origins and grounding were its central concern, the manner of argument, on all sides, suggests that the participants were largely assuming what was to be proved, in the way that Wittgenstein's 'form of life' is the silent condition in which all language communities function. Proponents of feeling would appeal to moral values as natural, while those committed to social rationality would take these same values as products of reason. The early eighteenth-century appeal to the values of sentiment could be made only because these values had already found widespread, largely unreflective acceptance. They had come to seem, and therefore in a sense to be, natural. A major change of feeling preceded a change of mind, while the mind had initially no adequate language in which to recognize or express this. This inference can be drawn from broad descriptive studies such as Geoffroy Atkinson's *The Sentimental Revolution: French Writers 1690–1740* (1965) and Jean Hagstrum's *Sex and Sensibility* (1980). A European-wide change was occurring here as large, and as elusive to single explanation, as the massive spiritualization of sexual feeling in the Middle Ages reflected in the cult of courtly love.

To see the cult of sentiment as not so much the invention as the coming into consciousness of a new sensibility focuses the import of the debate. David Hume saw this at the time in his insistence on morality being a matter of 'taste' as opposed to 'reason', but the pursuit of a chimerical grounding for moral values and motives is perennial and is one of the ways in which the eighteenth-century argument extends into our own time.[8] Yet it has reached us by culturally diffused means objectified above all in imaginative literature. With different truth claims from philosophy, such literature does not ground a way of life so much as represent it in a complex and dynamic form of self-knowledge largely eluding conceptual translation. What follows, therefore, is a brief summary of the eighteenth-century philosophical debate on moral sentiment highlighting not just the problems it threw up but why these were most fruitfully explored in literature.

Shaftesbury remains the invaluable starting-point. His impact depended on a Deistical belief in a rational and harmonious universe. He opens his *Enquiry Concerning Virtue or Merit* by denying the necessary dependence of virtue on religion yet goes on to argue that 'the perfection and height of virtue must be owing to the belief in a just God'.[9] This is not a contradiction but an affirmation of mutuality. Whenever it became necessary to invoke first principles, Shaftesbury would appeal, persuasively enough, to empirical experience and a generalized psychological probability. Only gradually over the course of the century would the instabilities of this conception become conscious and a source of anxiety. The central problem can be expressed in the formula: sentiment as 'principle and/or feeling'.

Sentiment as 'principle and/or feeling'

Shaftesbury's attempt to bolster social reason and the theological grounding of ethics with the supposedly natural feeling of benevolence was caught in what Jacques Derrida identified in Rousseau as the self-undercutting logic of the 'supplement'.[10] If feeling was merely supplementary, in the sense of being unnecessary, then why should it be adduced at all? Meanwhile, the very fact of its being adduced suggests the inadequacy of the supposedly grounding principles of social reason or religion and, far from strengthening the moral structure, the supplement begins to threaten its foundations. This is encapsulated in the shifting semantics of the word 'sentiment' in the middle decades of the eighteenth century.

The word combines the meanings of 'principle' and 'feeling'. When Samuel Richardson's characters, in the 1740s, referred to their 'sentiments', they usually meant the moral 'principles' by which they sought to live, whereas for Laurence Sterne in the 1760s the word had come to mean 'feelings'. Yet these two apparently distinct meanings are only the ends of a continuous spectrum of usage whereby the word had both meanings at once so that, even at the ends of the spectrum, it carried some implication of the whole and thereby focuses the hopeful instability of the whole project of sentimentalism. Sentiment as 'principle' was invoked as if it had the intuitive and spontaneous impact of feeling, while sentiment as 'feeling' assumed the universal, impersonal authority of principle.

Notoriously, however, feeling and principle are often in conflict and it is not surprising that the whole cult of moral sentiment led to much overblown rhetoric and was eventually discarded in its naive forms. At the same time, there was an important intuition, and a cultural work being done, in this debate and especially in its literary manifestations. For beneath the optimistic attempt to identify 'reason' and 'feeling' lies the deeper, as yet unformulated, intuition that, if they cannot be simply identified, neither can they be completely separated. In that respect, the problematic nature of moral sentiment lies not so much in the moral psychology itself as in a discourse which reified and polarized aspects of an integral whole. The new emotional wine is not recognized in the old rationalist bottles. But once we realize that the formal discourse is often at odds with the underlying implication, and with what is actually going on in much of the imaginative literature of the time, then the very failures of the project, at discursive and conscious levels, provide the analytic terms by which to understand the largely unwitting evolution of sentiment.

Richardson's use of 'sentiment', with its pre-sentimentalist meaning of general moral principle, indicates the externally statable axioms by which the characters sought to live. Hence the internal conflicts and emotional drama of the Richardsonian heroines. But a discourse of generality has even more radical consequences when it comes from the narrator and implies a way of conceiving human psychology as such. The entire functioning of the psyche is then understood in terms of general principles and laws, an effect which is clearer in Fielding. Fielding's first two novels, *Joseph Andrews* (1742) and *Tom Jones* (1749), are social comedies centred on male figures whose predicaments depend largely on imposed falsehoods which are eventually overturned. In *Amelia* (1752), by contrast, Fielding attempts a sentimental novel, based on a female central character, whose room for action is severely limited, and who is dependent on a final change of heart in her scapegrace husband, Captain Booth. Whereas Fielding's masterpiece, *Tom Jones,* has a perfect coincidence of form and meaning in presenting, from the opening paragraph, a broad social psychology in a discourse of generalized principle, in *Amelia* the difficulty is to present an individual change of heart, a reversal of feeling, which is not a matter of acquiring a new principle, and indeed it has to occur within someone who has repeatedly proved impervious to good principle. As with Augustine, who is likewise unaffected by further arguments of principle, the moment of conversion finally comes from a textual *tertium quid* as Booth reads in prison a sermon by the Latitudinarian divine, Isaac Barrow.[11] His circumstances as an imprisoned man help, in Dr Johnson's words, to concentrate the mind, but the difficulty of conveying the momentary and individual process of emotional deepening, the sudden reversal of feeling, as other than arbitrary pervades the narrative as in the following episode from earlier in the book.

A Miss Matthews, who is in love with Booth and, having been rejected by him, has incited a Captain James to attack him, suffers a reversal of feeling on hearing, albeit erroneously, that Booth has been killed.

> Now, of all the ministers of vengeance, there are none with whom the devil deals so treacherously as with those whom he employs in executing the mischievous purposes of an angry mistress; for no sooner is revenge executed on an offending lover, than it is sure to be repented; and all the anger which before raged against the beloved object, returns with double fury on the head of his assassin.
>
> Miss Matthews, therefore, no sooner heard that Booth was killed (for so was the report at first, and by a Colonel in the army) than she immediately concluded it to be James. She was extremely shocked with the news, and her heart instantly began to relent. All the reasons on which she had founded her love, recurred in the strongest and liveliest colours to her mind, and all the causes of her hatred sank down and disappeared; or if the least remembrance of anything which disobliged her remained, her heart became his zealous advocate, and soon satisfied her that her own fates were more to be blamed than he, and that without being a villain, he could have acted no otherwise than he had done.

In this temper of mind, she looked on herself as the murderer of an innocent man; and, what to her was much worse, of the man she loved, and still did love, with all the violence imaginable. She looked on James as the tool with which she had done this murder; and as it is usual for people who have rashly or inadvertently made any animate or inanimate thing the instrument of mischief, to hate the innocent means by which the mischief was effected (for this is a subtle method which the mind invents to excuse ourselves, the last object on whom we would willingly wreak our vengeance); so Miss Matthews now hated and cursed James as the efficient cause of that act which she herself had contrived, and laboured to carry into execution.

(Amelia, i, 239–40)

The passage is perfectly clear in its psychology mainly because it stays on a level of complete generality. Rationalism gives an effect of transparency. Miss Matthews's reversals of feeling are all instances of general principles which are separately enunciated and then applied to her particular case with a supposedly logical force of 'therefore', 'so', etc. The narrative is like oil and water in its constant interruptions of the action to introduce universal psychological principles by which to explain each new development. Indeed, as compared to the lucidly symmetrical prose of *Tom Jones*, the syntax frequently strains to fit the general psychological parentheses into the narrative sentences. For a comedic psychology this is not inappropriate, and it is quite sufficient for many other purposes too, just as one could describe a circle for most practical occasions by a series of short straight lines turning at the same angle at regular intervals. So here, the potentially infinite straight lines of universal principle are constantly interrupted to give the effect of a curve of feeling. But a new kind of emotional calculus is required to trace the curve as such. There is, of course, an intentional irony here about the processes of reason in the human mind as Miss Matthews reasons in different directions according to her mood, but Fielding himself cannot get beyond such terms except by a tonal condescension. That is a central problem with the discourse of sentiment in the eighteenth century. The language of generalized rationality cannot catch the shifts and rhythms of individual feeling which, in the ideology of sentiment, have become the basis of moral motivation. The difficulty of making principle do duty for feeling affects the moral psychology, and the narrative representation, therefore, at a more fundamental and intimate level than that of moral axioms. It is precisely the individual and the momentary which are now in question yet there is no discourse by which they can be properly thought, let alone represented. Comparing the vigour and wholeness of Nashe's prose one can see the force of T. S. Eliot's claim that the eighteenth century suffered a 'dissociation of sensibility' as intellect and feeling came apart. But it could be modified here to suggest not just a story of cultural decline but a philosophical reduction to elements. The coming apart is an unwitting form of analysis.

In this respect the discourse of sentiment, in seeking to illustrate a philosophical view, is significantly related to other contemporary forms: the philosophical tale and the moral essay. *Tom Jones* is a philosophical tale writ large with the embedded tale of the misanthropic Man on the Hill at the centre of the novel highlighting the different attitude embodied in the larger narrative. At the same time, the narrowness of the misanthrope makes Fielding's own narrative seem the more open and complete, more coterminous with life itself, and this points to a curious internal paradox of the philosophical tale which was to live on in the European novel. The philosophical tale was often devoted, as in *Candide* (1759) and *Rasselas* (1759), to challenging 'ideas' with 'experience'. Yet the form cannot give experience as such, only an idea of experience. What passes for experience in a fiction can only ever be an exemplary conception of it and one way of looking at the history of the novel form is as a continuing attempt to overcome this contradiction. The novel gives ever greater weight and complexity to the representation of experience, without ever fully escaping, so much as disguising, the form of the philosophical tale, the governing structure of a worldview. The term 'sentiment' is a microcosm of this overall tension. Straddling the divide between principle and feeling, it is both philosophical and anti-philosophical. If sentiment sits at the heart of this theoretical contradiction with such consequences for the novel form, it is an invaluable focus for seeing how theoretical contradictions are not necessarily stultifying. Contradictions can be illuminating and especially if the answer is not so much to overcome them as to learn to live with them as many great European novels show. Ultimately, the authority of the novel form is won by persuading the reader of the weight of experience implicit in the rhetoric, by an appeal to our own implicit knowledge. Taken in that way, *Tom Jones* and *Rasselas* are triumphs of the rhetoric of experience within the generalized mode of the philosophical tale and, in this regard, Fielding's sister Sarah's two-part novel *David Simple* (1744 and 1753) provides an instructive comparison in its critique of sentiment.

This morally exemplary novel promotes the importance of the bourgeois woman since 'the Welfare and Happiness of most Families depend in a great measure on Women'.[12] It is also a novel of sentiment in its appeal to tender feelings, and its presentation of anti-sentimentalists as decadent aristocrats or selfish egotists. Yet it also uses the form of the philosophical tale to question the theory of sentiment. It is a compendium of the internal problems of the sentimentalist ethic, as well as of its opponents. As with Henry's fiction, the characters have no great internal complexity and fall into broadly sheep and goat categories of sincerity and hypocrisy so that the engagement with the problematics of sentiment lies not at the level of true self-deception and opacity, as in Richardson, so much as in the hypocritical use of ideas. Mrs Orgueil, for example, is a woman of fake sensibility using her feelings to selfish ends, while her husband, Mr Orgueil, is an equally hypocritical anti-sentimentalist always happy to justify the limits of his benevolence. In other words, these contemporary theories or moral postures of senti-ment, precisely as theories and postures, can be alibis for selfishness. The effect of a philosophical tale arises from the use of the central figure, David Simple, whose innocently good-hearted curiosity leads him to investigate the many specimens of human nature he encounters. At the same time, he is very different from Candide. His unworldliness is a transcendental, Christian value and, like other figures of sentiment in the period, he resigns himself to successive misfortunes on the explicit model of Job.

If Henry Fielding's apparently confident Latitudinarian comedies are made possible by his generalized discourse, Sarah Fielding probes its darker underside in a way that points towards Dickens. But an incomparably richer and more intimate probing of the conflict between principle and feeling occurs in Richardson's *Clarissa* where the instability of sentiment becomes the dramatic subject-matter. Clarissa's formidable intelligence and honesty do not prevent, indeed they exacerbate, a certain blind spot at the level of feeling. She can think of herself only in terms of principle, of what she ought to be, and feel, and the fact that her life is so much a matter of public scrutiny, even before the tragic events of the novel, shows the positive importance and propriety of her doing so. Nonetheless it produces her curious reply to her friend Anna Howe's suggestion, when Lovelace first starts to visit Harlowe Place, that she is perhaps a little in love with him: 'Indeed, I would not be in love with him for the world!'[13] While her clear intention is to deny the charge, her phrasing expresses only what she should feel and leaves her actual, or possible, feelings in a limbo of the inconceivable, at least for her. The implication is not inconceivable to Anna Howe who is quick to seize on the revealing phrase, and Richardson's triumph as a novelist was to turn the limitations of his moral psychology and discourse, his very conception of sentiment as principle, to dramatic account. He built a complex tragic action out of its very problems.

The novel tests dramatically the capacity of principle to induce or compel feeling. Clarissa's own feelings are principled and her principles are charged with honest and delicate feeling. There is little room for a tragic flaw in her character, and Lovelace has eventually to take her by force and destroy her. The greatest dramatic tension, and test of the sentimentalist ethic as Richardson conceived it, therefore, lies not so much in her internal weakness as in the impact, or lack of impact, she has on others, including most importantly both Lovelace and her own family. In this respect, the epistolary form is crucial. As the letters which make up the novel are read by characters within the narrative, our own response is constantly compared with an internal one. Most obviously, this shows up the inadequacy of response of characters such as Lovelace in the face of Clarissa's distress. Emotionally, this defines his wickedness and inhumanity and our readerly solidarity is with Clarissa. Or that, at least, is Richardson's conscious effect, but subtextually a further level of immanent critique arises from this which can be seen in the contrast with Fielding. Fielding's Booth was thoughtless rather than bad-hearted and the conclusion of *Amelia* formally endorses the ideology of Shaftesburyan sentiment while unwittingly reflecting its weakness. By contrast, Lovelace's philosophically self-conscious refusal to be moved, as well as reflecting on him, also questions the power of the narrated distress to arouse the appropriate response. This is not so much a dramatic weakness as a dramatizing of the weakness. His readerly resistance extends the narrative logic into the realm of tragedy and throws into question the optimistic myth of sentimentalism itself. It is also not accidental, of course, that this is presented as a conflict between male and female.

The gendering of sentiment

What has been said of the Fieldings and Richardson shows the unstable rhetoric of sentiment to be highly gendered. Henry Fielding's narrative form is strained in dealing with a female central character in *Amelia* just as Richardson's form struggles, at least for most modern readers, to present a central male character in *Sir Charles Grandison* (1753). Sir Charles's principled moral life, and his exercise of social authority, are as effective as they are exemplary and for that very reason they are not sufficiently dramatic, while sentimental pathos is provided by the Italian Catholic, Clementina, who falls in love with him. So too, the older picaresque form, as used in *Tom Jones*, reflects the external orientation and freedom of a typically male experience while the epistolary form is classically suited to the female. Nancy Armstrong has shown how the creation of the modern bourgeois family was built on a changed construction of woman.[14] Whereas in earlier forms of social economy, based in the home, the woman contributed directly and equally, and therefore had a personal sphere of power, a new conception grew up in the seventeenth and eighteenth centuries reflected in conduct books which parallel the models promoted in the fiction of the period. As in *David Simple*, the woman now embodies both the moral values of domesticity and their fragility. In the era of sentiment, the woman placed in situations of distress, and presented with an overwhelming emotional charge, becomes a way of highlighting these values in themselves and the strength of character required for the woman as the centre of the domestic world. In that sense, of course, she is far from passive and may, like Richardson's Pamela, exert a decisive authority, emotional and educative, over the male. But her limited sphere of external movement means that everything hinges on the way she interiorizes the world; she has to understand and influence rather than directly control the external action. Her feelings become authoritative in so far as they are manifest as principled behaviour. Janet Todd has pointed out the difference in the characteristic fates of the man and woman of sensibility.[15] Once sentiment shifts from 'principle' to 'feeling', and modulates into full-blown 'sensibility', it becomes especially problematic for the male. As the socially authoritative male example of Grandison gives way to the softer, feminized model exemplified in Goethe's Werther or in Henry Mackenzie's Harley, these figures become socially ineffective and even destroy themselves. They represent a deep contradiction with a male social role. The woman by contrast has her true meaning, and her moral power, raised to mythic proportions by the sentimental ordeal, whether tragically tested, like Clarissa, or comedically vindicated, like Pamela.

But to say that the late eighteenth-century 'man of feeling' took on stereotypically female characteristics, is to distinguish cultural categories of masculine and feminine from the biological ones of male and female. Some feminist readers see this as another instance of repression since, even as the values of the feminine are exalted, they are usurped by men. Claudia Johnson shows that is undoubtedly what the late eighteenth-century man of feeling partly represents although, as Janet Todd's distinction also suggests, this is not necessarily an assumption of power.[16] Just as Nancy Armstrong's longer-term historical analysis resists a simpler kind of feminist *ressentiment* by showing the participation of women in the creation of the new bourgeois order, and their share in its class benefits, so the cult of sentiment was part of a more general feminization of culture.

The French feminist Hélène Cixous has coined the category of *écriture feminine*, or a female mode of writing, to indicate a set of characteristics which, while based on qualities associated with the female, are actually available for men or women, and may be avoided by either.[17] Eighteenth-century literary sentimentalism is an early form of *écriture feminine*. The ambivalence of feeling, its being at the 'heart' of the culture and yet constantly rejected or condescended to, is reflected in its association with the female. Apparently marginalized because it is female, it is perhaps seen as female because it is marginal. Once again, the circular logic of the supplement is reflected in the symbolic relations between the sexes. The emotional qualities of the female are necessary, yet they must be controlled by social reason to which they appear to be a threat. Hence it is precisely as feeling is ostensibly privileged that the structure of principle can be most coercive.

A striking instance is Rousseau's educational treatise, *Émile* (1762), in which a principled psychology is combined with a commitment to 'natural' feeling. The paradoxical outcome is that the pupil's education for freedom requires the most rigid direction and restriction. The preceptor, a suggestive term in itself, wishes the pupil to learn from experience but the effects of chance would take a long time and would be unpredictable. Experience has to be educatively concentrated into meaning. The preceptor, therefore, arranges meaningful scenarios such as letting the boy plant seedlings on a patch belonging to the gardener so that he will learn about property when they are torn up.[18] What might have been educative had it occurred through chance becomes manipulation. In effect, the pupil is surrounded with a coercive fiction which, although it is intended to protect him from social corruption in his early youth, becomes a kind of prison. This manipulation of experience by ideas to produce the effect of natural meaning reflects the ambiguity already noted in the novel form and renders more significant an effective slippage from treatise to novel that occurs within the text itself. The originally hypothetical and generalized pupil gradually becomes an individually named character and this precisely embodies the way the whole argument is conceived through general laws. The slippage does not matter to Rousseau because it is thought possible to predict, down to the last detail, what the pupil will feel. The same laws will apply whether in fiction or in life. Yet to speak so predictively of living persons is to elide the distinction with fiction for which such control is legitimate. As in the passage from *Amelia*, the underlying rational control can be seen not just at the level of moral maxims to be lived up to, but in a more pervasive discourse of psychological causality. The whole mode of thought is intrinsically coercive:

> So a child is naturally disposed to kindliness because he sees that everyone who approaches him wishes to help him, and he draws from this observation an habitually favourable view of his species; but as he extends his relations, his needs, his dependencies, active or passive, he becomes aware of his relation to others, and therefore of duties and preferences. Then he becomes masterful, jealous, deceitful, and vindictive. If he is obliged to obey, not seeing the use of what he is told to do, he attributes it to caprice, to an intention of tormenting him, and he rebels. If he is himself obeyed, as soon as something resists him, he sees it as rebellion, as deliberate resistance, and he beats the chair or the table for having disobeyed him. Self-love, which relates only to ourselves, is satisfied when our real needs are met; but selfishness, which compares ourselves to others, is never satisfied and could not be, because this sentiment requires that they should prefer us to themselves, which is impossible.
>
> (*Émile*, 276–7; *Emile*, 213–14, my trans.)

Even as this passage typifies Rousseau's acuteness and generosity in his thinking about early education, and recognizes the primary significance of feeling, it exerts the absolute control of its own rational and general principles. The founding distinction of 'self-love' and 'selfishness' submits the spectrum of feeling to the orderly analysis conveyed in the highly logical vocabulary of 'so', 'because', 'if' and 'then'. Feeling is not just submitted to rational control here, it is rationally conceived from the outset. Even his claim that feeling will be wild and unmanageable when only partly or inadequately socialized, is a function of this rational frame of reference. The boy's tantrums are rationally conceived and predicted while the behaviour itself is a direct obverse of reason. Whatever conflicts the child experiences, and most are in the secret control of the preceptor, the latter sees no conflict between universal reason and individual feeling; nor should Émile by the end of the process.

The implicit dominance of 'reason' over 'feeling' is reflected in the gender distinctions in the book at large. Despite his modernity in other respects, Rousseau keeps the doctrine of separate sexual spheres and does not extend to the woman the education given to Émile. Where Émile is educated for responsible freedom, his partner, Sophie, will exercise a becoming obedience. This resonates with the model of sentimental love expressed in *La Nouvelle Héloïse*, and in the *Confessions*, whereby sexual feeling is sublimated in explicit contrast to physical fulfilment. For the peculiarly ideal intensity of the feeling is so much a function of restraint that the overt order is effectively reversed. Instead of an illicit, but restrained, passion resulting in emotional intensity, the restraint seems rather the necessary condition for achieving the feeling. This model of sexual love shares with *Émile* the idealized otherness of the woman and although in the longer term Rousseau represented a step towards dissolving the traditional dualism of reason and feeling, the immediate internal dynamic of his emotional ideal is an investment in maintaining it. In this respect, he brought out what was only latent in Richardson. By stoking the pressures of feeling in the compression chamber of principle he raised the internal conflict of sentiment to its maximum sublimation. Furthermore, since Rousseau identified with women as much as he desired them, the gendered logic of desire was peculiarly enclosed within his own self-sublimating feelings.

Rousseau's genius lay partly in his heroic persistence in following out his own contradictions. Where Augustine's *Confessions* are modelled on the story of the prodigal son, with its undeserved and unexpected resolution, Rousseau is, to borrow a phrase from Diderot, a 'natural son': he combines the genuineness and integrity of nature with social illegitimacy, and has no divine intervention to overcome the contradiction.[19] But a crucial category which might have resolved his contradictions was art, or fiction, and this points to a less obvious aspect of his archetypal representation of contemporary sentiment. Because he wrote, in *La Nouvelle Héloïse*, the greatest novel of sentiment, his uneasy attitude to fiction, and to the imagination, is not always noticed. What makes his conception of fiction so much of its period is its literalism. Just as, in his own life, Rousseau's heroic persistency lay in the literalism with which he attempted to live out his values and beliefs, so his apologetic account in the *Confessions* of the composing of *La Nouvelle Héloïse* reveals the literalism with which he drew on his own feelings. He presents the composition of the novel as a slightly shameful, masturbatory overflow from his then emotional circumstances of being in love with Mme d'Houdetot and a friend of her accepted lover, Saint-Lambert. It may be that, with so much imaginative sublimation in his own emotional relations, he could not afford to indulge the further imaginative level of fiction even though this very proclivity was the source of his novelistic power. Rousseau's psychology was Lockean and his ambivalent view of the imagination marks another representative instability in the myth, and therefore in the fiction, of sentiment. The circular logic of eighteenth-century sentiment is that, even as it used fictional means, it constantly sought to deny the category of the fictional. To appreciate the force of this it is necessary to look more closely at the assumed psychology of sentimental response both in life and in fiction.

Moral sense, moral imagination and emotional literalism

The instability of moral sentiment, as caught in the mid-century ambiguity of the word 'sentiment', also provided the internal dynamic by which its contradictions were eventually, if not overcome, then more fruitfully understood. This happened in conjunction with a parallel instability in the model of fiction. Through most of the eighteenth century, there were two rival, although supplementary, explanations of sentimental response: the belief in an innate moral sense and an emphasis on the secondary process of imagination. These were both, at first, strongly governed by a literalistic conception but they were gradually merged into a more complex, indirect and imaginative one. Once again, both trains of thought can be picked up from Shaftesbury.

Shaftesbury is commonly credited with two important contributions to ethical philosophy: the idea of a 'moral sense' and the claim that the ethical and the aesthetic are exercises of the same faculty, although Gerhart Sauder has emphasized the earlier appeal to moral sense in the Cambridge Platonists and the word 'aesthetic', as will be seen, needs careful handling.[20] For present purposes, however, it is more important to note how Shaftesbury's way of introducing these claims reflects the earlier point about his going along with, rather than creating, the new culture of feeling for he does so not in a spirit of novelty so much as by an appeal to common sense, and common usage, as in his remark:

> When we say, therefore, of a creature 'that he has wholly lost the sense of right and wrong,' we suppose that being able to discern the good and ill of his species, he has at the same time no concern for either ...
> (*Characteristics*, ii, 259)

Shaftesbury's contemporary impact arose from his articulating what many were ready to believe and he does not lean analytically on the word 'sense' here in the way that later writers would seek to do. Francis Hutcheson, in 1725, gave 'moral sense' its stronger, but also more vulnerable, implication of an independent faculty contradistinguished from reason.[21] Moreover, by the early nineteenth century, as Laurence Lockeridge has noted, the expression 'moral sense' had faded back into common usage with much the same broad, unexamined import.[22] While it is proper to subject this usage to positivistic scrutiny, and to recognize that there is no separate psychological faculty to which the term 'moral sense' corresponds, it is fruitful to ask, in a more Wittgensteinian spirit, what shared worldview, or form of life, the use of such an expression implies. This applies even more importantly to the other major contribution attributed to Shaftesbury, his aestheticizing of the ethical.

In practice, this latter claim refers to Shaftesbury's view of the ethical life as a matter of educated, and socialized, taste; not, it should be noted, merely 'a matter of taste' in the modern relativistic sense for, in Shaftesbury's day, it would have been readily assumed that the appreciation of works of art was an educated capacity. The notion of ethical 'taste' was also to be subjected to philosophical analysis, most notably by David Hume, who saw that, given the absence of any purely rational or transcendental grounding for the ethical life, an absence which Shaftesbury, of course, had typically not insisted on, the ethical realm did indeed rest on a communal taste. As with Hutcheson's sharpening of 'moral sense', the notion of moral 'taste' took on a different implication when made to carry the whole burden of ethical meaning by itself. But the notion of 'moral taste' has not slid back into common usage along with the 'moral sense'. If we more readily think of morality as natural than as aesthetic, the difference is not just attributable to the subjectivizing, and weakening, of the notion of taste; it is also because something fundamental had happened to the idea of the aesthetic between the eighteenth and twentieth centuries.

From the time of Alexander Baumgarten's *Aesthetica* (1750), which is generally credited with first defining the aesthetic as a distinct order of significance peculiar to the sensory domain, it rapidly acquired the value of an autonomous realm in contradistinction to the cognitive and the ethical. Kant's three Critiques classically discriminated these orders although the subsequent nineteenth-century separation of the aesthetic should not be laid entirely at Kant's door. For many moderns, the aesthetic now designates a realm almost opposed to the ethical and if Shaftesbury aestheticized the ethical it is not with the strong modern implication of the term 'aesthetic'. It would take a further line of thought, culminating in Nietzsche and others, to produce an aestheticized morality in that sense. This is crucial since, although a gulf of intellectual history now separates us from Shaftesbury, the unproblematized conjunction of art and morality which he affirmed through the word 'taste' still corresponds to a common practical intuition about the moral value of art. If Shaftesbury's mode of argument, including the circular logic of the supplement, explains his philosophical eclipse after the age of sentiment, he nonetheless had an intelligent naivety and psychological shrewdness which anticipate something of the longer-term positive effects of sentimentalism. His best intuitions have been obscured as much as clarifed by the later tradition of speculative thought and his being in a measure epiphenomenal to a broader change in culture is precisely what makes him relevant to the present. In some respects he brought together, as an empirical matter of course, aspects which, once they were taken apart analytically, no one has managed fully to reassemble yet which we continue to recognize as in some way belonging together; or rather, perhaps, our behaviour shows us to be working on this assumption even if we cannot fully account for it. It may be that while the moral sentiment tradition underlies the *de facto* sensibility, or form of life, in which most people live, the very attempt to raise it to articulate self-consciousness, and find an objective grounding for it, reflects the loss of another kind of knowledge. Hence, although there would be little profit in returning to Shaftesbury for a reasoned solution to these questions as they are posed for a modern understanding, the origins of the movement of sentiment are nonetheless, in their capacious holism, closer to a true account of our relations to literary art, and its relation to ethical experience, than are some of the sophisticated systems of cerebration which have grown up since and are predicated on the separatist view of the aesthetic.

Shaftesbury also shows how, despite the problematic nature of a philosophical appeal to 'experience', the sentimentalist project seemed constantly to require it. This can be seen, for example, in Shaftesbury's use of his own personality as a moral exemplar. This was not merely a rhetorical device but part of the logic of the sentimentalist case which was to attain its strongest, and most evidently problematic form, in Rousseau's *Confessions*. Shaftesbury used the *ad hominem* argument against Hobbes that, since general reflections on human nature are necessarily based on the one case that can be truly known, oneself, then Hobbes's view of human selfishness was ultimately no more than a reflection on his own character. By the same token, the benevolent view must also be based on the individual's self perception and with an equal claim to be representative. This *ad hominem* argument was taken up by many later writers: the fictive 'Spectator' persona developed by Addison and his collaborators, or Henry Fielding's narrative voice, are versions of it. The Spectator's significance lies as much in his own character, his tolerant but shrewdly judgemental good-heartedness, as in his specific views and arguments. The *Spectator* paper of 1 September 1714, written by Henry Grove, a dissenting minister, makes the same charge against Hobbes:

> Now we will allow Mr. Hobs to know best how he was inclined: But in earnest, I should be heartily out of Conceit with my self, if I thought my self of this unamiable Temper, as he affirms, and should have as little Kindness for my self as for any Body in the World. Hitherto I always imagined that kind and benevolent Propensions were the original Growth of the Heart of Man ...[23]

The ideology of natural benevolence has deceived the real author's memory here if his use of the word 'original' can so completely overlay the traditional belief in original sin in which, as a Christian minister, he no doubt also believed. And he develops the point by invoking the unlikelihood that God would have made human beings essentially selfish: 'For what Complacency could a Mind, whose Love is as unbounded as his Knowledge, have in a Work so unlike Himself?' (*Spectator*, v, 11–12).

The appeal to common experience, the use of rhetorical questions and the general recourse to *ad hominem* and knock-down arguments here, all provide an insight into the ambivalence of the sentimentalist project. The rhetoric reflects its highly personal nature, its resistance to precisely the kind of universalist reflection by which its proponents sought to support it. It also reveals a half-witting insecurity, a desperate need to believe, whose very urgency suggests that the insecurity is inadmissible. The likely balance of real confidence or actual insecurity in any given case is largely imponderable but the importance of the question is more general and structural. At whatever level of awareness, sentimentalism seeks to present a conception of humanity as natural, intuitive and therefore beyond the need of argument, in a historical context in which this view had been strongly contested and was, by the nature of the case, beyond proof. It is, therefore, not just by the appeal to experience, but to experience seen in the right light, or within an appropriate mood, that the case was to be made persuasive. As Shaftesbury put it in his *A Letter Concerning Enthusiasm*, 'Tis not in every disposition we are capacitated to judge of things' (*Characteristics*, i, 11), and 'I very much question whether anything besides ill-humour can be the cause of atheism' (*Characteristics*, i, 17). Hence the sentimentalist case has constantly to go beneath the terms of philosophical argument, and when a directly principled defence is required it is typically asserted as a self-evident truth as in the final paragraph of the same *Spectator* paper:

> But to descend from Reason to matter of Fact; the pity which arises on sight of Persons in Distress, and the Satisfaction of Mind which is the

Consequence of having removed them into a happier State, are instead of a thousand Arguments to prove such a thing as a disinterested Benevolence.

(*Spectator*, v, 12)

Groves's appeal to self-evidence here links the question of personal response to the other important premise of sentimentalism already noted in Rousseau for what is called here a 'matter of Fact' is rather one of the sentimentalists' crucial beliefs: the supposed immediacy of response to the very 'sight' of distress. Even before knowing the circumstances, the heart is affected by the sheer spectacle or mere fact. This assumed immediacy of emotional response has a compelling implication for its literary representation: it encourages a comparable directness and literalism in presenting the distressful object. Accordingly, much sentimentalist fiction exploits precisely such a literalistic appeal to apparent fact, yet it proves to be fraught with pitfalls arising from its very immediacy. The dramatic treatment for which the sentimentalist beliefs seem to call has the effect of either exposing, or traducing, their spirit, and it was only by a more indirect understanding of emotional response as internalized in the imagination that the underlying intuition could eventually be fulfilled.

One problem, for example, that arises from this conception, when it is put in dramatic form, is that of presenting the immediacy of feeling as morally foundational. In fact, at this early, 'Shaftesburyan' moment in the tradition of sentiment, the Spectator is duly guarded about the ethical priority of the benevolent feeling. At the beginning of the paper he freely acknowledges the twin motives of self-interest and benevolence in human behaviour and towards the end he makes an equally important reservation:

the desire of doing Good . . . though Antecedent to Reason, may yet be improved and regulated by it, and, I will add, is no otherwise a Virtue than as it is so.

(*Spectator*, v, 13)

The phrase 'antecedent to Reason' casually combines a logical and a chronological meaning. Like Shaftesbury, the Spectator still sees feeling as supplementary to 'Reason' and he can therefore add quite innocently the very reservation which, in the authoritative voice of Immanuel Kant, was eventually to give sentimentalism its most decisive analytic dismissal. It is only in so far as feeling is regulated by reason that it *becomes* virtuous. For

Kant, writing after the excesses of sensibility into which the cult of sentiment was to descend, feeling needed to be isolated in an almost medical sense so as not to infect the ethical domain with a dangerous contagion. At the beginning of the century, however, before moral sense or feeling was separated from a traditional conception of reason, it seemed necessary to isolate it, in a celebratory sense, as a foundational motive. What is at stake is not just a personal psychology but a philosophical demonstration. And if the emotional response is to be isolated as a foundational motive, it may be hard to express this dramatically otherwise than as a literal coming first. In other words, within this Shaftesburyan model, the psychological priority of the emotional response is expressed as a literal priority in time. Hence the emphasis, in the literature of sentiment, on a leisured pausing over the moment of benevolent feeling.

One can see here the incipient logic of the internal contradictions which were to bedevil, and ultimately enrich, the evolution of sentimentalism. The appeal to experience rather than argument, and the primary importance of personality and mood, indicate why much of the burden of thinking through sentimentalism fell to literature, yet getting literature to do a philosophical job can create other problems. The analytic focus required to bring the point home to the reader produces a narrative self-consciousness which affects the underlying intuition. Translating a psychological idea into narrative or character terms may either distort it or reveal a contradiction at its heart. That is why much of the most significant critique of sentimentalism was to come not from external analytic attacks, such as Kant's, but from an immanent critique arising from the very attempt to give it imaginative realization. In the present instance, the desire to privilege the aspect of immediate feeling encourages a narrative lingering on the moment of response which may come over as self-indulgent and at the expense of the ostensible object of pity. Since this aspect has helped to discredit the whole project of sentimentalism it is worth recognizing that the problem does not necessarily lie with the underlying psychological intuition but with the philosophically driven need to separate out its elements. As a theory it does not entail the self-indulgence its dramatic rendering may imply.

The leisured lingering on feeling, therefore, points to a central crux of sentimentalism especially exposed by literary treatment: the question of 'complacency'. For the honorific use of the term 'Complacency', which the Spectator here attributes to the Deity, is a key to the structure of contemporary sentimentalism; and, as the subsequent steep decline in the meaning of the word implies, it also points to the aspect which is most remote from a modern comprehension. In modern usage 'complacency' is an even more damning charge than 'sentimentality'. Since we now have no term to indicate the legitimate moral satisfaction denoted by 'complacency' in the age of sentiment, and since the moral self-approval of the man of sentiment is the aspect by which he came to seem most obviously naive and questionable, it is particularly important to note its positive rationale, or indeed that it *had* a positive rationale. And the requirement of self-consciousness arises not just from the immediate literary/philosophical need but from the internal logic of sentimentalism as a crisis of articulation within a much larger cultural process.

If Shaftesbury raised a certain cultural formation into consciousness, then his emphasis on self-consciousness is of the essence. It was not enough that man should have a natural tendency to be social and benevolent. Like other natural faculties, this can atrophy if not exercised and an essential part of the exercise is the becoming aware of it. The awareness of one's own good feelings, and the appreciation of the feelings themselves as good, was just as vital, and as proper, as the appreciation of bodily health when practising a sport. Hence, where God may be permitted His 'Complacency', the man of sentiment is positively enjoined to exercise and appreciate the springs of benevolence within himself. Later in the same paper, the Spectator asks rhetorically, '. . . that charming Delight which immediately follows the giving of Joy to another, or relieving his Sorrow, . . . what can this be owing to but Consciousness of a Man's having done something Praise-worthy. . .?' And again, 'The Conscience of approving ones self a Benefactor to Mankind is the noblest Recompence for being so. . .' (*Spectator*, v, 13). These remarks express at the level of individual psychology the imperative of raising to consciousness which was an underlying historical dynamic of sentimentalism. But it will not readily translate into fiction without a damaging distortion of its spirit. Not surprisingly, these two aspects of sentimentalism, lingering on the moment of feeling and complacent self-consciousness, are the most notorious areas of weakness in the literature of sentiment. The problem is to determine to what extent this weakness reflects only a tactless fictional realization, or a falsity in the underlying idea, or admits of other, more creative, possibilities.

If the difficulty lies partly in a too-direct translation of an abstract conception into dramatic terms, it points to an unwitting significance in Groves's would-be patronizing ironic formula '..I always *imagined* that kind and benevolent Propensions. . .' (*Spectator*, v, 11, my emphasis). For the sentimentalist project, while partly basing itself, in a scientific spirit, on Locke's sensationalist psychology and contemporary physiological theory, was indeed heavily dependent, in both conscious and unconscious ways, on the imagination. It was, therefore, only as the internal complexities and constitutive function of the imagination came to be more appreciated that the sentimentalist response, both in literature and in life, acquired a more nuanced understanding. Addison's own series of *Spectator* papers on the 'Pleasures of the Imagination' was an important contribution to the upward movement of the imagination in the thought of the period.[24] He was one of the first to focus on the psychology of response to art, and anticipated much of the theory of the sublime. Nonetheless, his view of the imagination in the *Spectator* is still characteristically suspicious and delimited as is borne out by his opening declaration, in the first of the series on imagination, that he will use the terms 'Imagination' and 'Fancy' interchangeably, a sentence we cannot now read without recollecting the crucial significance Coleridge was to put into discriminating between them. In practice, Addison reflects common usage and already foreshadows Coleridge by tending to use 'imagination' for the positive and creative function while reserving 'fancy' for the more illusory or irresponsible effects, but his important assumption is that the one aspect inevitably involves the other and that imagination is to be closely disciplined by reality.

Locke's psychological model of the successive causal relations between 'impressions', 'ideas' and 'words' provides Addison with an explanatory model which can privilege the imagination without according it an excessive autonomy:

> Words, when well chosen, have so great a Force in them, that a Description often gives us more lively Ideas than the Sight of Things themselves. The Reader finds a Scene drawn in stronger Colours, and painted more to the Life in his Imagination, by the help of Words, than by an actual Survey of the Scene which they describe.
>
> (*Spectator*, iii, 560)

Since words are the index of ideas from impressions formed by the outside world, their proper power is an intense response to reality. And in like vein he goes on to argue that the poet can present more complex 'ideas' aroused by the scene than any one observer would be likely to take in from life. The poet, that is to say, is not adding to or changing the reality, but simply bringing out what would be there for an ideal observer. Addison indeed defines the ideal reader as follows:

> ... to have a true Relish, and form a right Judgment of a Description, a Man should be born with a good Imagination, and must have well weighed the Force and Energy that lie in the several Words of a

Language, so as to be able to distinguish which are most significant and expressive of their proper Ideas . . .

(Spectator, iii, 561)

A 'good imagination' for Addison implies verbal discipline and there is even a hint of resistance to mere fancy. A few lines later, for example, he remarks 'The Fancy must be warm, to retain the Print of those Images it hath received from outward Objects; and the Judgement discerning . . .' The merely receptive, potentially wayward, perhaps feminine, aspect of 'Fancy' is immediately counterbalanced by Judgement. The wax must be warm to take the impression but it must not, in another charged metaphor of the period, be melting; and the words, whose expressiveness is conceived atomistically in relation to their separate ideas, rather than collectively as modifying each other, cannot be allowed to merge in the spirit of what Coleridge would call the 'esemplastic' power.[25]

Addison's affirmation of the imagination, then, is not for its free creativity but for its responsiveness to reality. It is a vivid internalizing of external impressions as the basis for accurate and appropriate expression. Once again, this suggests why the literature of sentiment sought to arouse feeling in such a vulnerably direct and literalistic way. Even in fiction, one wants the impact of fact and Addison's repetition of the word 'Scene' reflects a significant ambiguity. In distinguishing the 'Scene' as described in 'stronger Colours' from 'an actual Survey of the Scene they describe', he distinguishes description from reality while using the same word for both. Tying words so closely to Lockean ideas and impressions, he allows for the fact of fiction while treating fiction as if it were fact. Similarly, sentimentalist writing typically seeks to move the reader by verbal heightening, as Addison acknowledges, even as the reader is supposed to be moved by the fact rather than the words. The rhetoric seeks to intensify the sense of fact rather than acknowledge the fiction and the *Spectator* papers constantly make use of real or fictitious occasions in which a sense of literal historicity is crucial to the response.

A common formula of the *Spectator* papers is to introduce an anecdote, or a letter from a correspondent, with an introductory suggestion of its proper emotional impact. The object is unchanged but the reader is prepared in advance to respond to it with a suitable emotional intensity. Hence these introductory comments amount to a theoretical definition of sentimentalist response. In his paper for 5 June, 1712, for example, Addison begins by affirming the value of compassion and disagreeing with the Stoic philosopher, Epictetus, who declared: 'If thou seest thy Friend in trouble . . . thou may'st put on a Look of Sorrow . . . but take care thy Sorrow be not real.' He then goes on to introduce Ann Boleyn's final letter from prison to Henry VIII with the following comments:

> Those who have laid down Rules for Rhetorick or Poetry, advise the Writer to work himself up, if possible, to the pitch of Sorrow which he endeavours to produce in others. There are none therefore who stir up Pity so much as those who indite their own Sufferings. Grief has a natural Eloquence belonging to it, and breaks out in more moving Sentiments than can be supplied by the finest Imagination. Nature on this occasion dictates a thousand Passionate things which cannot be supplied by Art.
>
> It is for this Reason that the short Speeches or Sentences which we often meet with in Histories, make a deeper Impression on the Mind of the Reader, than the most labour'd Strokes in a well written Tragedy. Truth and Matter of Fact sets the Person actually before us in the one, whom Fiction places at a greater distance from us in the other. I do not remember to have seen any Ancient or Modern Story more affecting than a Letter of *Ann of Bologne*, wife to King *Henry* the Eighth, and Mother to Queen *Elizabeth*, which is still extant in the *Cotton* Library, as written by her own Hand.
>
> *Shakespear* himself could not have made her talk in a Strain so suitable to her Condition and Character.
>
> (*Spectator*, iii, 486–7)

Addison's classical allusion suggests an ancient commonplace, and at a purely conceptual level he adds nothing to it. He nonetheless gives the familiar device a new inflection. In the incipient era of sentiment, the emphasis on 'affecting' the reader is attached to the immediacy of presence, the factual reality, of the distress. It is not just the claim that nature is more expressive than art so much as the underlying desire to believe that one is responding to the object itself, that we have 'the Person actually before us'.

Where Addison chooses a historical instance, Steele's paper for 10 March, 1712 introduces a letter from a distressed woman in the following way:

> It is often said, after a Man has heard a Story with extraordinary Circumstances, it is a very good one if it be true: But as for the following Relation, I should be glad were I sure it were false. It is told with such Simplicity, and there are so many artless Touches of Distress in it, that I fear it comes too much from the Heart.
>
> (*Spectator*, iii, 178)

Using a text of unknown provenance, Steele sharpens the implications of Addison's remarks. He begins by acknowledging that if the story were only a fiction it would not be remarkable, merely a blandly conventional narrative of distress. Hence his need to prepare the reader by insinuating its literal veracity. Yet although its factual reality is what justifies the response, this is only deducible from the qualities of the text itself, which is essentially what Addison was saying of his historical example. Although our encounter in both cases is with a text, it is assumed that, in some significant degree, what moves us is the very fact of the distress unmediated by art.

There is, then, a contradictory dynamic at the heart of sentimentalist fiction. The concentration on self-consciousness and intensity of feeling requires an overt rhetoric while the belief in immediacy requires a transparent access to the object. When Francis Hutcheson expounded in 1725 his notion of the 'moral sense' as a separate, innate faculty, he implied an immediate link between feeling and ethics, and thereby underwrote the literalistic psychology of sentimentalist fiction seen in these examples from the *Spectator*. Furthermore, since the notion of moral sense was entirely hypothetical it provided a blanket explanation which was likely to block closer examination, rather as in later physical theory belief in the 'ether' long prevented the right scientific questions being asked. The fictional mode and the assumed psychology were mutually reinforcing. Yet the self-fulfilling circularity of the ethical and literary psychology of sentiment suffered, as has been seen, from internal instability in both domains. The verisimilar presentation of distress could not enforce an appropriate response from Lovelace to Clarissa and the sentimental ideology itself, with its unstable merging of feeling and principle, focused the broader vulnerability of Deism. Even as it sought to supplement rational principle and theological authority it was uncomfortably close to a mere materialism. Not surprisingly, therefore, both the notion of moral sense and the literalistic response to fiction were subjected to closer scrutiny and increasingly gave way to more complex and indirect models.

Scepticism and sympathy: David Hume

David Hume, although influenced by Hutcheson, privileged sentiment from a different angle within his larger philosophical concern and dislodged the simpler model of moral sense. More intent on dispelling the illusions of reason, including its traditional claims in the ethical realm, Hume's philosophical scepticism led him to emphasize the realm of feeling not as the best, but as the only, basis for the moral life. His views are difficult to summarize since his arguments in the early *Treatise of Human Nature* (1736) were considerably changed in the later *Enquiries Concerning Human Understanding* (1748) and *The Principles of Morals* (1751). Moreover, the *Treatise*, although it is a less tidy work, proceeding in a digressive, partly exploratory, way and developing its arguments and reservations almost parenthetically at times, includes some of his bolder and more productive thought on sentiment. It also expresses a view which remained central to his thinking:

> Morality ... is more properly felt than judg'd of; tho' this feeling or sentiment is commonly so soft and gentle, that we are apt to confound it with an idea.
>
> > (*Treatise*, 470)

and again:

> To have a sense of virtue, is nothing but to *feel* a satisfaction of a particular kind from the contemplation of a character. The very *feeling* constitutes our praise or admiration. We can go no further...
>
> > (ibid., 471)

Yet Hume is hardly an enthusiast for sentiment. His scepticism applies not just to reason but to the realm of feeling too in so far as it claims to be the basis of the moral life. Hence in the *Treatise* he seeks to explain ethical feeling not in terms of a special faculty, a Hutchesonian moral sense, which precisely because it acts directly cannot be examined, but rather through the working of sympathy, a more oblique process whereby the subjectivity of another being is inferentially reconstructed in the imagination.

> To discover the true origin of morals .. we must compare some principles which have already been examined and explained.
>
> We may begin with considering a-new the nature and force of *sympathy*. The minds of all men are similar in their feelings and operations, nor can any one be actuated by any affection, of which all others are not, in some degree, susceptible. As in strings equally wound-up, the motion of one communicates itself to the rest; so all the affections readily pass from one person to another, and beget correspondent movements in every human creature. When I see the *effects* of passion in the voice and gesture of any person, my mind

immediately passes from these effects to their causes, and forms such a lively idea of the passion, as is presently converted into the passion itself. ... No passion of another discovers itself immediately to the mind. We are only sensible of its causes or effects. From *these* we infer the passion: and consequently *these* give rise to our sympathy.

(ibid., 575–6)

Although Hume's philosophical scepticism entailed the unknowability of another's subjectivity through any direct apprehension, in the ethical sphere he rightly recognizes that some general similarity of constitution has to be assumed for a relevant subjectivity to be in question at all. Where there is no commonality of being there is no ethical problem in the first place. But while it is clear that the emotional identification with the other is only by inference, the process is ambiguous in its detailed working. His physical image of the wound-up strings, which has lurking behind it in turn contemporary physiological theories, suggests an involuntary process almost of contagion. This would reinforce the sense of sensibility as an immediate, unreflected response to the very sight as in the 'moral sense' conception. And even as Hume gives it an ostensibly different inflection by insisting that these effects are reconstructed in the mind, the outcome is to form 'such a lively idea of the passion as is presently converted into the passion itself'. But instead of claiming that the idea is converted into 'the passion itself' Hume might better have recollected his philosophical scepticism about all perceptions. For strictly speaking, the observer's 'idea' can be converted only into a reconstructed equivalent passion which may or may not coincide with the original.

In fact, Hume goes on to stress the importance of imagination in this inferential process in a way which might seem to direct it away from a one-for-one reproduction of the original, and might even warrant thinking of the sympathetic reconstruction as a species of fiction, but his notion of imagination, like Addison's, still assumes impressions and ideas binding it to the external world. Accordingly, he goes on to remark:

'Tis certain that the imagination is more affected by what is particular, than by what is general; and that the sentiments are always mov'd with difficulty, where the objects are, in any degree, loose and undeter-min'd.

(ibid., 580)

This is in keeping with the sense of imagination as an immediate response to reality and therefore to specific occasions of compassion but, as Hume realizes, this in turn raises problems for the impersonal dimension of justice. For, whereas feeling is aroused by what is to hand, the demands of justice, which are also emotionally motivated, involve giving equal moral weight to persons entirely unknown to us. That suggests limits to sympathy as an ethical motivation. He, therefore, distinguishes 'sentiments' and 'imagination':

> Sentiments must touch the heart, to make them controul our passions: But they need not extend beyond the imagination, to make them influence our taste... The imagination adheres to the *general* views of things, and distinguishes betwixt the feelings they produce, and those which arise from our particular and momentary situation.
>
> (ibid., 586–7)

Here he rather reverses his earlier emphasis linking the sympathetic imagination to the particular object and suggests that moral sympathy, by means of imagination, must extend beyond what can be explained by the immediacy of a distressful occasion.

The digression which has brought him to this last conclusion has in fact stressed the limits of sympathy by anticipating an objection to his sympathy-based system:

> ... we give the same approbation to the same moral qualities in *China* as in *England*. They appear equally virtuous, and recommend themselves equally to the esteem of a judicious spectator. The sympathy varies without a variation in our esteem. Our esteem, therefore, proceeds not from sympathy.
>
> (ibid., 581)

He answers this objection by accepting the psychological fact that sympathy is stronger for those close to us but, since our emotional subjectivity is so shifting and unstable, he claims:

> ... we fix on some *steady* and *general* points of view, and always, in our thoughts, place ourselves in them, whatever may be our present situation.
>
> (ibid., 581–2).

This may seem to bring us back to a traditional ethic based on general social and rational principles but Hume has already inverted the derivation of these. The principles are themselves now derived from sympathy even if in practice our immediate sympathies remain in traditional conflict with 'reason':

> Here we are contented with saying, that reason requires an impartial conduct, but that 'tis seldom we can bring ourselves to it, and that our passions do not readily follow the determination of our judgement. This language will be easily understood, if we consider what we formerly said concerning that *reason*, which is able to oppose our passion; and which we have found to be nothing but a general calm determination of the passions, founded on some distant view or reflexion.
>
> (ibid., 583)

The outcome is that Hume's deconstruction of the claims of reason shifts the basis of the ethical life onto the affective realm, since 'reason' itself is now understood as only a given mode of feeling. At the same time, the feeling has to pass through the indirection of this reconstructive model of sympathy and adopt an emotionally distanced vantage-point. His reference to a 'judicious spectator', and his emphasis on achieving emotional distance, temper any enthusiasm for feeling as a simple motive and criterion of ethical life. This more complex argument, advancing a sympathy-based ethic while alert to its problems, was the element that largely disappeared in the later *Enquiry Concerning the Principles of Morals* as Hume moved closer to a moral-sense conception of sentiment and it was Adam Smith who was to develop this line of thought in one of the period's most summative and magisterial treatments of moral sentiment: *The Theory of Moral Sentiments* (1759).

Sympathy as fiction: Adam Smith and Lord Kames

Smith was a friend and admirer of Hume as well as a successor to the Chair of Moral Philosophy at the University of Glasgow once held by Francis Hutcheson. His strategic contribution to the theory of sentiment was to develop the notions of 'sympathy' and of the 'impartial Spectator' with a different inflection from Hume's use of seemingly similar terms. Part of the difference was that, whereas Hume's detached viewpoint was a corrective to the immediate workings of sympathy, Smith's two corresponding conceptions came closer to being aspects of the same function. Smith posed two great, opposite motives of human behaviour: the instinct of self-preservation, and therefore a measure of self-love, was as primary and legitimate as the motive of benevolence. There was a constant conflict of interest, therefore, that made feeling as such no adequate criterion or motive. Hence the importance of the 'impartial Spectator' whom Smith posed as the internal monitor of the ethical life. Ethical judgements were a matter of imagining how a disinterested observer would view the case. Sympathy likewise took on a more neutral implication. For Smith, sympathy was the capacity to reconstruct imaginatively the inner state of another person irrespective of what that state might be. It applies to vicious and happy states as much as to virtuous or painful ones. Furthermore, if sympathy is an exercise of the imagination, it is not just a means of reconstructing the subjective states of others; it is equally necessary in creating the viewpoint of the impartial observer within the self, and even creating oneself as the object of such observation.

Smith, who formed his view before the excesses of sensibility in the latter decades of the century, absorbed the strongest currents of sentimental ethics and was able, from his new vantage-point, to dismiss rather more cogently the earlier views that everything comes down either to Hutchesonian compassion or Hobbesian self-love. On the latter he was particularly scathing. Since he freely admitted self-love as a legitimate motive, his conception of sympathy was more readily defensible from the charge of being merely a secret form of it.

> Sympathy ... cannot, in any sense, be regarded as a selfish principle. ...though sympathy is very properly said to arise from an imaginary change of situations with the person principally concerned, yet this imaginary change is not supposed to happen to me in my own person and character, but in that of the person with whom I sympathize. My grief ... is entirely upon your account, and not in the least upon my own. .... A man may sympathize with a woman in child-bed; though it is impossible that he should conceive himself as suffering her pains in his own proper person ... That whole account of human nature ... which deduces all sentiments and affections from self-love ... seems to me to have arisen from some confused misapprehension of the system of sympathy.[26]

In Smith, sympathy shifts its centre of gravity. It is less a movement of individual feeling and rather an imagined arena in which the subjectivities of all human others, and of the self, are reconstructed in a manner which has to be both emotional and judgemental at once. The compelling analogy is with the novel.

The analogy with fiction is reinforced by a corresponding aspect of Smith's conception which can be highlighted through comparison with

Kant's *Critique of Practical Reason*: the other single great treatise on ethics produced in the period. Smith's 'impartial Spectator' is the equivalent function to Kant's 'categorical imperative' that you should always act in such a way that you could wish your action to be made into a universal principle. Both are a means of transcending the merely subjective or emotional viewpoint yet they have quite different purposes. Kant's transcendental philosophy sought to define the nature of the ethical as such whereas Smith was more concerned with the practical principles and workings of the moral life. Hence Kant states his position *as* a universal principle, and speaks as if a universal principle could be located within any moral action. Smith, by contrast, denies that general moral principles are of much use in the practical occasions that constitute the moral life.

> The general rules of almost all the virtues, the general rules which determine what are the offices of prudence, of charity, of generosity, of gratitude, of friendship, are in many respects loose and inaccurate, admit of many exceptions, and require so many modifications, that it is scarce possible to regulate our conduct by a regard to them.
>
> (*TMS*, 174)

There is a difficulty in referring synoptically to Kantian ethics as he produced three major treatments of the subject: *Grounding for the Metaphysics of Morals* (1785), *The Critique of Practical Reason* (1788) and *The Metaphysics of Morals* (1797). While the third, which could have removed some common misconceptions, was published late in life, the earlier ones established a view of Kant's inflexible formalism which has persisted to the late twentieth century. The first treatises defined the transcendental conditions of possibility for the ethical as such, while the *Metaphysics of Morals* was concerned with practical application in a way that would dissolve some of the sharp contrast with Smith.[27] For present purposes, however, the historically perceived Kant is the most relevant and the difference between the traditions they embodied emerges sharply in two testing examples. Kant argued that the principle of telling the truth must apply even in the case of an intending murderer who comes to your house and asks if his victim is there. The interest of truth must be upheld, Kant says, even at the cost of revealing the victim's presence. Kant's austere formalism has always struck readers as both admirable and appalling but he stuck to his guns and was scathing in his dismissal of Benjamin Constant's objection that the murderer has no right to expect a truthful answer.[28] Smith, on the other hand, imagines the situation of a traveller who promises to pay a highwayman a sum after being released. Opinions on the matter will vary, he says, from those who would deny any obligation to those who would see it as dishonourable to break the promise but, in fact, most observers would lean to one side or the other according to the circumstances (*TMS*, 331–2). If the sum was very large, and would constitute a serious loss to the individual and his dependents, then it would generally be considered an extravagant gesture to pay it. If, on the other hand, it could be easily paid, then there would be some meanness in not doing so. At the same time, Smith says, whatever the circumstances there would always be a measure of shame in not paying. To that extent he acknowledges the force of Kant's point: all derogation from truth is damaging and shameful even when circumstantially justified.

The problem with the Kantian position from the Adam Smith point of view is its apparent assumption that all moral occasions are to be understood in the light of a single principle, or at least do not involve conflicting principles. Unfortunately the moral life is largely made up of conflicts of precisely that kind which both these imaginary situations exemplify. Where Kant sees only the principle of truth at stake in his example of the murderer, we may see the more urgent principle of protecting the weak and innocent. Indeed, from Smith's point of view, the very word 'principle', in Kant's sense, would be misleading here. Just as Hume saw 'reason' as being, when closely examined, only a certain phase of feeling, so 'principle', rather than denoting an *a priori* and universal requirement, would mean the summary statement of a given weight of consideration with its limitation built in. It is the very act of weighing, of judging how much, which Kant's commitment to absolute principle prevents him from doing. Without naively espousing feeling, Smith significantly diffuses the notion of 'principle'. It may be that the traditional dualism of feeling and principle gave a specious clarity to the latter, and as the dualism is dissolved in the figure of the internalized spectator, so the internal instabilities of principle itself become apparent. Smith is explicit that, as far as moral conduct and judgements are concerned, there is no recourse but to consider circumstances as fully as possible in the light of goodwill, past experience, and the likely outcome. By the same token, while benevolent sentiment will often provide the motive for action, it cannot provide guidance; this arises from a larger view of present and past circumstances, which means in turn that the novelistic imagination implied in Smith's conception of sympathy also has to take on the totality, or holism, that increasingly characterized the novel form.

Smith's impartial spectator, situated within the head, suggests a historical specificity in the novelistic parallel. For his ambiguous posture between inner and outer, as a kind of internal theatre, is more precisely an image of how eighteenth-century fiction internalized the forms of theatre. The larger shift by which the novel became the dominant form in the nineteenth century was not simply by replacing theatre but by internalizing it. In eighteenth-century fiction the psyche is constantly conceived as a stage, a publicly observable arena, so that even where it is intensely private it can be imaged, as by Richardson's heroines, as open to scrutiny. Theatre was part of a world of public meanings: executions, social status defined by costume, etc. The internalizing shift is initially a reflection of that world of public values within the individual. In the first instance, it is anti-subjective. Gradually, however, the meaning of this structure would be reversed as the outer world would increasingly be significant only *as* it is internalized by the individual. From being a microcosmic arena replicating the outer world in a one-for-one imaginative reflection, the inner world would itself become a standard of judgement.

For the purposes of a philosophical understanding of ethics, Smith's impartial spectator solved no substantive problems. The underlying motives of the moral life remain mysterious and all theories which seek to rationalize this have an irremovable circularity. Its merit is to know this and as a way of imaging the intrinsic proportions of the moral life, the internalized responsibility that is required as theological sanctions and rational principles cease to provide the assumed support, it is compellingly true to its moment. Most importantly, it gave a new inflection to existing ideas by its constant recourse to imaginative examples bristling with aesthetic implication. Within this, the central figure of the Spectator, with such deep roots in the century's attempts to understand ethical life in social terms, becomes the focus of an internal fiction in which the imagination plays a constitutive part.

If Smith's theory is finely balanced between inner and outer and depends on an imaginative transposition of sentiment, the literary implications of this shift can be seen more clearly in Henry Home, Lord Kames's, *Elements of Criticism* (1762). Kames, another aristocrat, whose work is dedicated to the new king, George III, is squarely in the tradition of Shaftesbury. He makes the same assumption that taste and feeling, whether in art or in ethics, are socially educated, and a desire for order and rank is assumed to be innate: 'we are framed by nature to relish order and connection.'[29] But Kames, like Smith, sought to understand the workings of feeling and taste in a more practical and 'scientific' manner. His claim was that 'the fine arts, like morals, [could] become a rational science; and, like morals, may be cultivated to a high degree of refinement' (*Elements*, i, 8), and the work includes a great deal of what we might now call practical criticism. On the one hand, therefore, Kames believed in the innate and immediate response: 'Such is the constitution of our nature, that upon perceiving certain external objects, we are instantaneously conscious of pleasure or pain' (ibid. 47), and did so in a way that might well reinforce the assumed immediacy of sentiment and the corresponding literalism of response to fiction. He was also open to the running together of fiction and actuality that so frequently characterized sentimentalism: 'if, in reading, ideal presence be the means by which our passions are moved, it makes no difference whether the subject be fable or reality' (ibid., 114). But his desire to understand the more detailed workings of fiction led him, in the most original part of his argument, to define the response to fiction more closely as fiction. In this respect, his phrase 'ideal presence' was a careful balance between immediacy of the response and the imaginative status of the object.

He retains the sentimentalist assumption that 'it is present distress only that moves my pity' (ibid., 115) and that this impact will be weakened if the occasion is known to be fictional. Yet he also believed that literal fact was not the crucial element but rather a reality effect, and hence the parity of emphasis in the phrase '*ideal* presence'. As with Addison on Ann Boleyn, he argued that even history impresses us only by its similarity to fiction. But the object is now more internalized. With an incipient hint of Proust, he suggested that emotional memories conjure up past occasions with exceptional vividness, so that we lose our sense of their pastness in an imaginary present. Fiction capitalizes on this psychological proclivity and, as 'ideal presence', it is a compelling but fragile mode which must not collapse into being perceived too simply as either fact or as fiction. So too, while he was typical of his time in believing that 'Of all the means for making an impression of ideal presence, theatrical representation is the most powerful' (ibid., 116), he disapproved of elaborate stage machinery, on grounds similar to Diderot's arguments for a new bourgeois 'serious' drama, that 'Fictions of this kind ... never move the sympathetic passions, because they cannot impose on the mind any perception of reality' (ibid., 125). A reality effect, rather than literal historicity or present fact, was the vital point. He begins thereby to define a positive meaning for fiction as such which escapes the circularity of the 'seen' and the 'scene' in the *Spectator* passages.

Kames also suggested a less literalistic conception of literature's moral effect by linking the ideality of fiction to a more nuanced account of moral psychology. He distinguished 'passion' from 'emotion' by defining passion as an emotion with a specific object and he laid it down 'as a general law of nature, that every passion ceases upon attaining its ultimate end' (ibid., 148) But in so far as emotion can be experienced *per se*, without an immediate object, it constitutes a 'curious piece of mechanism in the nature of man' such that a work of literature could produce 'a desire to perform acts of gratitude, without having any particular object' (ibid., 71). On this argument, 'Virtuous emotions of this sort, are in some degree an exercise in virtue' (ibid., 75). Furthermore, their ideality creates a kind of vacuum in reality. Sympathy is an imaginative and emotional identification with another which, as Shaftesbury had argued, is a source of pleasure in itself, but that does not make the distress as such enjoyable. On the contrary, it creates a conflict of enjoyment and distress and therefore the need to alleviate the condition: 'Mutual support, the shining attribute of society, being essential to the well-being of man, is not left upon reason, but is inforced even instinctively by the passion of sympathy' (*Elements*, ii, 143). In this way, Kames, like Adam Smith, kept faith with the underlying impulse of sentimentalism while transposing it into a less literalistic understanding of its psychological premises and of the moral impact of fiction.

Individual feeling versus social reason: Jeremy Bentham

Kames, like Smith, formed his views before the lurch into 'sensibility' which began in the 1760s with *La Nouvelle Héloïse* and Sterne's *A Sentimental Journey*. After the delicate balance between feeling and principle in the mid-century use of the term 'sentiment', feeling was privileged at the expense of social reason. For some observers, then and now, this development was the natural outcome of sentiment. John Mullan has argued the damagingly private nature of the sentimentalist conception of virtue *per se* and revives the view that Smith's *Wealth of Nations* (1776) is a corrective to the *Theory of Moral Sentiments* in that the later work shows the benign effects of the social economy bypassing, and thereby rendering inconsequential, personal motives such as benevolence.[30] Yet Smith brought out five revised editions of the *Theory* over the period. It seems that for him his study of personal ethics was not discounted but complemented by that of the larger social process since the two scales involve different orders of question. The supposed contradiction between the two works is rather a confusion of orders. Even if a selfish pursuit of commercial interests had a socially beneficent effect, that would not change the moral status of selfishness as such.

Nonetheless, the 'Adam Smith problem', real or imaginary, points to an important historical shift. As modern society developed it became increasingly apparent that social questions could not be dealt with in simply personal terms, such as benevolence to the deserving in distress, or by conceiving of the poor as a god-given estate for the reception of charity. A comparable duality of orders is suggested by Smith within the *Theory* itself when, having affirmed the circumstantial nature of most moral decisions which renders them unsuitable to general rules, he then emphasizes the need to follow precisely such rules in matters of justice, including economic relations such as borrowing money. He presents these different orders of consideration as a matter of degree which, at a certain point, becomes a difference in kind, without either order denying the validity of the other. The role of sentiment in personal relations, and as a motive to the ethical, is not undermined by this even if, tragically, it cannot be simply transposed onto the social scale. If the order of personal ethics is both inseparable from, and yet incommensurable with, the political and social orders, this is not so much a theoretical problem as a predicament of modernity. It is no adverse reflection, therefore, on Smith that his two major theses collectively express, rather than resolve, this divide.

The increasing recognition of this predicament has consequences both for the novel as a form seeking to encompass an overall understanding of society and for the efficacy of moral sentiment. On the one hand, the novel, like the tradition of sentiment, could continue to see individual feeling as primordial and seek to accord it the general value of example or efficacy. But contemporaneously with the later editions of Smith's *Theory*, a different conception was being developed. While sentimentalism is the effective ancestor of much modern ethical discourse on the personal plane, the last two decades of the eighteenth century saw the creation of the other major, complementary aspect of modern ethical thought on the social scale: the utilitarian principle of the greatest benefit, or happiness, for the greatest number. It is worth noting how this radical alternative to the sentimental tradition is a curious mirror image of it, and, as Charles Taylor points out, is partly dependent on it.[31] Jochen Barkhausen goes further in seeing them as two aspects of the same tradition.[32]

Their ambivalent relation is significant and permanent. Utilitarian principle still governs most thinking about legislation just as feeling is the common basis of personal ethical relations. Yet both are usually implicit, and where they are obliged to become self-conscious are often disavowed. Educated citizens of the twentieth century rarely define themselves as either sentimentalist or utilitarian *tout court*, although few, when subjected to objective analysis, would escape these descriptions. Even many who view themselves as religious actually live in this composite humanist formation. Sentimentalism and utilitarianism share an almost instinctive ill-repute although, by the continuing logic of supplementarity, the way of avoiding the one is usually by shifting momentarily to the other so that the general degree of dependence on both remains undetected. In view of this complementarity, it is highly suggestive that, just as the evolving tradition of moral sentiment was inextricably involved with changing conceptions of fiction, so Bentham placed at the heart of his thinking on jurisprudence a theory of fictions. Although he did not actually write his *Theory of Fictions* until 1813–15, he meditated on this theme from 1780 as a part of his larger argument. Bentham, of course, used the term 'fiction' in a diagnostic and depreciatory sense quite remote from the novelistic, yet his preoccupation with it parallels the fictional transformations of sentiment.

Bentham believed that philosophical errors arise from mistakes about words, and assumed that all words must correspond to existing entities. With a Lockean ambition of precision, he sought to identify terms whose meanings, although indispensible, were fictitious, such as, in one of his own recurrent examples, the word 'motion'. We might prefer to regard this rather as an abstraction than a fiction but there was clearly something at stake for Bentham and I will return to this example in relation to Wordsworth for whom 'motion' was likewise a crucial term. Bentham's Preface to *An Introduction to the Principles of Morals and Legislation* (1789) indicates the danger he saw in fictitious entities. The truths at the basis of political and moral science

> ... will not compress themselves into epigrams. They recoil from the tongue and the pen of the declaimer. They flourish not in the same soil with sentiment.[33]

As an early social scientist, insisting on scientific criteria in the study of society, Bentham sees fictitious entities as the point through which sentiment, and therefore implicit, uncritical judgements, can enter. He gives the example of the term 'purity' whose simply technical meaning of 'unmixed' is likely to be overwhelmed by a moral judgement arising from common usage. Bentham's disturbed recognition that even the most scientific language has to use fictitious entities, and is therefore porous to inappropriate incursions of sentiment, reflects the way sensibility was being questioned as part of a larger choice of myths by which society is to be understood and its ethics grounded. Instead of reason and feeling being competing or supplementary elements within an overall model of the self that still assumed a broad cultural assent, in the 1790s 'Reason' and 'Sensibility' became polarized into rival political myths. The figure who most illuminates the resulting conflict was Mary Wollstonecraft.

Mary Wollstonecraft and the politics of sensibility

By the 1790s the unstable synthesis of sentiment had given way to a polar contrast between sensibility and social reason, a culture war which was then sharpened by divided political reactions to the French Revolution. Reason, in the figures particularly of William Godwin and Thomas Paine, came to be associated with the radical cause while sensibility, especially in Burke's *Reflections on the Late Revolution in France* (1790), was thought of as conservative. These terms had no necessary political alignment, as Chris Jones has shown in his tracing of 'radical sensibility' in the 1790s, but once established the identification took on a cultural reality and, as a number of critics have noticed, Mary Wollstonecraft embodied the resulting conflict both in her life and in her writing.[34] She suffered the conflict damagingly but, in *A Vindication of the Rights of Woman* (1792), she turned it into a source of ideological understanding.

Her first substantial work, *Mary, a Fiction* (1788), was a novel of sensibility aimed against the contemporary conception of marriage. The newly married heroine, living for a long period apart from her unsuitable husband, meets her true soulmate in an appreciative man of sensibility who dies. Wollstonecraft's last work, the unfinished and posthumous *Maria, or the Wrongs of Woman* (1798), is similarly a critique of marriage from the standpoint of a heroine of sensibility. These novels reflect Mary Wollstonecraft's own life as a strong-minded and courageous heroine of sensibility. Like Rousseau, she enacted in herself, and in a publicly representative way, the cultural contradictions which others avoided by leaving them unconscious or keeping them private. William Godwin's *Memoirs of Wollstonecraft* (1798), published after her death, presented her to the public as a heroine of sensibility but drew much criticism, both of her for her improper conduct in formerly cohabiting with Gilbert Imlay and bearing his child, and of Godwin himself for exposing his deceased wife's behaviour. Godwin's purpose, as the grief-stricken widower of a maligned public figure, was not to present an apologia, but to give a frank account to which fair-minded readers would respond with a measure of respect and sympathy. She was largely denied this response just as her heroine is denied it in the sketched ending of *Maria* when the judge to whom she pleads her case disallows it on the general grounds that female pathos is no basis for legal judgement. There is a teasing symmetry between her novels, the first of which uses her own name in its title while specifying a fictional status, and Godwin's account of her life, and one might speculate whether, if the substantive narrative of the *Memoirs* had been recounted in the form of a novel, readers who were censorious of the real woman might have been sympathetic to the inner integrity and pain of a fictional heroine, much as Werther's illegitimate love for his friend Albert's fiancée could be read, as a fiction, under the sign of tragically doomed passion rather than immoral behaviour. But this thought experiment really points to a more essential problem.

Godwin describes Wollstonecraft, towards the end of the *Memoirs*, as a 'female Werter' which, in the gendered context of sensibility, is a richly ironic formulation.[35] Werther, as a man of feeling, has the self-destructive weakness of the feminized man; he has abnegated social virility and resents Albert's exercising of responsible authority. Wollstonecraft reversed this: instead of killing herself for love, which she nearly did on two occasions, she lived out her sensibility with demonstrative courage. The phrase 'female Werter', therefore, in her case, means not a doubling of the supposed weakness of sensibility but living it as an exercise of, or challenge to, 'male' authority. And the phrase has already been prepared for by Godwin's describing Mary's first meeting with her friend Fanny Blood as like that of Werther and Lotte, so that Mary is already constructed as the male, and in their subsequent relationship Godwin brings out the tough-minded and affirmative outlook of Mary in supporting the more sterotypically female weakness of Fanny. But there is the rub. The heroine of sensibility is essentially passive, not in terms of courage, principle, intelligence and feeling, but in terms of social power. In this respect, Mary was the opposite of a Werther, a reversal of the man of feeling. Mary's strength, her true self, was in her feeling for which sensibility provided the contemporary model and discourse. Yet the exercise of her strength was undercut by its perception as sensibility, and as female.

In her first treatise, *A Vindication of the Rights of Men* (1790), written in opposition to Edmund Burke's *Reflections*, this conflict comes out more symptomatically than otherwise. She attacks Burke for his sensibility and offers herself in contrast as the voice of reason. Yet it is the affectation of sensibility, rather than feeling itself, which she criticizes in him while her own criteria are hardly rationalist. When she asks rhetorically if Burke's is 'the language of the heart', she is invoking a criterion of genuine feeling yet it is hard to identify positively what true feeling is and it would have been tactically unwise for her to acknowledge it as her own basis (*VRM*,

38). For if that were the basis of her argument, there would be no authoritative standpoint, comparable to that traditionally accorded to reason, and her position would have all the weakness of the conventionally female. On the same principle that sees the Jewish commitment to reason as the strategic response to anti-Semitism, she needed to keep up the claim of an impersonal reason opposing the political weathervane of Burke's supposed sensibility. In the event, although Gary Kelly has gallantly suggested that her manner is feeling its way towards a different style of argument, her treatise comes over as something of a tirade beside which Burke's seems the more reasoned.[36] But when it came to her second, and more major, treatise she turned the gendered conflict of sensibility to account by understanding it *as* a cultural and discursive formation.

In *A Vindication of the Rights of Woman* (1792) her chosen object of attack was Rousseau who provided her with a more self-reflective locus of cultural contradiction. Whereas she had felt personally opposed to Burke, in the case of Rousseau, whom she admired and identified with, she could experience their area of disagreement, the nature, education and social role of women, in its deeper contradictoriness.

> But all Rousseau's errors in reasoning arose from his sensibility, and sensibility to their charms women are very ready to forgive. When he should have reasoned he became impassioned, and reflection inflamed his imagination instead of enlightening his understanding. Even his virtues also led him further astray; for, born with a warm constitution and lively fancy, nature carried him toward the other sex with such eager fondness that he soon became lascivious. Had he given way to these desires, the fire would have extinguished itself in a natural manner, but virtue, and a romantic kind of delicacy, made him practise self-denial; yet when fear, delicacy or virtue restrained him, he debauched his imagination, and reflecting on the sensations to which fancy gave force, he traced them in the most glowing colours, and sunk them deep into his soul.[37]

She sees Rousseau, as man of sentiment, experiencing a conflict of sensibility which is, in some respects, a mirror image of her own although without the analytic grasp that his case perhaps helped her to achieve. She sees the secret collusion by which the principle of virtuous restraint in him served to inflame the feeling. She seems also to detect that his idealization of woman as 'other', enshrined in the different education of Sophie from Émile, is not just an accidental element of conservatism falling outside the progressive thrust of this thought, but is actually essential to it. Male and female are the gendered dualism, of social reason versus feeling, on which the internal energy of the system depends. This is partly disguised in *La Nouvelle Héloïse* by the fact that St Preux is a man of feeling and Julie a woman of principle, but both the lovers enact this dualism within themselves as well as being mutually subjected to the social reason of M. de Volmar and Julie's father. The outcome is that Wollstonecraft has understood what would now be called the ideological construction of 'woman', and especially as this is intensified in the myth of sensibility.

The nub of the matter for her is to deny 'the existence of sexual virtue', that is to say any virtue exclusively appropriate for one sex (*VRW*, p. 140). Having seen the constructed and relative nature of supposedly impersonal principle, she attacks Adam Smith's conception of the impartial spectator:

> ... it is not sufficient to view ourselves as we suppose that we are viewed by others, though this has been ingeniously argued, as the foundation of our moral sentiments. Because each by-stander may have his own prejudices, besides the prejudices of his age or country.
>
> (*VRW*, 250)

And her alternative, like Rousseau's, is a radically protestant appeal to the omniscient eye of God modulated into a metaphor for intensely secular, individual conscience.

> We should rather endeavour to view ourselves as we suppose that Being views us who seeth each thought ripen into action, and whose judgement never swerves from the eternal rule of right.
>
> (*VRW*, 250)

In many ways, Wollstonecraft is a descendant of Clarissa who could also have expressed this sentiment. She likewise wishes to protect her integrity from a false authority before which she is vulnerable specifically as a woman. But the ground has shifted beneath the argument. Clarissa sought by exemplary behaviour, and the exercise of personal authority in language, to hold the social community up to its proper self against the licentious philosophy of Lovelace and the greed of her family. Its falseness in the given instance was personal and adventitious, it lay in the cupidity and ambition of her family, and she therefore submitted to paternal authority despite her legal right, as her uncle's heiress, to assume her fortune and be independent. Her tragic endeavour was to maintain the criterion of personal feeling and sincerity within the order of social principle.

In effect, Wollstonecraft, in Godwin's account, accords with mid-century sentiment by combining feeling with principle, and allowing neither the downward collapse into sensibility nor the reification of reason. Yet her mode of internal unity reverses this, as Godwin bemusedly recognizes. He concludes his *Memoirs* by reflecting on this quality in her from which he himself had learned the limitation of his own long-standing 'attempt at logical and metaphysical distinction' (*Memoirs*, 195).

> The strength of her mind lay in intuition. She was often right, by this means only, in matters of mere speculation. Her religion, her philosophy ... were ... the result of feeling and taste. She adopted one opinion and rejected another, spontaneously, by a sort of tact, and the force of a cultivated imagination; and yet, though perhaps, in the strict sense of the term, she reasoned little, it is surprising what a degree of soundness is to be found in her determinations.
>
> (*VRW*, 197)

This recalls Rousseau's account of Mme de Warens whose heart was so pure and tactful that, even when the disingenuous casuistry of her philosophy tutor misled her at the level of principle, her behaviour was still essentially right because of the quality of feeling which motivated it.[38] But Wollstone-craft trusted her own heart and was not confused by the spurious authority of 'reason' as a supposedly separable principle. Although her temperament is completely different, Godwin's description essentially corresponds to what Friedrich Schiller, Mary's coeval, defined as the 'beautiful soul', one in whom principle is in complete harmony with feeling.[39] Schiller saw this model as peculiarly female and the gendering of reason and feeling is still evident in the residual touch of condescension in Godwin's loving acknowledgement. It is hard to say whether this reflects a continuing emotional ambivalence on Godwin's part or that his conceptualization continues to lag behind his own intuition as well as hers.

As it happens, Schiller provided, in his conception of the 'aesthetic', one of the most significant resolutions of the sentimentalist dilemma, the cogency of which is not generally recognized even today. His continuing pertinence emerges by placing him more fully in his historical context and most especially in contrast to the literalism of the eighteenth-century literature of moral sentiment but it is helpful to look first at how, along with the philosophical debate, much of the important 'thinking' about sentiment was done within the fiction itself.

2
Feeling and/as Fiction: Illusion, Absorption and Emotional Quixotry

The preceding survey of the eighteenth-century debate suggests fiction was more intrinsically related to sentiment than being merely its vehicle. As the theories of sympathy increasingly defined it as a response to imagined objects so it took on the character of an internal fiction. Meanwhile the inherent instability of sentiment left the pros and cons of the debate largely unresolvable in the abstract, as it has remained ever since. Each side speaks, with abstract consistency, from its ideological bunker. But fiction could dramatize the same questions more holistically by exploring the liminal area between these categories. Some eighteenth-century fiction subjected the internal instabilities of the sentimentalist project to an immanent critique and, increasingly, this was to became a means of dealing with the complexities and deceptions of emotional being as such. Such works did not just passively reflect the weaknesses of a theory, but actively explored the condition of ethical life by breaking down the discursive dualisms of emotion and reason, feeling and principle, fact and fiction, truth and illusion. In this context, even the generic shift from theatre to novel becomes significant as the dualism of stage and spectator is elided into an internally imagined action.

It has been seen how the assumed psychology of sentiment as an immediate, even visceral, reaction to the fact of distress encouraged a literalistic mode of fiction. At the same time, the concern for arousing a properly sentimental response within the narrative was inextricable from the reader's response to the narrative itself. The fictional ordeal of the hero, or more likely the heroine, was also a testing of the reader. Hence, along with the motive of affective literalism was a counter-motive of readerly reflexivity. That could give rise to dull sermonizing and self-congratulation but also to some remarkable moments. The memorable instances of fictional self-reflexivity in the period are not usually in a spirit of postmodern relativity *avant la lettre*, as is sometimes supposed, but are closely bound up with a contemporary critique of sentiment as in the reading of Macpherson's *Ossian* in Goethe's *Werther*.[1] Although Werther and Lotte read a poem, and their archetype is Dante's poetic episode of Paolo and Francesca, this classic critique of excessive sensibility, and inappropriate emotional identification, occurs within an epistolary novel in the mode of affective verisimilitude.

Illusionism as such, of course, was not new and Cervantes provides a historical benchmark to highlight the epochal element in the fiction of sentiment. Don Quixote is the extreme case of the reader who takes fiction as fact, but Cervantes explores the theme of illusion in more familiar and realistic ways in a multiplicity of subnarratives. Elena Percas de Ponseti, elaborating Cervantes's concept of art, analyses the illusion theme in the episodes of Master Pedro's puppet show and the braying aldermen from *Don Quixote Part II*.[2] Master Pedro, who turns out to be the bandit Gines de Pasamonte in disguise, comes to the town with his puppet show and a supposed talking ape. The ape astonishes the inhabitants when Master Pedro interprets its chattering as snatches of personal local gossip which he has actually picked up on the way to town. The centre of the episode is Don Quixote's destruction of the puppet theatre when he enters the illusion so completely that he attempts to rescue the puppet princess from her pursuers. But this episode of staged illusionism is framed by the real-life incident of the two braying aldermen. Each is proud of his ability to bray so perfectly as to deceive a real ass. Hence, when one of them loses his own ass, they spend the night wandering separately on the hillside to see whose braying will attract it. In the morning it is discovered that the ass was dead all along while they have been braying at each other. Within these farcical actions Ponseti elucidates a subtle critique of illusionism in art. Artistic meaning lies in the gap between reality and imitation. Perfect imitation, or illusionism, is a pointless achievement; to imitate an ass perfectly is to be an ass indeed just as the talking ape is a witless parody of the human. Ponseti further notes that the word 'retablo', meaning both 'altar' and 'stage', along with the reference to the remains of the puppets as 'reliquías', or 'relics', brings in a theological suggestion. Not only does artistic mimesis lose its point if it becomes indistinguishable from reality but perfect imitation is a blasphemous rival to God's creation.

Whereas for Cervantes the instructive value of art involved a resistance to illusionism, in the era of sentiment a new value accrued to the compelling affectingness which he had deprecated. The sentimental reader, however, is an *emotional* rather than an *ontological* Quixote.

Whereas Don Quixote thinks the object is real, the sentimental response takes the emotion as real. The difference may not always be apparent but there is a significant shift in the centre of gravity of emotional Quixotry. The fiction of sentiment, in its more complex and productive forms, was ultimately just as critical of Quixotry but it could not so readily dismiss it by appealing to external reality or a theological criterion. Any critique of illusionism had to be developed within a new aesthetic and psychological conception. The figure who most significantly explored the problems of an aesthetics of sensibility was Denis Diderot, partly because of his intellectual and emotional volatility. His chameleon-like capacity to shift ground, to see either side of any case with equal force, reflects the way sensibility itself was a widespread set of assumptions open to opposing interpretations. Diderot campaigned for a new aesthetic of sentimentalist verisimilitude while showing a sharp sense of its problems and dangers. Above all, he had an endless fascination for the liminal experiences which get between the rigidities of conventional understanding, and for this purpose prose fiction was especially fruitful.

Absorption or illusion

Michael Fried corrects a traditional misinterpretation of Diderot and, although his argument largely concerns Diderot's discussion of painting, it has implications for literature in which Diderot was a practitioner as well as a connoisseur and theorist.[3] Fried distinguishes the principles of 'theatricality' and 'absorption' which have commonly been mistaken for each other. In praising the sentimental genre artist, Greuze, and in promoting his own new style of bourgeois sentimental drama, Diderot has been understood as wishing to impose emotionally on the spectator whereas, Fried points out, it is rather that he wishes the spectator to be as if absorbed into the work, to disappear altogether as a separate focus of emotional consciousness.

While theatrical tragedy was still the most prestigious and continually theorized form in the period, Diderot argued for a new mixed form of serious drama based on everyday life and proposed that the ideal play in this style would encompass the maximum number of emotional tableaux.[4] This might seem to suggest precisely the intention of freezing the action and directing its effect out onto the audience. But Diderot contrasts the tableau to the *coup de théâtre*, by which he means a sudden turn in the action implying an emotionally manipulative wrenching of probability. The tableau, by contrast, is meant precisely *not* to be stagey; it is rather a moment when the collective emotion on stage is so completely absorbing to the characters that they, as it were, lose consciousness of the audience and seem most completely within their own world. The spectator then sees them as through an imaginary fourth wall and at such a moment the stage characters might even break theatrical, though not painterly, decorum by turning their backs to the audience (*Entretiens*, 1137). In this conception the work does not make the observer conscious of itself *as* a work but rather absorbs the observer emotionally into its world.

The context gives Diderot's argument an exemplary force. It occurs in his *Entretiens sur Le fils naturel*, three dialogues accompanying the text of his play of this name which, though written in 1757, had a single performance in 1771. An introductory narrative nests the text of the play within a fiction. A young man of sentiment, Dorval, has been at the centre of a painful situation which was finally resolved with the return of a long-lost father who has subsequently asked him to write up the action so that the family may perform it in private every year. Hence the play was not only unperformed in public for years, but even in the fictional narrative only the family members are present enacting their roles. In the fiction, however, Dorval, learning of Diderot's interest, permits him to be secretly present at a performance. In this way, the play as witnessed by 'Diderot' becomes the living image of the principle of absorption, a play without an audience, while his subsequent discussions of the play with Dorval are placed in the bottomless regress of reality and fiction which never ceased to fascinate Diderot. The events are moving because they have actually happened to these individuals, and the play is a ritualized repetition of them, yet the play seeks to give them an artistic concentration and clarity which is why Dorval seeks the critical opinion of 'Diderot'.

The fictive discussions proved more substantial than the play itself and, if absorption was Diderot's aim, he may have been right to spell it out in the framing fiction rather than leave it to the vagaries of an actual audience's response. Even an ideally responsive audience would require a given dramatic quality in the work. In that respect absorption is a self-conscious version of affective verisimilitude, or emotional Quixotry, in that the accent falls not so much on moving the observer as on giving the observer something to be moved by. It may still be sentimentalist literalism from the point of view of the spectator but not from that of the artist who will need experience and technique to achieve the effect. Diderot's invoking of the tableau suggests the significance of his art criticism, and of painting itself, in his conception of theatre. Historical painting and dramatic tragedy were the prestigious genres of the period, and much of the fiction we now prize was comparatively unregarded, in many cases seen as a mere sport. Not surprisingly, therefore, Diderot invoked the tableau and worked out his aesthetic of absorption in contrast to the theatricality and self-conscious-ness of the baroque and rococo modes.

But if it has been difficult to see that Diderot was after absorption rather than theatricality it may be because he was seeking it precisely in theatre where, as we might now think, he was running most directly against the grain of the medium. Diderot's image of the tableau as theatrical absorption places drama between painting and narrative in a way that highlights the fundamental ambiguity of theatre as an art object. What we see in the art of acting is a specific individual enacting a character. Theoretically, therefore, there should be no problem. The actor is the art object and the character is what is represented. But discussion of the theatre, including Diderot's, commonly treats the actor's gestures and voice etc. as part of the emotional representation or dramatic illusion. The physical presence of the actor is taken as an aspect of realist content and, in a sense, this is perfectly correct since we are indeed responding to Irving's Hamlet or Olivier's Richard III; there is no abstract character on stage before us. But this means that theatre, although it is properly the form in which consciousness of artistic representation is most unavoid-able and of the essence, is also the form in which the distinction, at the level of discussion, is most commonly collapsed. It is spoken of as compelling realism. Actually, of all the media in question here, it is realistic prose fiction, recreated through a private act of reading, or in a theatre of the mind, which allows for the greatest absorption, the maximum elision of categories. Yet in true eighteenth-century style, even as he affirmed the power of absorption in Richardson's fiction, for example, Diderot expressed it in theatrical terms of feeling like a naive spectator tempted to call out a warning to the character on stage.[5] In the age of sentiment the expectation of affective verisimilitude collapsed the very nature of theatre and, by forcing theatre against its own grain, Diderot helped to absorb it into the aesthetics of prose fiction from which it did not fully escape till the turn of the twentieth century.

Absorption, then, is a sophisticated form of emotional Quixotry or affective verisimilitude distinct from ontological illusion. Marian Hobson, in tracing the minute arguments about art and illusion in eighteenth-century France, distinguishes two fundamental attitudes of 'soft' and 'hard' illusion to be found in representational art at all times.[6] 'Soft' illusion is only provisional and to be seen through by the observer. In renaissance literature, as in Cervantes, this may imply a realm of eternal values beyond the phenomenal world. 'Hard' illusion encourages the observer to respond with maximum forgetfulness of its artifice. In this latter conception it is difficult to avoid aesthetic collapse into illusion and the polar imperatives of producing absorption without deception continued to bother, and to fascinate, Diderot as in his *Paradox on the Actor*.[7] Hobson also observes that while there was a main line of principled debate on other arts such as painting and theatre, the less prestigious form of prose fiction shows a less consistent pattern either in theoretical argument or in practice. Once again, its comparatively informal status allowed it to get under the wire as a medium of possible experiment and innovation, not least in the case of Diderot himself who wrote substantial, and highly self-reflexive, novels on the English models of both Richardson and Sterne.[8]

By concentrating on the status of the object, the question of whether it is illusory or not, this debate rather subsumes, or elides, the question of its emotional impact. Of course, the emotional impact is implicitly subsumed in all discussion of fictional illusion since that is what the illusion is for. But its being subsumed is precisely the problem, for the emotional response of the observer has a different logic from the questions of cognitive or ontological status with regard to the object. In the liminal area of emotions aroused by fiction the significance of the emotional response is not contingent on the status of the object. Where the quality of the emotion is the primary concern, the imaginary nature of the object is a recognized condition hardly requiring the negative sign of illusion. When Kames remarked, '. . . if, in reading, ideal presence be the means by which our passions are moved, it makes no difference whether the object be fable or reality', he was not merely eliding the categories but distinguishing their orders of significance.

It is not accidental that this commonsensical remark, undercutting the whole pother about illusion and deception, should come from a British source for, lurking in the background of the question of aesthetic illusion in France is the French myth of feeling *per se* as being the sphere of illusion. That is the underlying locus of the anxiety. The term 'myth' here does not imply this conception is untrue. It merely indicates the deep-lying formation through which this culture perceives emotion. Denis de Rougement and René Girard, writing from within a francophone history, offer this view of emotion as a universal of western culture which is what makes it culturally specific.[9] Meanwhile Hobson quotes La Place, the translator of Shakespeare, on the English in a way that confirms a contemporary perception of the national cultural distinction. He claims that the English being

> naturellement mélancholique, sont moins disposés que d'autres à se prêter à l'illusion. La constante étude du vrai rend souvent le coeur indocile et rebelle à la vraisemblance.

(Hobson, 151)

What is perhaps at stake here, however, is not a phlegmatic refusal of the English to lend themselves to theatrical illusion so much as a relative absence, for them, of any special significance in the category of illusion. The French focus on the illusion theme in aesthetics derives from a suspicion of the emotional object because emotion itself tends to be thought of as unreliable, subjective and the sphere of illusion. Hobson indeed remarks that *La Nouvelle Héloïse* is arguably the 'only tragedy written in eighteenth-century France' because the preoccupation with illusion in the aesthetics of the eighteenth-century French novel uniquely coincides with the heroine, Julie's, central recognition that:

> 'Le pays de chimères est en ce monde le seul digne d'être habité, et tel est le néant des choses humaines, qu'hors l'Être existant par lui-même, il n'y a rien de beau que ce qui n'est pas.'
>
> (ibid., 119)

Julie's conclusion is echoed in French fiction through La Fayette, Senancour, Stendhal, Flaubert, Proust and Sartre. In the British tradition, on the other hand, emotion is treated critically, but not with this ontological distrust because emotional discrimination can be conducted irrespective of the ontological status of the object. Indeed, the internal critique of emotion would be undermined by general ontological scepticism and needs protection from any direct interference from reality. Real people can never be objects of complete judgement in the way that fictional characters properly can. On this model, the reader's emotion, far from requiring an ontological guarantee from the object, lends the object whatever in the way of a provisional reality it needs.

Hence in the 'British' tradition any question of illusion in the aesthetics of affective verisimilitude, an equivocation between the 'scene' and the 'seen', or between emotional rhetoric and distressful object, is likely to be part of a more intrinsic analysis of emotional response. Literalism likewise should not be taken too literally. Affective verisimilitude, even when carrying the full burden of sentimentalist response, clearly did not mean that readers were literally unaware of reading a fiction. On the contrary, those who urged Richardson to save Clarissa were in the grip of emotional Quixotry yet were manifestly aware of his authorial control. Hobson, indeed, argues a 'bipolar' response in which all fictional illusion is self-conscious and she challenges the previous scholarly account of the run of memoir novels produced in France around the turn of the eighteenth century. In her view, far from representing a genuine desire to deceive the reader into accepting their actual historicity, their asseverations of veracity signal their fictional status (ibid., 87–8). It is a legitimate scholarly question what these authors and their readers thought, but maybe this argument points to something more fundamental about the nature of reading as intrinsically 'bipolar'.

The perennial doubleness of absorption is relevantly analysed in Janice Radway's study of modern readers of escapist romance.[10] Her interviews with readers, combined with analysis of texts, suggests that a double consciousness is normal in responding to sentimental fiction. Even as the readers are absorbed by the emotions, and identify with the heroine, the text maintains a conventionalized patina of literariness, such as idioms slightly removed from the norm, which are not merely accidental survivals in an inappropriate context, but signals of its fictitious status. It is an obvious point that fictionality is a condition of the popular romance's appeal of escapist identification, but the implications may be more far-reaching. For even Radway, who wishes both her romance readers and their fiction to be taken seriously, presents it as a feature of naive reading. George Orwell invented the term 'double-think' for the bad faith induced by political propaganda and ideology and one could think of such sentimentalist reading as an equivalent in the realm of feeling, as a kind of 'double-feel'.[11] The emotion is knowingly indulged in an unreal object. It may be, however, that we should think of it the other way round. Instead of sentimental 'double-feel', in relation to fiction, being the naive version of the act of reading, it is rather the archetype. Its formulaic naivety only reveals with stark clarity what sophisticated fiction rather conceals than transcends. In the intrinsically liminal experience of reading fiction a continuity with the reader's own life of feeling is always crucial although it is only at the minimal degree of literary interest that this presents itself as the primary motive and effect. The occlusion of the sentimental structure within more sophisticated occasions of reading may be one of the most important senses in which the apparent naivety of sentimentalism has been substantively assimilated, while being theoretically excluded, in mainstream culture.

As has been seen in Addison, even when the ideology of sentiment most privileged the sense of reality in the text, the textual mediation was a silent condition of the experience. Yet precisely because it is inescapable and needs to be minimized in consciousness during the act of reading, the silent premise of fictionality is constantly overlooked in the discursive accounting, although that is the most telling witness to its fundamental significance. In this respect, the sentimental response throws into relief the emotional dynamics of literary response at large. Moreover, the continuity which lends real emotions to fiction works equally in reverse: it silently acknowledges the fictive element in feeling.[12] This fruitful liminality might be expressed in the formula 'fictive emotion' as the phrase could denote either an emotion engendered *by* a fiction or that the emotion *is* a fiction. As a thought experiment, one might ask whether we could now propose the categories of sentimental and unsentimental, or of false and genuine feeling, if our culture had no category of fiction. If fiction, that is to say, has the capacity to be emotionally educative, it is not just at the level of content and theme but through an underlying ontological commonality. Since feeling always lives in the imagination, fiction is not a special case to be explained, but the essential instance to contemplate. In responding to fictional beings, we acclimatize to the elusive and imaginative dimension of all objects of feeling.

Seen in this light, affective verisimilitude, in seeking to elide the distinction between fiction and life, got the right point the wrong way round. There is an emotional continuity between object and observer but it works most significantly under the sign of fiction rather than of fact. This shift in focus from the status of the object to the quality of the feeling has vital long-term consequences. The two questions of reality status and emotional quality have no single, necessary relationship and, although they were to develop remarkably over the period covered by this study, analytic understanding still lags behind. This can be seen in a recent critique of Martha Nussbaum by John Horton. Nussbaum, as a moral philosopher, has rediscovered the traditional humanistic value of imaginative literature at a time when many literary academics, for whatever reasons, have been actively denying it.[13] Horton questions several of her arguments including her stress on the imaginative dimension against which he instances the 'all too common ... responses of a man who is moved to tears by a dramatisation of *The Ragged-Trousered Philanthropist* but is stonily indifferent to the vagrants he passes on his way from the National Theatre.'[14] Horton's question is of perennial pertinence yet, despite the example from a modern novel, it rehearses a standard objection to the eighteenth-century man of sentiment. Horton exercises an emotional and ethical judgement without seeing this as part of the literary occasion. Critical reading is a test of the reader as well as the work. Historically, this critical awareness arose precisely from the kind of discomfort Horton finds in the simple model of sentimental response. Above all, although imaginative occasions can exercise and educate the moral feelings, they cannot supply them where they are lacking. An emergent consciousness of such questions can be seen in episodes from Richardson and Sterne. Whereas most sentimentalist writing merely reflected its myths naively, some exercised a critical self-scrutiny within the sentimental narrative itself.

The slippage in Addison's *Spectator* essay, whereby the word 'Scene' refers first to the verbal creation and then to the reality 'surveyed', reflects the assumptions of sentimental verisimilitude. These are put under pressure in *Clarissa* when Lovelace's former companion, Belford, now reformed by witnessing the distress of Clarissa, writes to the unrepentant villain with a view to reforming him. Since Clarissa is in a bailiff's garret after the rape and refuses to see any man, especially Lovelace, Belford, who does manage to visit her, is the only means of conveying the reality of her situation to Lovelace. Ideally, Lovelace should simply see what Belford sees and he would relent. Belford therefore feels an acute burden of writerly responsibility in putting the reality of the 'scene' before Lovelace and wishes that he had Clarissa's own 'affecting pen' with which to do so (*Clarissa*, iii, 425). Belford's respect for Clarissa's writing matches her family's fear of her power of expression which they see as an insidious force of rhetoric rather than the sober truth. Belford, therefore, unwittingly touches on a fundamental and pervasive ambiguity of the whole narrative caught in the ambiguity of the 'scene' and the 'seen'. Is it the sheer reality that would move the observer, as in the sentimentalist belief, or is it an affecting description, a merely rhetorical power as her family claim? He does not want to play on Lovelace's emotions, which Lovelace would in any case despise and resist, yet he wishes the situation to do so. He needs to be both a transparent and an intensifying medium, and his narrative of distress preserves this ambiguity in that he minutely details the circumstances of the house, the garret room and finally Clarissa herself in an extended description reflecting the 'leisure' with which, as he himself remarks, he initially paused to survey the scene. It is a classic moment of sentimental lingering on the effect. As Diderot would have appreciated, he creates a painterly tableau in which Clarissa's linen, astonishingly white despite her not having changed since coming to the house, forms the central focus against the dingy background of the room.

Belford's account of his emotional absorption is one of the great *narrative* climaxes of the book although not one of its strongest moments of *writing*. We feel too much the straining after effect, the 'palpable design' upon the reader. But this precisely exemplifies how the novel continually transcends its own psychological and narrative premises. By delegating the authorial function to Belford, Richardson's epistolary method makes the very straining of the description part of the larger action. Almost unawares, and without rupturing the verisimilitude, we have been submitted to an important self-reflexive device of sentimental fiction: the tale within the tale. To see how this device can introduce a fictive self-scrutiny without disrupting the response, it is worth revisiting one of the most famous, and still controversial, examples.

The sentimental tale within the tale: 'The Story of Le Fever'

Sterne's 'Story of Le Fever' in *Tristram Shandy* is one of the most celebrated instances of the sentimental tale within the tale.[15] Since this device was usually the most naive expression of the sentimental aesthetic, an invitation to emote, it was also the point at which the sentimentalist assumptions could be most significantly tested by a sceptical spirit. Of course, the interpolated narrative is an ancient device already familiar in Homer and it may be no more than a mechanical way of incorporating more material. That motive undoubtedly survives, for example, in Sterne's master, Cervantes, but he already uses it to explore the ingestion of narrative, the process of its internalizing within the reader or listener and, in that respect, he provides a benchmark for Sterne's use of it.

In the first part of *Don Quixote*, the 'Story of the Impertinent Curiosity', which is almost certainly a ready-made insertion from Cervantes' desk, is a found manuscript listened to precisely out of 'curiosity' by a group of young lovers whose own concerns are obliquely reflected in the story.[16] Only when the story is over are the damaging obsessions, particularly of the male characters, sufficiently overcome for the tangle of their relationships to be resolved. Writing before the development of modern subjectivity, Cervantes gives no internal, psychological analysis but reflects the characters' inner lives in a story outside themselves. Their relationship to the narrative is emotional yet far from emotional identification in the Wertherian way. Indeed, Cervantes' fugue-like structure of simultaneous narratives enforces on the reader a constant forgetfulness of these listening characters which reflects their own fruitful forgetfulness of themselves. The fiction exerts its effect on them while their own emotional preoccupations are apparently suspended.

In the age of sentiment, however, the characteristic effect of the tale within the tale is directly opposite to this. The listener within the fiction is aroused to sympathetic compassion as a surrogate for the real reader who is thereby offered an intensifying model of response. Such a naive example occurs in Henry Brooke's *The Fool of Quality* (1770). A man of sentiment, Mr Clinton, has just lost his beloved young wife, Matilda, in childbirth and, while telling the story to his aristocratic relative, he interrupts himself to remark:

> There is surely, my cousin, a species of pleasure in grief, a kind of soothing and deep delight, that arises with the tears which are pushed from the fountain of God in the soul, from the charities and sensibilities of the heart divine.
>
> True, true, my precious cousin, replied the countess, giving a fresh loose to her tears. O Matilda! I would I were with thee! – True, my cousin I say; even now I sink under the weight of the sentiment of your story.[17]

In its more naive forms, the fiction of sentiment was indeed to sink under its own excessive emotional weight, and especially over the course of the 1770s, although no such irony is intended by the speakers here. The fictional listener offers the response expected of the reader. Yet writers, like Diderot, Goethe and Sterne, who dramatically examine rather than simply reflect sentimental ideology, focus on precisely this moment of dramatized response to probe its sentimental premises.

Sterne's episode was subtitled 'The Story of Le Fever' within the original text as if inviting its subsequent excerption for separate publication and there is no doubt that, like the Henry Brooke example, it solicits the response it received from its contemporaries. Yet in context the story is shot through with a more quizzical awareness of its own narrative process. In fact, the story is placed at several removes since it is set in the distant past at the time of Tristram's narrative, as well as being originally narrated to Toby by Corporal Trim. Uncle Toby heard that Le Fever, a young ensign of his regiment, was dying in a nearby inn but, despite his concern at this news, he was confined with gout so that he could only hear of Le Fever from Trim. We likewise, therefore, only experience the event through Trim which creates the familiar ambiguity as to whether it is the occasion of distress or Trim's narrative which moves us. But what gives this episode its peculiar flavour, and ambiguity, is the Sternean humour constantly glancing across it. Does this intensify the emotional effect by a tonal contrast and highlighting, or does it throw the quality of the feeling radically into question?

From the original publication down to the present time, readers have been divided about the effect of the episode. If few modern readers would respond in the classically sentimental way, there is little consensus as to how to take it. One reading sees the episode as ultimately sentimental in the dismissive modern sense; for these readers it is tastelessly self-indulgent. Such readers are often governed, however, by an anti-sentimental persuasion. Anthony Nuttall, for example, has analysed the weakness of the episode as representative of the whole contemporary project of moral sentiment but this depends on prior assumptions about the relation of literature to sentiment. Since this literature is so closely linked to the theories of moral sentiment there is a tendency to suppose that if the literature shows these theories to be unsatisfactory, then the work itself is a failure. But *Clarissa* is not only a work of psychological complexity and power, it develops a tragic logic precisely out of Richardson's ideology of 'sentiment as principle'. The fiction of sentiment produced neither a coherently articulable view of the moral life based on sentiment, nor for the most part works of great formal compression and control. It did, however, work on the unresolved problems of moral feeling in a way that later generations could put to use.

Nuttall's sharply analytic reading of Sterne's episode provides a useful template. He first sets up a radical polarity dividing not only eighteenth-century but all ethical outlooks into a choice between '. . . those who see morals as essentially a matter of rational insight . . . and those who feel that morality is properly a matter of passion . . .' (Nuttall, 73). Although he quotes Hume's insistence that moral passion is not opposed to reason, he nonetheless maintains the underlying polarity in his discussion of Sterne, proposing for his opening question: 'The . . . danger of anti-rationalist morality is that it should degenerate into mere sensibility, the ethic of warm feelings. Has this already happened to Sterne?' (ibid., 73). But Hume was precisely questioning the dualism of terms like 'rational insight' and 'anti-rationalist'. 'Rational insight' is an obfuscation here since it does not explain how reason enters the sphere of the ethical in the first place. It takes for granted what the other side of the debate is at least recognizing to be a problem. Nuttall's reading then highlights the quaint subjectivity and ineffectuality of Uncle Toby's feelings while omitting Toby's summary response, at the end of Trim's narrative, in taking out his purse for Le Fever. Sentimental feeling was open to the charge of self-indulgence and giving the purse signifies the practical application of the feeling in benevolent action. Of course, we might now question the charity of the well-off, and see dependence on private benefaction as a social evil in itself. But leaving these anachronistic responses aside, the quaintness of Toby's expression and the sheer concentration on his feeling are set against his decisive charitable action. Furthermore, with the benefit of the flashback, we know that Toby not only succoured Le Fever but took over the boy's education till he could be placed in a profession.

Nuttall also objects to the focus on Toby's own feelings at the expense of Le Fever's distress. But Sterne has also legitimated this in the narrative situation. Since Trim will not be able to return to Le Fever till the next day, there is no urgency of practical response, and the concentration on Toby is not in the face of Le Fever's suffering since he is not present. As was remarked earlier, the sentimentalist need to focus on the moment of response can readily seem self-indulgent in fictive presentation but Sterne has engineered a situation in which the lingering on Toby's reponse, however one responds to it at the level of personal taste, is at least not at the expense of action. Also, although Toby is certainly concerned with his own feelings, he is not enjoying them and it is not he but the narrative which lingers on them. Unlike Richardson's handling of Belford in the bailiff's garret, Sterne has created a special space for dwelling on the moment of feeling within the larger enacting of its charitable outcome.

Nuttall's more important charge, however, is that we are invited to enjoy Trim and Toby as comic characters even while supposedly sharing their compassion for Le Fever but, far from being awkward or manipulative, this now touches the heart of the question. For the tonal mixture highlights a deeper distinction: although Toby and the reader listen to ostensibly the same story, they do so within different orders of consideration. While Toby learns of a real occasion of distress requiring a moral response in the form of action, the reader enjoys a fiction about Toby's response. The reader is not called upon to act, and has, as it were, the legitimate leisure to attend sympathetically to the workings of sympathy in Toby. His feelings are an object for us in a way they are not for him and some significant consequences flow from this distinction. The duality of feeling in the reader reflects the appropriate responses to a distressful occasion, on the one hand, and a distressful fiction on the other. By a deceptively simple, non-analytic means, Sterne distinguishes the ethical and the aesthetic modes of response to the same tale.

Compared with Henry Brooke's naive version of the embedded tale, Sterne's episode opens a significant discrimination within the sentimental response. In Brooke's case, different qualities of feeling were run together in an unlikely and possibly complacent way. The grieving husband affirmed a 'species of pleasure' in grief while the fictional listener sank under the 'weight of the sentiment of [his] story'. Sterne's episode, on the other hand, distinguishes these emotions by the different orders of response for which they are appropriate. Toby, the listener within the fiction, is oppressed by the weight of feeling to the extent, as he quaintly puts it, of wishing he was asleep, while we, as readers outside the text, can enjoy a 'species of pleasure' in contemplating him. The pleasure, moreover, is not just that of appreciating his amiable quaintness; it includes the recognition, as with Brooke's Mr Clinton, of a spring of benevolent feeling, a source which, for Toby too, implies a connection with something beyond the self. Hence, although we and Toby appear to listen to the same story, he is required to respond ethically while we are invited to respond aesthetically. As we are not called upon to act, that is to say, we have a legitimate leisure, or freedom, to reflect on the values rehearsed in the narrative. At the same time, however, our aesthetic response occurs through Toby's ethical one and cannot exist without it. The aesthetic order here is distinguished, but not separated, from the ethical. In the very act of opening the distinction, the embedded tale enforces the common root in feeling.

The force of this point can be seen by comparison with Nuttall's reading. Nuttall rightly recognizes that the question of the aesthetic is raised by the episode but he links Sterne back to Shaftesbury as one whose reliance on taste makes him a 'moral aesthete':

> For Shaftesbury's morally cultured man, virtue is in a very real sense its own reward.
>
> Such an ideal ... could never survive realisation. Let us suppose...a novel in which ... is presented to us... a man who behaves virtuously because he believes that thereby he will become happy. The novelist ... would discover, pragmatically, that he had not portrayed a good man. It is not that goodness and happiness are incompatible; it is just that the goal of happiness must not be allowed to appear among the motives for goodness.
>
> (Nuttall, 77)

Nuttall dismisses sentimentalism by imagining its fictional realization. The fiction is taken to be the working out of a set of ideas, thereby revealing their inadequacy. This knock-down argument would apply in many instances. Yet even if one accepted his judgement that it could not work in a novel, we could not assume that its psychological or moral truth is invalidated just because it does not readily translate into fiction. And surely Shaftesbury's underlying point could be represented in fiction without a complacent self-consciousness in the character concerned. With elementary novelistic tact, the fiction could communicate the *effect* of a good action within the self without making it a *motive*. As has been suggested earlier, the problem with sentimentalist fiction was not that this was intrinsically impossible, but that the ideology of sentiment, combined with a philosophical and didactic purpose, led writers into this naive model. In that respect, Nuttall's own hypothetical fiction is remarkable for its sentimentalist literalism. It is a striking example, along with John Horton, of the way in which the original formulations of sentimentalism have lodged in the cultural consciousness at the expense of the more complex, and implicit, culture of feeling to which they gave rise, Sterne himself being part of this latter process.

Meanwhile, Nuttall's charge that Sterne has 'inherited the taint of aestheticism' rests on a more significant anachronism (Nuttall, 76). As was indicated earlier, this description refers to Shaftesbury's assumption that moral and artistic taste are the same faculty so that the one necessarily affects the other. In so far as Nuttall's target here is the emphasis on feeling rather than the objective needs of the situation, the link with Shaftesbury is fair enough, although one might say that in many situations the sheer awareness of another's sympathy is indeed an objective need. But the phrase 'moral aesthete', used as a self-evident and sufficient disparagement, draws its critical power from the modern assumption that the aesthetic is an autonomously separate realm (Nuttall, 75). It sees as an improper yoking what for Shaftesbury had still not come apart. Shaftesbury was not an aesthete in this modern sense and would not have understood such a conception. That in turn suggests the true historical interest of the Sternean episode.

We need not suppose that Sterne consciously thought through the implications I am attributing to the episode. He enjoyed playing on the liminal region between fiction and life and he explored the instabilities of sentiment with an opportunistic and quizzical receptiveness to contemporary shifts in taste and sensibility. Like Diderot, he was divided on the question of sentiment although, unlike Diderot, he was little given to discursive reasoning and rather expressed his ambivalence in constant shifts of tone and feeling inextricable from fictional self-consciousness. Yet in some ways, Sterne's emotional doubleness and fictional play got closer to the heart of the matter. Just as he anticipated, in his largely implicit critique of Locke, the essential elements which later romantic thought would systematically identify as the areas of weakness of Lockean thought, namely humour, emotion and creativity, so his self-conscious play with the fictional representation of sentiment led him to intuit the difference that might be at stake in an aesthetic, as opposed to an ethical, consideration within the 'same' experience. This was precisely the consciousness which was growing up, and getting philosophically articulated, in the latter part of the century and it is no accident that the German romantics were drawn to this aspect of Sterne albeit he himself might not have understood the significance they attributed to him. Sterne did not so much 'inherit' aestheticism, therefore, as anticipate it. Or more strictly, he anticipated emotionally rather than in principle a conception of the aesthetic which would at a much later point transpose into aesthetic*ism* for he still adhered, as Nuttall rightly suggests by invoking Shaftesbury, to an older conception in which the aesthetic is not yet divorced from the ethical. Sterne's tale within the tale opens up the possibility that feeling may be variously modulated for different orders of meaning. He thereby anticipated those in his own century, such as Friedrich Schiller, who were to transform the cruder models of sentiment through a growing recognition of the aesthetic.

3
Friedrich Schiller and the Aestheticizing of Sentiment

Schiller's attempt to resolve the contradictions of sentiment produced one of the best accounts we have of the relation of the moral and the aesthetic. His immediate point of departure was Kant. Kant's *Critique of Practical Reason* (1788), along with his *Grounding for a Metaphysics of Morals* (1785), had provided a radical criticism of the tradition of moral sentiment including the notion of moral sense. He argued that morality is a 'categorical imperative' independent of feeling so that, even if an impulse of feeling should lead to moral action, it is only the recognition of the imperative which makes the feeling moral. To speak of 'moral feeling', therefore, is at best a potentially misleading shorthand and, since feeling in itself is not merely unreliable, but is actually outside the realm of the ethical, it is dangerous to accept it even as a supplement to the ethical which it may actively undermine.

The aim of Kant's 'transcendental' philosophy in his three major critiques was not to analyse empirical experience, but to determine the nature of the cognitive, the ethical and the aesthetic realms as such. In the cognitive domain, his *Critique of Pure Reason* (1781) overcame an earlier tradition of scepticism about the ability to know the outside world by accepting that the ultimate nature of reality, what he called the 'noumenal', is indeed unknowable while at the same time showing that the phenomenal world of experience is constructed out of necessary categories of thought such that it partakes of their intrinsic certainty. He reaffirmed the authority of reason by defining its limits, and in a similar way, he sought to define the nature of the ethical rather than to explore its psychological workings. His thought, however, was best suited to the topic of cognition for, as Kant himself recognized, the moral life includes a psychological and affective dimension which he had to exclude in principle from his definition. He puts the point explicitly in the *Critique of Practical Reason*:

Thus there remains nothing to do except to determine in what way the moral law becomes a drive, and to see what happens to the human faculty of desire as a consequence of this motive. For how a law in itself can be the direct motive of the will (which is the essence of morality) is an insoluble problem for the human reason.[1]

This suggests why Kant's transcendental method, as applied to the ethical sphere, has caused so much disquiet. For rather than defining a given realm as unamenable to reason and not our concern, he acknowledges that the rationally 'insoluble problem' is at the heart of the subject. In the ethical sphere, the noumenal is within and of the essence.

The enduring power of his argument was that, whereas much ethical thought in the tradition of Shaftesbury and Hutcheson had sought to naturalize and domesticate it, Kant maintained a properly naive wonder at the sheer fact of the ethical. His comparatively brief treatise arrives at the ethical not by a gentle gradient but by a sublime abruptness. He even brought God back into this critique: only an idea as sublime as the traditional Deity is commensurate with the awesome imperative of the ethical. Moral freedom in the individual capable of reason requires recognizing the same autonomy in others which is why they must be used as ends rather than means. Any priority accorded to feeling only obfuscates the absoluteness of this imperative. From the transcendental viewpoint, Kant was surely right and there is no point in objecting to his austerity; indeed his temperamental hostility to contemporary sentimentalism was a partial source of his power. While recognizing the empirical role of feeling in the moral life, his emphasis was that of 'sentiment as principle' in its strongest form: feeling was to be entirely subservient to the moral imperative.

By the same token, on the plane of everyday action, the absoluteness of Duty can provide virtually no guidance. Duties conflict and are of different weights, so that the sublimity of the categorical imperative is not readily translated into practical behaviour, yet what Adam Smith saw as responsibility Kant is more likely to see as conceit. Just before his central address to a deified Duty, Kant refers to

... the moral teaching of the Gospel that, through the purity of its moral principle and at the same time through the suitability of its principle to the limitations of finite beings, ... first brought all good conduct of man under the discipline of duty clearly set before him, which does not permit him to indulge in fancies of moral perfections;

and ... set limits of humility (i.e., self-knowledge) on self-conceit as well as on self-love, both of which readily mistake their boundaries.

(*CPR*, 90)

Kant's reading of the Gospel is as idiosyncratic, in the opposite direction, as the Latitudinarian interpretation of the Deity seen in Grove's *Spectator* paper at the beginning of the century. Indeed, the ideal of 'good conduct ... under the discipline of duty' seems better to reflect the Mosaic ten commandments than the teachings of Jesus which focused on love as unmeasurable, as likely to challenge the law and to conflict with conventional duties. For Christ, God is seen in the unfathomable sublimity of love as much as of duty and in that respect his teaching points to the greater mystery of their combination with which the sentimentalist tradition, however inadequately, was grappling. It would seem that the two wings of the debate, the emotional and the rationalist, are mutually necessary but each constantly decries the other by seeing it only in terms of its vicious extreme, as in Kant's reference to 'self-conceit' and 'self-love'. Kant's transcendental definition, therefore, throws a genuinely critical light on sentimentalist attempts merely to identify feeling and principle, yet is unable to account for our entry into the ethical domain, or to guide our conduct very closely within it.

Schiller's *Letters on the Aesthetic Education of Man* (1795) seek to combine the Kantian analysis with the sentimentalist impulse by something other than the logic of the supplement. His opening letter acknowledges the Kantian structure of his thought while an epigraph from Rousseau affirms the link with sentiment: 'If reason makes man, it is sentiment which guides him.'[2] But Schiller's crucial point of departure is not so much Kant's moral as his aesthetic thought. In his *Critique of Judgement* (1790), Kant had distinguished the realm of the aesthetic from the cognitive and the ethical and, once again, his 'transcendental' distinction was reinforced by an empirical observation running directly counter to the optimism of sentiment:

> ... those persons who refer all activities to which their inner natural dispositions impel men to the final purpose of humanitiy, viz. the morally good, have regarded the taking an interest in the beautiful in general as a mark of the good moral character. But it is not without reason that they have been contradicted by others who rely on experience; for this shows that connoisseurs of taste not only often, but generally, are given up to idle, capricious and mischievous passions, and that they could perhaps make less claim than others to any

superiority of attachment to moral principles. Thus it would seem that feeling for the beautiful is not only (as is actually the case) specifically different from the moral feeling, but that the interest which can be bound up with it is hardly compatible with the moral interest, and certainly has no inner affinity therewith.[3]

Even by the end of the eighteenth century, the assumed continuity between the aesthetic and the ethical, as embodied in Shaftesbury's notion of 'taste', had become problematic. The modern scandal of the 'cultured' concentration camp officer, or of Henry James's Gilbert Osmond in *The Portrait of a Lady*, was already theoretically with us and it was this division which Schiller was seeking to resolve. He did this not by merging the moral and the aesthetic but by carefully discriminating between them.

The 'modernity' of the issue is worth emphasizing since a major mystery concerning Schiller's treatise is the relatively little attention it receives outside specialist Germanist circles given that it is the most cogent expression of a view which still underwrites the less articulated belief held by many people in the value of art. Apart from his outdated idealism and optimism, the explanation for this may lie in the principle enunciated by Schiller himself in a footnote. He remarks that the initial effect of philosophical enquiry is commonly to undermine, and to estrange itself from, the commonsense view of a given topic, but that a full understanding is shown precisely in a return to common sense at another level of appreciation (*AEM*, 127). There are many good and critical readers of literature who feel, perhaps rightly, little need for such a complex justification of what to them is self-evident. Others who are puzzled to account for the value of art often seem unaware of Schiller's nuanced argument which could save many anguished paradoxes. Meanwhile, some who do read him have philosophical commitments unsympathetic to this commonsense view. As with A. D. Nuttall in relation to Sterne and Shaftesbury, a modern conception of the aesthetic is then read back onto Schiller. A recent instance is Terry Eagleton whose *The Ideology of the Aesthetic* is likely to be read by many who have not read Schiller and will not, on the basis of his account, feel a need to do so. But if Schiller's optimistic eloquence is not to modern taste, that should not obscure the robust coherence of his thought and what follows is largely a matter of restating his argument against such modern misreading.

Kant's most positive view of sentiment came in his discussion of the aesthetic. It is as if, when describing directly the nature of the ethical, he had to keep a careful distance from moral sentiment, yet as he seeks to define aesthetic taste and judgement, he has to acknowledge, not just feeling as its subject-matter, but moral sensibility as its precondition. Hence, in an appendix, if not to say supplement, directed to the more practical questions of the teaching of art and the origins of creativity, he argues that since

> there neither is nor can be a science of the beautiful ... the true propaedeutic for the foundation of taste is the development of moral ideas and the culture of the moral feeling, because it is only when sensibility is brought into agreement with this that genuine taste can assume a definite invariable form.
>
> (*CJ*, 202)

He is referring here to general, educative preconditions, not the nature of aesthetic experience or judgement in themselves which, in the spirit of transcendental definition, he keeps separate from moral feeling. None-theless, 'moral feeling' and 'sensibility' are in some broader way necessary. Likewise, following the passage quoted above in which Kant denies the connection between artistic connoisseurship and 'attachment to moral principles', he goes on to distinguish sharply between an appreciation of the beauty of nature and of art. For 'to take an *immediate interest* in the beauty of nature (not merely to have a taste in judging it) is the mark of a good soul' (*CJ*, 141, his emphasis). Once again, a door is left open to sentiment as long as it is placed firmly outside the house of the aesthetic. Schiller, however, while accepting the transcendental separation of realms, argues a more active mutuality between aesthetic experience and moral sensibility, and it is here that his argument has to be followed in its full precision for he is sometimes seen as hopefully combining what his own logic has separated whereas the true purpose of the transcen-dental separation is to establish the limits of the aesthetic precisely as the basis for its positive mode of working. To follow his thinking it is helpful to note his radical redefinition of sentiment as set out in another essay written just after the *Aesthetic Letters*.

The naive, the sentimental and the aesthetic

Schiller's generation benefited from J. G. Herder's attempts to understand culture historically. Hence Schiller, like Hegel after him, understood sentimentalism not in personal and ethical, but in collective and historical, terms as a phase of cultural evolution. In his essay 'On Naive and Sentimental Poetry' (1796), Schiller followed a line of European philosophical thought about cultural evolution whereby an early stage of spontaneous, whole and unselfconscious human life has given way to a state of self-consciousness from which, once it is attained, it is impossible to escape. For Schiller, the term 'naive' refers to the original whole condition of consciousness, for which Homer was a poetic exemplar, while 'sentimental' referred to the modern condition of self-consciousness. Rather than its being a matter of personal choice, desirable or otherwise, to privilege a universal possibility of the psyche such as 'emotion' or 'reason', he saw the 'sentimental' as the general condition of a specific phase of cultural development. Schiller thereby turned the word 'sentimental' into a neutrally technical term denoting a particular relationship of those elements of feeling and reflection which an earlier notion of sentiment had sought merely to merge. Although 'naive' and 'sentimental' were not, in principle, evaluative terms, and Schiller strove to honour the incommensurability of their respective advantages and disadvantages, modern self-consciousness was prone to internal division and self-alienation for which the naive wholeness provided a nostalgic contrast. In the sentimental state, wholeness is harder to achieve. By recognizing the sentimental as a specifically modern condition, and one in which it became vital to distinguish qualities of feeling, Schiller set the stage for a modern culture of feeling even if his particular model has not become central.

Schiller's definition of the 'sentimental' not only gave it a philosophical rather than a moral value, but saw it as objectified largely in artistic texts. It was, therefore, already some way towards being an aesthetic term and it is worth noting that the literary genres by which Schiller sought to understand his philosophical conception were no longer prose fiction or theatre, which had been the primary vehicles for thinking through the aesthetics of moral sentiment throughout the century, but epic and lyric poetry. Between the age of sentiment and the generation we now think of as the romantics, there was a generic shift whereby poetry became the crucial arena for devising aesthetic paradigms. The concentration on epic and lyric poetry allowed Schiller to emphasize the artist's own state of feeling rather than the problems of absorption or illusion which arise when an emotionally compelling effect upon the audience was the primary concern.

By giving the 'sentimental' a philosophical definition through artistic models, Schiller was able to make the necessary internal discriminations by which to distance his conception from the fashionable excesses of contemporary sensibility. His principal point was that, for the sentimental condition, everything, including the objects making up the natural world, was experienced in terms of an 'idea':

It is not these objects themselves, but an idea they represent, and which we love in them. We love in them their quietly creative life, their peaceful self-functioning, their way of being after their own laws, their inner necessity, their eternal unity with themselves.[4]

This enables him to distinguish the truly sentimental perception of nature from its debased forms

Since this interest in Nature is grounded in an idea, it can only show itself in temperaments sensitive to ideas, namely moral ones. Most people merely affect it, and the popularity of this sentimental taste in our time, especially since the appearance of certain writings, sentimental journeys, gardens in the same style, country walks and other such hobbies, is absolutely no proof that this response is widespread.

(*NSD*, 696; *NSL*, 22–3)

Although fashionable sensibility is an excess to which the sentimental condition is prone, it represents merely its vice, not its essential definition. Only in that sense does Schiller warn youth against the vogue for the poet Klopstock, who was a favourite of Goethe's misguided young hero of sensibility, Werther. Klopstock epitomizes the sentimental spirit in his extreme idealism, his capacity to turn the bodily into the spiritual at all points, and hence:

Youth, which always strives beyond the limits of life, which flees all forms and finds all boundaries too narrow, plunges with love and pleasure into the infinite spaces which are opened by this poet.

(*NSD*, 736; *NSL*, 55)

Schiller's critique of fashionable sensibility as a self-induced state of overwhelming feeling suggests the crucial turn in his notion of the aesthetic: a central concern of his *oeuvre* is freedom but it is manifest here in a metaphysical rather than a political sense. For Schiller did not just seek to overcome the conflict of feeling and reason in 'sentiment'; he argued that both instinct and reason are forms of compulsion and it is only because there is a conflict between them that human beings, uniquely, have freedom from either. But such freedom can only be glimpsed theoretically since, in the ordinary course of events, human beings are always subject to one 'drive' (*Trieb*) or the other. Hence, he developed Kant's notion of the aesthetic as a higher form of play. In play we obey rules in a spirit of free choice. Where an earlier notion of sentiment had sought moral efficacy on a model for which anything less than compulsion was a problem, Schiller privileged the freedom from compulsion, the ability to appreciate values and feelings as such. The emphasis on freedom, therefore, cut against much of the intrinsic drift of sentimentalism. Likewise, just when the fashion of 'sensibility' was enacting the apparent dissolution of thought into bodily sensation, Schiller stressed the opposite aspect, the transposition of feeling into consciousness, as the very definition of the sentimental. And by transposing feeling into specifically aesthetic consciousness, Schiller implicitly met the earlier 'complacency' problem which had arisen from combining an idealized self-reflection with a criterion of practical benevolence. The aesthetic state, by contrast, was a quality of conscious-ness created within an objective context but with no burden of immediate efficacy. In so far as the problems of sentiment arose from its literalism, both psychologically and artistically, it is not surprising that Schiller turned to an aesthetic transposition of feeling.

It is important to see the error of literalistic efficacy that Schiller was leaning against since a later history has developed the opposite error and then saddled him with it. He emphasized the indirection and separateness of the aesthetic against the didactic literalism of earlier conceptions but he was equally far from a modern notion of aesthetic autonomy. Whereas Kant had restricted the purview of the aesthetic to artistic experience while acknowledging its cultural and emotional preconditions, Schiller saw the specialness of the aesthetic experience as a distinct phase of feeling which, once it has been recognized in that way, can then be seen to apply to feeling at large. The life of feeling precedes the aesthetic experience as its necessary condition, and continues to be affected by it afterwards. Schiller took from Kant the disinterestedness of art and the analogy with play, but saw them as forming a necessary moment in every developed life of feeling. Even the most practical person, Schiller argues, needs some reflexive awareness of the values motivating action, and prior to every important action is a moment, however fleeting, notional or unconscious, in which values are held in the balance. As he puts it:

> truth and duty... must owe their determining power to themselves alone ... the pure logical form, namely the concept, must speak directly to the understanding, the pure moral form, namely the law, to the will. .... But for them to be able to do this, for such a thing as a pure form to exist for sensuous man at all, this, I insist, has first to be made possible by the aesthetic modulation of the psyche.
>
> (*AEM*, 161)

The aesthetic, as embodied in art, privileges this more general, and largely unconscious, 'modulation of the psyche' by placing it within a conventional frame. Outside the aesthetic frame it might be complacency; within the frame it is the experience of the responsible self as such.

On this account, the 'autonomy' of the aesthetic is always and only aspectival. No one could live entirely within such a frame, nor could it enclose something completely unconnected from the outside world, if only because the aesthetic object is necessarily experienced from outside the artistic frame. Likewise, Schiller recognized that the aesthetic cannot of itself produce non-aesthetic values. Where moral values and sensibility are lacking, no aesthetic experience can provide them, even for someone, like the concentration camp officer, who is an artistic connoisseur. It is precisely the clarity of the transcendental separation which should prevent this prevalent modern confusion about the morally educative claims of art. The capacity of art to enlighten emotions and values does not rest on a claim to give the morally stupid and the pathologically brutal what they lack. Similarly, Schiller argued that the contemplative reflection on values and feelings is conditional upon art being disinterested in the sense that the experience of great art, such as a performance of *King Lear*, is a pregnancy of moral feeling but it does not direct the onlooker to any specific course of action such as a religious conversion or joining the socialist party. A given individual, following the impulse of the artistic experience, may perform such actions, and that would be entirely in the spirit of Schiller's argument, but it is not the function of the aesthetic as such to provide practical guidance.

The distinction is crucial. Terry Eagleton quotes this caveat from Schiller that if 'we find ourselves disposed to prefer some one mode of feeling or action, but unfitted or disinclined for another, this may serve as infallible proof that we have not had an aesthetic experience...' and Eagleton goes on to comment: 'As the very taproot of our moral virtue, the aesthetic is apparently invalid unless it predisposes us indifferently to murder or martyrdom.'[5] But Schiller has not presented the aesthetic as the 'taproot' of moral virtue, only as a crucial phase of it, as 'a modulation of the psyche', and the firm boundary he sets to the aesthetic is to prevent the confusion Eagleton exemplifies. Just as Schiller does not claim that the aesthetic as such is moral so, for him, moral sentiment without aesthetic self-knowledge is likely to be inadequate. Both exist independently, but inadequately, by themselves and it is the transformative relation between them which he sees as vital. Our relation to art is intrinsically liminal: art has its meaning in both the continuity with, and the separateness from, life. Eagleton's elision of the crucial discriminations here is more than a momentary slip: it is the basis for his larger argument in which the supposed ethical vacuity of Schiller's aesthetic conception becomes a repeated point of reference and a synecdoche for the status of the aesthetic in Western thought at large. It is also self-fulfilling in a typical way: he reads into Schiller what he expects him to be saying. A later tradition of thought about the aesthetic has given it an autonomous force which is now routinely read back into this earlier moment. Schiller's conception, however, is clearly not 'autonomous' in that later sense and his lasting importance lies in his refusal to confuse a vital distinction with a senseless and impossible separation, however common the latter may have become at the level of theory.

Of course, this is not to say that Schiller's account is without its problems and Marc Redfield, for example, offers a sophisticated ideological objection to Schiller's humanism as necessarily placed within a set of social relations.[6] Historically, the disinterestedness of the humanist has tended to serve conservative interests. Hence Schiller's investment in the aesthetic has been seen as a withdrawal from progressive thought in reaction to the disillusion of the French Revolution. His reliance on the educative effect of the aesthetic would then be an alibi for putting off the political pursuit of social amelioration. The political fortunes of sentiment in this period have already been touched on and the relevant emphasis here is that Schiller's conception of aesthetic education seeks to dissolve the literalistic and doctrinaire commitment to one's own values which the revolutionary period had shown to be, on all sides, a major evil in itself. He sought to overcome the compulsion of thought as well as feeling so that, whatever his own ideological awareness may have been, the compulsion of ideology is itself open to aesthetic recognition. The contemplative concentration of value within the aesthetic experience is anti-dogmatic and, for a certain style of progressive thought, the real Schiller is a truer, and more damaging, opponent than the aesthete he is conveniently accused of being.

The aspectual nature of the aesthetic is not a merely 'theoretical' point, then, since it reflects on the moral domain as much as on the understanding of art. Walter Benjamin's often-cited description of fascist propaganda and public life as the aestheticizing of politics is anticipated in Schiller's insistence on distinguishing artistic from non-artistic 'semblance'.[7] Confusion between them is symptomatic of something more than an aesthetic error:

> ... single individuals, as well as whole peoples, who either 'eke out reality with semblance, or (aesthetic) semblance with reality' – the two

often go together – give evidence alike of their moral worthlessness and of their aesthetic incapacity.

(*AEM*, 199)

This is no bad definition of fascist politics and national socialist art, the relation between them and their symptomatic significance, but for present purposes the emphasis lies on the relation of the aesthetic, as a 'modulation of the psyche', to moral sentiment. Just as the aesthetic does not exist separately from ethical feelings and values, so the moral feelings themselves require this modulation via the aesthetic.

Schiller's conception of the aesthetic, then, does not just resolve the antinomies of moral sentiment: his emphasis on moral freedom turns their very instability to positive account as a definition of responsibility. And Schiller's criticism of an ambiguous leakage between art and reality would apply to the unstable emotional literalism of the fiction of sentiment. Likewise, Schiller's insistence on the self-conscious 'semblance' of art detaches the question of emotional *participation* from that of *illusion*. His dismissive reference to 'the apelike capacity for mere imitation' recalls the Master Pedro episode from *Don Quixote* but his concern has shifted from illusion as such to an emotional quality conditional precisely upon a conscious illusion or artistic semblance (*NSD*, 755; *NSL*, 70). In effect, Schiller infuses the emotional Quixotry of affective verisimilitude with a new self-consciousness by articulating in principle the discriminated mutuality of the aesthetic and the ethical already hinted at in Sterne's embedded 'Story of Le Fever'. His 'aesthetic modulation' encompasses Kames's principle of 'ideal presence', in that the emotions of art are no more or less 'real' than those of everyday life, even as the object of art is now firmly discriminated as a fully conscious 'semblance'. When Schiller thinks of aesthetic experience as intrinsically educative he echoes what has been said about the emotional awareness enabled by fiction. In life, emotions are deceptive, possibly self-indulgent, even an unwitting fiction, but overt fictiveness puts the focus critically, and educatively, on the quality of the emotion as such. Emotions within fiction are objects of judgement in a way that emotions in the infinitely receding conditions of real life never can be.

Schiller's aesthetic transposition also sharpened Rousseau's thought. It is sometimes objected that Rousseau's social contract is merely a myth. Rousseau was aware of this without wishing to stress the fact. Schiller, however, argues more positively that society could *only* develop uncritically until it arrived at the point of rational self-critique which the notion of a social contract embodies. In other words, we have not just omitted, by some historical oversight, to establish such a contract, it is inconceivable that we could have done so at any earlier stage of historical development. By the same token, however, a people must be culturally ready for such an order, a case that could be argued from later modern history (*AEM*, 11–17). Likewise, Schiller's emphasis on aesthetic education ameliorates the 'bootstraps' problem in Rousseau whereby man has to be socialized into the good life in order to create the kind of society which would effect such a socialization. We have already noted how Rousseau's attempt to resolve this circularity through education was itself still very literalistically and rationalistically conceived in a way that answers to Schiller's general criticism of his mode of thought which is worth quoting at length:

> Rousseau, as Poet as well as Philosopher, has no other tendency but either to seek nature or to take vengeance on art. When his feeling has dwelt with one or the other we find him by turns elegiacally soothed, stirred to Juvenalian satire, or, like his Julie, drawn into the realm of idyll. His fictions have undeniably poetic content, since they treat of the ideal, except that he does not know how to handle them in a poetical manner. His serious character never allows him to sink to frivolity, but nor does it allow him to rise to poetic play. Pulled between passion and abstraction, he rarely or never achieves that aesthetic freedom which the poet must have toward his material and share with the reader. Either his sick sensibility dominates him and drives his feeling to the point of pain, or else his power of thought enchains his imagination while its conceptual strength destroys the grace of the picture. Both qualities, which in their succession and combination form the poet, are present in this writer to the highest degree, and nothing is lacking but that they truly unite: that his self-affirmation be more mingled with his sensibility, and his susceptibility with his thought. ... His passionate sensibility is to blame that, in order to be free of dispute with humanity, he would rather see it led back to the monotony of its original condition than see the conflict carried through in the spiritual harmony of a complete education. He would rather see art never begin than have to await its completion; in short, he would rather set the target lower, and bring down the ideal, in order to reach it so much faster and more surely.
>
> (*NSD*, 730–1; *NSL*, 49–50)

Even allowing for Schiller's tendency to understand everything through radical dualities, he catches an important limitation not just of Rousseau but of eighteenth-century sentiment generally. 'Thought' and 'feeling' may be reifications but, in so far as they govern discourse, they have an important kind of reality so that the sentimentalist attempt to overcome their duality constantly reinforced it. For Schiller, Rousseau's essential incapacity for the aesthetic is the symptom of a more fundamental conditon. And Schiller is undoubtedly right to see that Rousseau, who represents the major, and mythic, step towards modern affective individuality, still conceived of feeling in highly rationalist and universalist, as well as literalistic, terms. He sees Rousseau as possessed by, rather than truly possessing, his own feelings. Whether or not he is fair to Rousseau, Schiller's notion of the aesthetic, coupled with his analytic definition of the 'sentimental', provides a means of discriminating in principle those failures of emotional truth we now refer to as 'sentimentality'.

Aesthetics, judgement and sentimentality

The philosophical argument of the *Aesthetic Education* relates closely to Schiller's critique of the vices of sensibility: emotional indulgence, excess and falsity. In this respect he points forward to the modern definition of sentimentality whether in artistic criticism or more generally. The important elements of his thought in this regard, along with the inner freedom and responsibility he found in the aesthetic, were his attempts to resolve both the internal antinomy of principle versus feeling and the external problem of feeling's relation to its object.

To take the internal antinomy first, in his earlier essay 'On Grace and Dignity' (1793) he sought to reconcile principle and feeling more directly although with strong hints of continuity between the moral and the aesthetic. Ironically enough, even as he proposes the resolution of a deeply gendered dualism, he does it in two gendered forms. Dignity is the male form in which feeling is contained within a consciously principled, and socially authoritative, behaviour for which a judge might be an example. Grace, on the other hand, is the feminine quality in which moral principle is so fully absorbed into the life of feeling that, while only the feeling seems to be expressed, it communicates an embodied life of principle. A particularly tactful and intuitive hostess might exemplify this spirit. Whereas Kant saw such a reconciliation as practically impossible, or as the attribute of God alone, Schiller saw it as an ideal possibility which might be approached by some rare human beings, an ideal which he called the 'beautiful soul'. The phrase *'beautiful* soul' focuses the aesthetic resonance in his governing concepts of 'Grace' and 'Dignity' but this conception quickly began to get a bad press in a way that has distorted the record ever since.

In *Wilhelm Meister's Apprenticeship* (1796), which was written in close contact with Schiller, Goethe included a whole book, the sixth out of eight, devoted to 'The Confessions of a Beautiful Soul', the memoir of a deeply spiritual woman in the mode of German pietism. The ethos of the novel as a whole is highly masculine: Wilhelm is a kind of Tom Jones endowed with cultured interests and inner life, and he enjoys a largely affectionate irony from the narrator. The sixth book, by contrast, is a female novella narrated in the first person. The central figure, an aunt of the young woman, Natalie, whom Wilhelm eventually marries, inhabits a world of spirituality which, by reading her own account of her life, Wilhelm is led to appreciate. But Wilhelm does not himself adopt her values and her story suggests between the lines, and particularly in its contrast with Wilhelm's own life, a measure of repression and self-enclosure.[8] Schiller's idea of the 'beautiful soul' was subjected to pertinent critique by Goethe's imagining its possible consequences in 'real life', yet it was intended more as a regulative and philosophical ideal such as Schiller articulated to him in a letter discussing the 'Confessions of the Beautiful Soul':

> I find in the Christian religion the disposition towards the highest and noblest, and the very different manifestations of it in life seem to me so adverse and repellent because they are failed representations of the highest. The essential characteristic of Christianity, which distinguishes it from all monotheistic religions, lies in nothing other than the *cancelling of the law* or of the Kantian imperative, in place of which Christianity puts a free inclination. It is, therefore, in its pure form, the representation of a *beautiful* ethic, or the becoming human of the sacred, and in this sense it is the only *aesthetic* religion; which is also why this religion brings so much happiness to female nature, and is only found in a tolerable form in women.[9]

As well as the limits of 'the Kantian imperative', this answers the Kantian perception of the Gospel as quoted earlier. And as Schiller remarks in a later letter, the truly beautiful soul in Goethe's novel is not the aunt but Natalie herself 'who alone has a purely aesthetic nature. How beautiful, that she is absolutely unaware of love as an exclusive and special feeling because love is her very being, and permanent character' (ibid., 190) Likewise, Natalie is not especially pious, nor interested in artistic pursuits. It is precisely her moral completeness, her emotional wholeness, to which

Schiller applies the word 'aesthetic'. Here the word 'aesthetic' denotes an identity of moral feeling and principle at the opposite extreme from the separatist conception of aestheticism.

Yet it was the aunt's case, rather than Natalie's, which became exemplary of the beautiful soul and perhaps helped to obscure Schiller's more substantial and dynamic conception of the aesthetic as a crucial modulation of moral sentiment. Goethe's sympathetic, but sardonic, view of the Beautiful Soul's ideal of inner perfection was taken up more critically again by Hegel, and through him in turn by Marxist thought, and has become inscribed in the left philosophical tradition as an image of false consciousness. Yet as Godwin's memoir of Mary Wollstonecraft implicitly suggested, there could be other, less auratic, more feisty, versions of the beautiful soul but they would then hardly be recognized as being such. The subsequent fate of the idea of the 'beautiful soul', coupled with the relatively modern appreciation of Wollstonecraft, may stand as an emblem of the larger impulse of sentimentalism itself which has continued to affect European culture in incalculable positive ways while remaining, in the discursive tradition, merely a byword for the inauthentic. The moral ideal has *consciously* survived principally in the form of its attendant vice.

Goethe himself shared many of Schiller's preoccupations, albeit with constant, fundamental disagreements. The difference includes an avoidance of his younger friend's intellectual systematizing so that he often worked out similar questions in creative terms which might not admit of discursive translation, and this could apply even when his thought appeared in ostensibly discursive form. R. H. Stephenson, for example, has concluded that even Goethe's wisdom literature, consisting of moral generalizations, is an essentially 'aesthetic deployment of language' thereby vindicating' 'Schiller's claim that the aesthetic can set us free'.[10] On this reading, even sentiment in its earlier sense of general maxims has been aesthetically transposed. Likewise in Goethe's two novels of education, in which the aesthetic interests of the heroes are a central motif, the supposed outcome of the educative process is itself to be understood aesthetically rather than doctrinally. Many moments of illumination are attained but no 'conclusion' is final. This echoes Schiller's sense of the aesthetic as a 'modulation' of feeling and thought which is inseparable from the wholeness and continuity of a life. Just as we accept feeling to be shifting and relative, so are the intellectual recognitions of which feeling is an integral part. In this respect, Goethe's works, precisely by being in such a pervasively aesthetic spirit, also express the pervasiveness of the aesthetic within the texture of life. At the same time, Goethe's practice of art equally reaffirms Schiller's insistence that the aesthetic affects the moral by not being confused with it. Karl Viëtor has remarked on Goethe's correction of a 'philistine half truth' in Herder who expressed the conventional eighteenth-century view that art must acknowledge the moral order and serve it. As Goethe puts it:

> It has always done, and must do, the former, because its laws, as much as those of the moral order, spring from reason; but if it did the latter, it would be lost.[11]

Art, for Goethe too, has a moral effect only by refraining from direct moral purpose.

Hence in Goethe, too, emotional and aesthetic quality are distinct yet intimately intertwined so that the one is constantly understood through the other. Goethe's career as a novelist began with *The Sorrows of the Young Werther* (1774) in which the critique of Rousseauvian sentiment was linked with an aesthetic theme: Werther's emotional errors have as their repeated symptom a non-aesthetic literalism. The sign that Werther is not a real artist is that his intense feelings allow him no detachment from himself or his world. Precisely by experiencing the world so much *through* his feeling, he is unable truly to invest it *with* feeling. In a less naive and destructive way, the later hero, Wilhelm, suffers from the same vice of dilettantism, of mistaking aesthetic *sensibility* for the rarer faculty of artistic *creativity*. Although Schiller's description of Rousseau does not quite say so, it suggests that just as he might have become a great artist so, by the same logic, he might have proved to be a dilettante if he had sought to enter a properly aesthetic realm. Werther is precisely a Rousseauvian figure who does seek, mistakenly, to achieve the aesthetic without overcoming his sentimental identification with the object. In this sense, the aesthetic is far from being a blanket answer to the problems of sentiment or of false feeling. Indeed, the realm of the aesthetic replicates internally to itself the whole problematic of authenticity endemic to sentimentalism but the special advantage of the art work in this respect is that its achievement or failure is objectified, and can be more objectively assessed, at least by those fit to judge. The condition of Werther was critically objectified in *Werther* even if it took another few generations to see the point.

If the adequacy of the object is a key to the quality of the feeling, in both art and life, the adequacy lies not in the object as such but only as it is invested with significance by feeling. The difficulty was to ensure that the feeling was truly invested in the art object, and not just an inartistic supplement drawn from the observer's feelings. That was the topic of another exchange between the two poets. Goethe had written to Schiller of his puzzlement over the apparently excessive responses produced in him by a recent journey. He offered the incipiently Proustian surmise that his states of emotional reflection were a product of memory somehow triggered by external impressions. Punning on Sterne's title, he refers to his own experience as a 'sentimental journey' in Schiller's redefined sense of the term. Schiller replies:

> The sentimental phenomenon in you does not disturb me at all, and it seems to me you have already explained it. It is a need of poetic natures, if not rather of the human mind generally, to suffer as little emptiness as possible, and to have, through feeling, as much world as possible around them; to seek out the depth of all appearances and to furnish a human whole. If the object in itself is empty and poetically lacking, the faculty for ideas will attempt to grasp it from its symbolic side, and make out of it a human language. But the sentimental (in the good sense) is an effect of the poetic striving which, for reasons either in the object or in the mind, is not completely fulfilled. Such a poetic aspiration, without a truly poetic mood or subject, seems to have been your case, and what you are experiencing is nothing but the general story of the sentimental mode of feeling, and proves everything we agreed together about it.
>
> Only one thing I must remind you. You speak as if it is the object that matters, which I cannot admit. Certainly, the object must *mean* something, just as the poetic object must *be* something, but ultimately it depends on the *mind* whether an object means anything to it, and so the emptiness or richness lies more in the subject than in the object. It is the mind which sets the limits here, and it is the treatment, not the material, which makes something either commonplace or interesting. What the two places were for you, any street, or bridge, or ship, or plough, or any other mechanical tool, would perhaps have been in other circumstances and in a more open poetic mood. So do not reject these sentimental impressions: give them expression as often as you can. Nothing, except the poetic, so cleanses the mind of the empty and commonplace as the appearance of such objects. A world is placed thereby into the individual thing, and flat appearances take on an infinite depth. If that is not poetic, it is, as you yourself say, human; and the human is always the beginning of the poetic which is but the summit of the human.[12]

The interest, then, has shifted from the internal sincerity of feeling in relation to principle and focused on the adequacy of the object to the feeling. The poetic nature, as an essential version of the human, is seen as that of the man of sentiment, the one who brings feeling to the occasion. But while the value, or feeling, is recognized as coming from this internal source, the mood in itself is not aesthetically valuable. Only when it achieves an adequate object, what T. S. Eliot was to call the 'objective correlative', will the feeling acquire artistic significance. Until then the feeling or mood is only of potential significance, what the dilettante might mistake for art. The literalism of the earlier model of sentiment has now modulated into the more subtle need for an object that is no longer supposed to carry its own intrinsic charge of meaning. The secret subjectivity of sentiment is now the acknowledged point as it seeks adequate objectification. That may be difficult and whether it is achieved is a matter of aesthetic or critical judgement. The possible disparity between object and feeling is an important underlying significance in the diverging meanings of the word 'sentimental'. When the object and the sentiment fail to combine adequately, the result is merely 'sentimental' in our modern pejorative sense. And as Schiller emphasized, modern 'sentimental' self-consciousness is especially prone to mere sentimental-ity. It is a creative achievement to close the gap between feeling and object. At the same time, as with all his aesthetic thought, the poetic condition is the purest version of the human so that these critical analyses have a much broader moral implication.

The emphasis on investing feeling in an object might also suggest an especial poetic worth, if not necessarily the greatest poetry, in common-place occasions since these would most clearly depend on artistic achievement. The compelling English instance of this, a poet who deliberately sought out the poetic challenge of the banal and the sentimental, is Wordsworth. He is an inverse parallel to both Goethe and Schiller in that, despite his constant meditation on the nature of poetry, especially his own, he did not privilege the category of the aesthetic so much as feeling itself. In that respect, he typifies the English sentimentalist inheritance.

4
Wordsworth: the Man of Feeling, Recollected Emotion and the 'Sentiment of Being'

Wordsworth is the fulcrum on which a significant turn into poetic modernity occurs and his reputation and significance remain controversial. There are two 'Wordsworths' reflecting the bifurcated inheritance of sentimentalism itself. Behind the softer, popular image of Wordsworthian love of Nature and of man is a more austere philosopher of Being, and of moral feelings, whom critics have repeatedly found to be disturbingly unsentimental. These two Wordsworths exemplify how the most obvious impact of sentimentalism is the least substantive while the true inheritance of sentiment became not so much lost, as lost to view; the deeper current of feeling began, like certain rivers in Coleridge and Wordsworth, to flow increasingly underground.

The historical watershed which occurred in Wordsworth was that, while he was steeped in the poetic tradition from Chaucer through Spenser to Milton, and maintained the Renaissance and Enlightenment belief in poetry as a means of public moral instruction, he pre-eminently established the modern understanding of poetry as an expression of personal feeling. The relation between these dimensions is a matter of continuing debate. The historical meaning of Wordsworth has been examined in a remarkable series of critical studies over the last thirty years. While critics such as John Beer, Geoffrey Hartman and Jonathon Wordsworth have elucidated the poetic and philosophical achievement, others such as James Chandler, Jerome McGann, Marjorie Levinson and Alan Liu have analysed the ideological mystification whereby Wordsworth mythologized his own recollected feelings and suppressed his earlier radicalism.[1] The general force of this critique is incontrovertible and I am indebted to this remarkable period of Wordsworth criticism. The negative emphasis in these latter readings, however, often leaves the decade of acknowledged great poetry in a critical limbo. What exactly is left after the demolition?

I wish to emphasize that Wordsworth's *mode* of emotional recollection has an intrinsic value and that if he did not satisfactorily hold the orders of public history and personal feeling together the significance of this transcends his individual instance. His well-documented case throws a more general condition of modernity into sombre relief. He is an index of what happens to the value of feeling itself: even as it becomes a more fundamental criterion in the life of the modern individual its relation to the public realm becomes problematic. The individual and the social realms are not separable but the means of understanding them have become so and the word 'sentiment' continues to focus this development. James Chandler quotes Burke's privileging of moral sentiments against what he saw as the damaging impact of the ideologues:

> ... the moral sentiments of some few amongst them do put some check on their savage theories. But let us take care. The moral sentiments, so nearly connected with early prejudice as to be nearly one and the same thing, will assuredly not live long under a discipline which has for its basis the destruction of all prejudices, and the making the mind proof against all dread of sequences flowing from the pretended truths that are taught by their philosophy.
>
> (Chandler, 1984, 55)

Meanwhile Chandler himself remarks, in a critical spirit, that 'the cultural past survives in moral sentiments' (ibid., 197). The eighteenth-century quotation and the modern comment demonstrate how the ground has shifted under the phrase. Used positively by Burke and pejoratively by Chandler, 'moral sentiment' denotes a feeling once justified by being part of a social order but now an empty piety.

As the critical debate shows, once this bifurcation has occurred, it is difficult to acknowledge simultaneously both the power of Wordsworth's personal myths of feeling and their questionable bases. This points to the coming apart of the original sentimentalist project: the attempt to base a moral order on feeling through an identification with social principle. Yet even as feeling becomes radically privatized, Wordsworth partly recognizes this and enacts a critical transformation of feeling with positive consequences for the future. As with much eighteenth-century sentimentalist literature, an artistically uneven achievement is compatible with a significant engagement with the problematics of moral sentiment, and, through that, of the moral life. A fruitful lesson can be drawn here from Jonathon Bate's study of Wordsworth's 'romantic ecology'.[2] Bate defends Wordsworth, in broader political terms, by reaffirming the nineteenth-century reception of him as a 'nature' poet and linking this in turn to late twentieth-century ecological concerns. Many of the passages Bate quotes with respect to Nature, however, give almost equal emphasis to the feelings, which was Wordsworth's other great area of significance for nineteenth-century readers. Of course, the inner and outer, the cosmic and the emotional, are inseparable in Wordsworth, that was his great theme, and this insight retains a fundamental value, emotionally and ontologically, even as the political significance of feeling becomes radically problematic.

The artistic implications of the shift from a public mode of poetic meaning to a concentration on personal feeling can be seen in Wordsworth's reflections on the pastoral. In *The Prelude* he records how, within his own sensibility, the public form of the pastoral suffered an inner dissolution as a significant category. Without deriding pastoral convention from the outside, as Dr Johnson did with 'Lycidas' in his *Life of Milton*, Wordsworth rather relives from the inside the historical process of its decline, a process which is perhaps also suggested, in the Cambridge episode, by the difference between Spenser's poetic serenity and Milton's besieged singleness.[3] The pastoral form not only belonged to a public, didactic conception of poetry, it depended on a set of shared conventions which were explicitly not realistic. The pastoral is rather a form of public allegory. By contrast, Wordsworth's shepherd is the solitary figure numinously glimpsed in the mountains and the mists.

> ... suddenly mine eyes
> Have glanced upon him distant a few steps.
> In size a giant, stalking through thick fog,
> His sheep like Greenland bears; or, as he stepped
> Beyond the boundary line of some hill-shadow,
> His form hath flashed upon me, glorified
> By the deep radiance of the setting sun.

(*Prelude*, viii, ll. 264–70)

Here we partake in the creation of a personal myth. This shepherd is an actual individual, and a social type, initially set against the literariness of the pastoral convention, yet he is even more forcefully rendered as a creature of the Wordsworthian imagination, glimpsed at a given moment in a chance play of light. And as he is created for us now in Wordsworth's blank verse lines, the pre-eminent and naturalized form for dramatic speech and poetic self-communing in English, the shepherd is a product of poetic art but with an effect of reality set off by the contrast with an outmoded literary convention of pastoral. Even as Wordsworth goes on to insist on his social reality, the shepherd is

> Far more of an imaginative form
> Than the gay Corin of the groves, ...

(ibid., viii, ll. 284–5)

He takes on the deeper ambiguity of status which Cervantes creates in *Don Quixote*. At first glance, the romance of Don Quixote contrasts with the real world of the deluded provincial gentleman, Alonso Quijano, who imagines him. Only slowly do we realize that Alonso Quijano is equally fictional, albeit in a world of realism, and that Cervantes is juxtaposing not just fiction and life but different kinds of fiction.

The elusively poetic, or mythic, status of such Wordsworthian figures parallels the aesthetic modulation of feeling in Schiller and links with the problematics of response in sentimental fiction. For Wordsworth's notable achievement lay in a critical transformation of moral sentimentalism for which the crucial first step, the unnoticed prior condition, was an escape from its literalism. Feeling, in Wordsworth, is no longer explained as an immediate response to an object but becomes quite explicitly the stuff of imagination and reflection. Without quite appealing to the category of the aesthetic, Wordsworth finds an equivalent meaning to Schiller's through reflection on feeling, particularly in the process of poetic creation. The break from the literalism of earlier models of sentiment, therefore, comes not from a poetic or imaginative transposition *per se* but through the internal logic of Wordsworth's naturalistic recognition of the importance of time in relation to feeling. In so far as the object, such as the shepherd, is remembered at some distance in time it is inevitably an imaginative creation and Wordsworth's famous account of the creative process indicates the doubleness of his relation to sentiment. On the one hand, poetry is the 'spontaneous overflow of powerful feelings' yet on the other hand it 'takes its origin from emotion recollected in tranquillity'.[4] The basis in feeling is fully acknowledged, and, like Schiller, he stresses the greater importance of the feeling over the ostensible object.[5] Yet it is never simply the feeling as such. It is feeling as it lives on in the memory, both consciously and unconsciously. Wordsworth's great insight lay in his way of understanding feeling within the process of personal time although this inevitably increased its privatization and weakened its relation to the public sphere. There is an intrinsic logic to this bifurcation, and the gain is not separable from the loss. The gain in understanding, however, was that the emotional sublimities, which for Rousseau had been a matter of nostalgia and illusion, became for Wordsworth a continuing process in the psyche for which these categories were themselves part of a critical dynamic. They were part of the nature of the case rather than a self-evident point of critique. Or to take a more distant comparison again, Augustine's emotional intensities were typically in conflict with time as his ultimate yearning was for eternity, and time presented itself to him as a recalcitrant mystery as long as conversion was delayed. In Wordsworth, by contrast, feeling merges inseparably with the flow of time itself. The poetic formula of recollected emotion points, therefore, to a more general psychological one. Emotions acquire their significance in time.

If Wordsworth's emotional internalizing parallels Schiller's thought on the aesthetic, and both grew from the problematics of sentiment, his emphasis seems opposite to Schiller's. He rarely discusses the 'artistic' as a value in itself. But this is because, as in Schiller, the poetic is valued only *as* a modulation of the life of feeling. When, for example, he records in *The Prelude* his earliest boyhood awareness 'Of words in tuneful order' and how he 'found them sweet / For their own *sakes*' (*Prelude*, v, ll. 555–6, Wordsworth's emphasis) he goes on to attribute this to the untutored 'wish for something loftier, more adorned, / Than is the common aspect, daily garb, / of human life' (ibid., v, ll. 575–7). He even suggests something that may sound like Schiller's emphasis on 'play':

> ... sounds
> Of exultation echoed through the groves!
> For, images, and sentiments, and words,
> And everything encountered or pursued
> In that delicious world of poesy,
> Kept holiday, ...

> (ibid., v, ll. 577–82)

But this is naive boyhood experience and, although Wordsworth always honours the principle of relaxation, we do not imagine him committing himself to Schiller's formula that 'Man is only fully a human being when he plays.' Whereas play for Schiller is an intense formal concentration, Wordsworth's term 'holiday' suggests his half-witting ability to let experience wash over him precisely so that he will, while remaining alert, not be too deeply touched by the inessential. The 'good-natured lounging' of his Cambridge years underlay what he later understood as a 'wise passiveness' (*Lyrical Ballads*, 104). His extraordinary ability was to let the longer-term process of emotional time flow beneath consciousness while retaining a capacity, at given moments, to bring it to the reflective surface. Accordingly, in the present context, he goes on precisely to emphasize that his being 'stirred to ecstasy, as others are, / By glittering verse' would have been empty without the earlier, formative intimacy with 'living Nature'. Only for that reason is there for him a 'Visionary power ... / Embodied in the mystery of words' (*Prelude*, v, ll. 588–97). Similarly, when he argues, in the 1800 Preface to the *Lyrical Ballads*, for the importance of poetic metre, he justifies it as a psychological means of preventing the feelings from being overwhelmed by the immediate event (*Lyrical Ballads*, 264). In short, Wordsworth is opposite to Schiller in practically eliding the category of the aesthetic, yet he is, for that very reason, more deeply at one with him in not dividing art from the general life of feeling.

The emphasis on the internalizing process of recollection and reflection indicates why much of the critical problem posed by Wordsworth is encapsulated in Keats's phrase, derived from Hazlitt, 'the egotistical sublime', and the inverse parallel with Schiller helps to hold it in focus.[6] Given Wordsworth's commitment to compassionate sympathy, readers have always been disturbed by his love of solitude and his imaginative preoccupation with his own feelings. Such criticism of his poetic self has seemed to be endorsed by his apparent self-enclosure, his willingness to take others for granted, in his personal life. On this model, Wordsworth is a great poet whose creative concentration, like Tolstoy's, was at the expense of ordinary human relations in a way that, given the autobiographical emphasis in his work, throws the artistic achievement into question. Wordsworth's 'egotism', however, bears a more intrinsic relation to his subject-matter. As Hazlitt put it:

He is the greatest, that is, the most original poet of the present day, only because he is the greatest egotist. He is 'self-involved, not dark.' He sits in the centre of his own being, and 'there enjoys the bright day.' He does not waste a thought on others. He stamps that character, that deep individual interest, on whatever he meets.[7]

Schiller, by developing the notion of the aesthetic as a special transposition of feeling, as a state of emotional intensity within a condition of disinterestedness, avoided conflating it with practical moral feeling. He presented it as a phase of feeling which affects the capacity for moral action only by, at least metaphorically, preceding it. Wordsworth understood equally well, and consummately practised, the principle of artistic disinterestedness, but he did something more challenging in carrying disinterestedness directly into the moral sphere. If this was partly a matter of temperament, it was nonetheless essential to his investigation of the moral life of feeling. It may be that, because of his peculiar temperament, he did not need the aesthetic state to achieve disinterestedness. In a succinct formula, his egotism was for Wordsworth what the aesthetic was for Schiller. To give Wordsworth's egotism an honorary aesthetic sign, however, is to challenge the notion of the aesthetic as a disguised form of self-indulgence for the force of the formula works the other way. A certain detachment, a meditative passivity, even at moments of compassion, is part of the human, as well as the aesthetic, relation. He recovered within sentimentalist occasions the affirmation of St John of the Cross: 'Love consists not in feeling great things, but in having great detachment and in suffering for the Beloved.'[8]

Much traditional criticism of Wordsworth has emphasized his *avoidance* of sentimentality while the recent appreciation of sentimentalism has led to an emphasis on his *continuity* with it. Both emphases are correct and I am indebted to several critics who have discussed his relation to late eighteenth-century Sensibility.[9] Yet such discussions pass over the ways in which Wordsworth transforms the models of moral sentimentalism from within and, instead of its impact on him, I wish rather to consider his impact on it. The older style literary history, which spoke of 'pre-romanticism' as the harbinger of romanticism, while it helpfully kept the lines of continuity in focus, had the effect of making the earlier moment seem merely ancillary and discardable. Where the present theme is concerned, it is more helpful to think of continuing transformations of a problematic which can never be resolved, for the problems of moral sentiment, its indulgence, its possible insincerity, its concealed egotism, are the intrinsic problems of the moral life and the life of feeling.

Whether or not he always got his feelings right, Wordsworth's remarkable achievement, arising from his reflective internalizing of emotional response within a process of personal time, was to grasp the nettle of egotism at the heart of the tradition of moral sentiment. Instead of being the badly disguised secret underlying, and therefore undermining, the project of moral sentiment, the ego becomes in Wordsworth the primordial condition. This had two relevant effects. First, his reflective egotism transformed sentiment by challenging the absoluteness and immediacy of momentary compassion. But its deeper effect, growing out of that, was that his emotional intensities eventually transcended the ethical domain entirely for the sake of an ontological vision. In both these respects, Wordsworth had critically to rework not just the ideology and psychology of sentiment, but its characteristic reliance on a literary mode of affective verisimilitude. Once again, the response to a distressful object is explored through the 'tale within the tale' but the focus now shifts to an examination of the *response* as mediated in *time*. Wordsworth builds a new emotional significance from the ruins of sentiment.

The sentimental tale and the ruins of sentiment

In the Preface to the 1800 *Lyrical Ballads* Wordsworth attacked the poetic diction of the Augustans, but in seeking the 'real language of men' he may be criticizing, as Jerome McGann has argued, a contemporary poetry of sensibility, the Della Cruscans.[10] The dangers of sensibility are his more immediate and creative preoccupation because he is keeping faith with its underlying endeavour. Yet it is instructive that, if it is a poetry of sensibility which is disapproved as artificial, the instances of a too unmediated emotional impact are from sentimental fiction and drama: the 'distressful parts of *Clarissa Harlowe* or *The Gamester*' (*Lyrical Ballads*, 264). For his internal methods in the *Lyrical Ballads* are those more commonly associated with prose fiction. The oxymoronic formula of the title, its combination of the impersonality of the ballad with the 'subjectivity' of the lyric, has always been recognized but only in a series of comparatively recent studies has the importance of narrative voices and multiple framings in a number of Wordsworth's poems of pathos, including some of the *Lyrical Ballads*, been appreciated.[11] As was remarked before, it was in the comparatively open, informal, less prestigious medium of prose fiction that much of the self-criticism of sentiment was conducted, whether self-consciously, as in Diderot, or less consciously, as in Richardson. John Beer notes that the only work of modern literature Wordsworth commented on having read before their composition was *Tristram Shandy*.[12] Whatever weight is placed on this, Wordsworth's narrative poems often highlight not so much the object of distress as the sentimental response itself. The response becomes the primary dramatic element. His own emphasis on the *Lyrical Ballads* being a series of 'experiments', linked to his later comments on following the 'man of science' wherever his speculations might lead, is to the point. For these poems are not just literary experiments so much as experiments in what he calls the 'moral feelings' (*Lyrical Ballads*, 255).

More specifically, the references to Richardson and Edward Moore suggest how his relation to an earlier sentimentalism involves rethinking the question of affective verisimilitude. When Wordsworth asks, in the 1802 Preface, 'What is a Poet?' his reply, like Schiller's, starts with the characteristics of the man of sentiment: 'a man ... endowed with more lively sensibility, more enthusiasm and tenderness ...' But the poet's unusual readiness 'to be affected' is given a different inflection by his specifically poetic ability: he can conjure up

> in himself passions which are indeed far from being the same as those produced by real events, yet (especially in those parts of the general sympathy which are pleasing and delightful) do more nearly resemble the passions produced by real events, than anything which, from the motions of their own minds merely, other men are accustomed to feel in themselves.
>
> (ibid., 255–6)

Unlike the earlier literalism of sentiment, the poet does not confuse the emotions of the poem with those produced by real events yet he reproduces something very like it at the level of artistic semblance. Indeed, as part of the creative process, Wordsworth even acknowledges as legitimate the

> wish of the Poet to bring his feelings near to those of the persons whose feelings he describes, nay, for short spaces of time perhaps, to let himself slip into an entire delusion, and even confound and identify, his own feelings with theirs ...

Wordsworth invokes here the kind of emotional identification seen in Rousseau, and more playfully in Diderot. And some such emotional identification with characters has been attested by many great literary artists, yet Wordsworth keeps it clearly distinct as a creative moment from the final outcome in artistic semblance. At the same time, an ontological discussion of its status *as* semblance, which was central to Schiller, is almost studiously avoided by Wordsworth. Instead, he covers this aspect in directly emotional terms by his discussion of metre. Having refused the distinction of prose and verse as a general quality of language, which is his way of denying the separateness of the poetic experience, he goes on to affirm the crucial working of metre upon the feelings. Metre tends

> to divest language, in a certain degree, of its reality, and thus to throw a sort of unsubstantial existence over the whole composition, there can be

little doubt but that more pathetic situations and sentiments, that is, those which have a greater proportion of pain connected with them, may be endured in metrical composition, especially in rhyme, than in prose.

(ibid., 264)

A still controversial endurance of the painful can be seen in one of Wordsworth's most challenging reworkings of the sentimental tale: the story of Margaret, or 'The Ruined Cottage', which, after existing for many years in different manuscript versions, was eventually published within the first book of *The Excursion*. The pathetic tale of this woman who loses in turn her husband and both sons, falls into a decline and dies is told, in all its versions, to the poet figure by a narrator met at the site of the cottage. Although the core poem about Margaret is one of Wordsworth's crucial achievements, the reason it never saw separate publication was presumably that it always existed, for him, in a problematic relation with the narrator, initially the Pedlar and finally, in *The Excursion*, the Wanderer. The meaning of the story for him does not lie simply within the story itself but in the exact discrimination of response. In reworking the sentimental formula of the tale within the tale Wordsworth shifts the centre of gravity from an exemplary intensity of feeling for the sufferer to an examination of the quality of feeling it arouses in the listener. It inverts the tradition of sentiment from the inside.

This is signalled from the outset by the Pedlar/Wanderer's hesitation in telling the tale since it can only be justified by an adequate response in both teller and listener. Already there is an ambivalence: is the hesitation about whether the poet/speaker will make an adequately sentimental response, or is it the whole tradition of sentimental voyeurism which is being questioned?

> It were a wantonness, and would demand
> Severe reproof, if we were men whose hearts
> Could hold vain dalliance with the misery
> Even of the dead; contented thence to draw
> A momentary pleasure, never marked
> By reason, barren of all future good.[13]

As with the story of Le Fever, the retrospective framing means that neither the poet-figure nor the internal narrator now faces Margaret's distress directly. Hence, unlike the discharged soldier, for example, she raises no question of immediate moral action, and any distinctions to be made are entirely within the realm of feeling as mediated by time. Of course, she is no mere fiction for them either, and the poet's feelings are aroused, as in so many sentimentalist occasions, by the literal actuality of her life, yet his feelings may still, which is the other side of the sentimentalist ambiguity, be a response to the narrator's tale rather than to the person:

> In my own despite,
> I thought of that poor Woman as of one
> Whom I had known and loved. He had rehearsed
> Her homely tale with such familiar power,
>
> . . .
>
> that the things of which he spake
> Seemed present; . . .

(ibid., ll. 612–18)

Margaret's distress is both vividly present and highly mediated. She tells her story to the Pedlar/Wanderer who retells it to the poet/speaker who is in turn our surrogate in the reading. The resulting combination of emotional immediacy and temporal distance, as in 'The Story of Le Fever', allows a discrimination between different aspects of response. In the original unpublished version, the poem's structure is like Keats's 'Ode on a Grecian Urn' in that it begins with an overall distanced serenity, is drawn into an emotional intensity, and then withdraws to a new version of the original distance. Even here, however, Wordsworth eschews the absolute, aesthetic distance of the urn. He rather develops a similar implication naturalistically from inside the action. The opening scene is picturesquely framed by the 'impending branches' of an oak to become 'More soft and distant'.[14] Meanwhile one of the Pedlar/Wanderer's first remarks, in all versions, is to approve how

> The Poets, in their elegies and songs
> Lamenting the departed, call the groves,
> They call upon the hills and streams to mourn,
> And senseless rocks; nor idly; for they speak,
> In these their invocations, with a voice
> Obedient to the strong creative power
> Of human passion.

(*Excursion*, I, ll. 475–81)

Poetic convention is invoked only to be dissolved into its underlying, naturalistic emotional meaning.

The poem's challenge comes at the end as the Pedlar/Wanderer enacts a comparable withdrawal from inside the emotional action. Readers have constantly been troubled by the moment when, explicitly detaching the pathos of Margaret's story from a larger sense of life, he concludes:

> I turned away,
> And walked along my road in happiness.

> (ibid., ll. 955–6)

This astonishing moment fixes indelibly a certain image of Wordsworth's own self-enclosure. Critics have objected to a comparable instance in 'The Old Cumberland Beggar' where Wordsworth's argument that the old man should not go to the workhouse rests not on the inhumanity of the workhouse itself so much as on his ethical value as an object of charity and contemplation in the local community. The narrator's unironized attitude in these poems is uncomfortably close to what a Marxist would call the 'aestheticization of poverty' and A. D. Nuttall sees its damaging self-enclosure as a direct descendant of the complacency of the man of sentiment (Nuttall, 1974, 129–35). But there is some reductiveness in this account for the sentimental tradition, far from being the poem's unthinking premise, has become its critical subject-matter. The delicacy here, however, as with the transformation of the pastoral, is that Wordsworth is not merely satirizing the tradition from outside but is seeking another significance from within it.

In both poems, the reader is challenged with an unexpected viewpoint and, even if Wordsworth's human and artistic judgement are open to question, he makes a serious point against the grain of a sentimentalist expectation which still lives on for modern readers. The common objection to the man of sentiment was that in the face of distress he indulged his own feeling of benevolence, sometimes even as an alternative to personal assistance or social reform. Wordsworth, however, offers not a defence of the man of sentiment *despite* this complacency but a defence of the 'complacency' *itself*. He deliberately privileges the notorious blind spot of sentimentalism. The spirit of it is akin to his images of Newton, Spenser and Milton in the Cambridge section of *The Prelude*. They are all imaged as solitaries: Newton 'for ever / Voyaging through strange seas of Thought, alone'; Spenser moving 'with the moon's beauty and the moon's soft pace'; and Milton who 'Stood almost single' (*Prelude*, iii, ll. 62–3, 283–7). Each discovered universal truths, or performed profound acts of human solidarity, by entering a lonely world of contemplation. Wordsworth's meditations have a similar impact in seeking to understand the life of feeling not just as it should be but as it is, and not just in its immediate human relation but in its longer-term effects. In a spirit of enquiry closer to Freud's would-be scientific self-analysis than to Rousseau's apologetic *Confessions*, Wordsworth sought to understand the life of feeling within himself not just through self-regard but because it was the one case directly available for inspection, and it is not so much the egoistic remove as the impersonality with which he conducts this enquiry which gives it its uncanny power to disturb our moral expectations.

In effect, the story of Margaret engages the traditional theological problem of evil within a creation that is believed to be good as if this were ultimately an affective question, and Wordsworth prepares for this in several ways. First, the blend of presentness and mediation preserves throughout a double time. However vividly recalled, Margaret's distress is always experienced in a peculiar combination of narrative present and past. The conflation is typified in the description of her offering to passers-by, 'the cool refreshment drawn / From that *forsaken* spring' (*Excursion*, ll. 504–5, my emphasis). Second, the Pedlar/Wanderer's final 'affirmation' that he walked his road 'in happiness', although it could not be more challengingly bald in itself, is dramatically placed with a care comparable to the affirmation that ends Yeats's 'Lapis Lazuli':

> *Their* eyes, mid many wrinkles,
> *Their* ancient, glittering eyes, are gay.[15]

> (my emphases)

It is the character's statement, not the poet's. Hence, although the Pedlar is in some sense Wordsworth's spokesman, the poet has placed himself within the poem as one listening to the remark with something of our own astonishment. And the Pedlar/Wanderer, while clearly offering his response as exemplary, attaches it to this one occasion in a way that suggests it is an unusual and surprising response even for him.

> ' ... I well remember that those very plumes,
> Those weeds, and the high spear-grass on that wall,
> By mist and silent rain-drops silvered o'er,
> As *once* I passed, into my heart conveyed
> So still an image of tranquillity,
> So calm and still, and looked so beautiful

> Amid the uneasy thoughts which filled my mind,
>
>   . . .
>
>   I turned away,
> And walked along my road in happiness.'

(ibid., ll. 942–56, my emphasis)

The moment is not simply recalled for its immediate and exemplary normality, it is rather confided for its uncanny, almost mystical, strangeness. It is akin to the lover's experience in 'Strange Fits of Passion I have Known' in that we intuit something of its psychological origin, and in the present case we can also see its general philosophical justification, yet it came to the speaker himself, like certain Proustian moments, irrationally and as a surprise. So too, the ending of the poem, as the poet and story-teller are both 'admonished' and then move on 'together', is itself as much outside this privileged moment of happiness as it is a partial withdrawing from the compassionate feelings aroused by the tale.

The conclusion contains several levels of recognition. The first concerns the appropriate degree of compassionate response. At the end of Margaret's story, the Wordsworth figure '. . .was moved' and from 'that low bench . . . turned aside in weakness' (ibid., ll. 918–19) but the response of the Pedlar/Wanderer, who observes this, gives a force to the word 'weakness' undercutting the amiable softness of the man of sentiment which we are at first inclined to read into it. The poetic speaker's immediate response is humanly fitting in itself, but he is not allowed to indulge it for long. After revisiting the cottage ruins in the light of Margaret's story, and blessing 'her in the impotence of grief', a phrase which itself implies the possible vacuity of sentiment, he returns to the Pedlar/Wanderer who instructs him:

> My Friend! enough to sorrow you have given,
> The purposes of wisdom ask no more:
> Be wise and chearful, and no longer read
> The forms of things with an unworthy eye.

(ibid., ll. 932–5)

It is not given to human beings to grieve for ever, nor is it healthy to do so, to see life only under this single emotional aspect. And grief itself, like Schiller's aesthetic state, is 'impotent' although its longer-term effect may similarly be to motivate the ethical life. But when and how we should leave off grieving is difficult to say, and this is the first level of the question

Wordsworth raises. There are, of course, experiences by which individual human beings are completely, irrecoverably crushed. Margaret is such an instance and the discomfortable challenge of the poem lies in its affirming its counter-truth so directly after her story. Rather than keeping the two, in themselves acceptable, moods separate, it enforces the consciousness of one within the other. On the site of a concentration camp most people feel silenced by a boundless compassion which is, in the old sense, sublime. The occasion beggars both feeling and reflection. Yet if one is not a former inmate or relative, this moment of feeling will not remain at that intensity indefinitely, and, more significantly, the change can be anticipated at the time, although that does not mean the response is inadequate or insincere.

The belief that such a feeling should be sustained, that anything less is a dishonour to those who have suffered, imposes an impossible, and therefore falsifying, burden on the feelings. The earlier tradition of sensibility had strained after such intensities and, at one level, the Pedlar/Wanderer's instruction is to cut off the infinite ambition of sentiment and to seek a proportionality of feeling. But the question of proportionality of response, although important, is ancillary to the underlying issue of an emotionally based theodicy enforced by this double time in the realm of feeling. As the Pedlar/Wanderer's broader reflections on experience underwrite the emotional insight into his final happiness, it is hard to say whether the tale should be seen as a tragedy or as a diffusion of the tragic possibility. Because of its double perspective in time, the Dostoevskeyan concentration on unjust suffering in the tale is inseparable from the Tolstoyan placing of it in a broader span of experience in the telling. The paradoxical logic at the heart of the situation is that the compassion and fellow feeling aroused by the tale, and which is predicated on suffering, is inseparable from the feeling that binds the Pedlar/Wanderer to his communal and natural world. The most intense sympathy for Margaret's distress gives the fullest sense of the blessed oneness on which his moment of happiness is based. As with 'The Story of Le Fever', the two levels, precisely in being discriminated, are shown to have a common root. The double time of the narrative mediation enforces the underlying logic of this connection as a shocking conjunction, somewhat as Shakespeare, to focus a psychological investigation, allows Macbeth to be simultaneously evil and remorseful as notoriously does not happen with his counterparts in life.

But the challenging conjunction points to another level of significance in the poem extending beyond its immediate moral or human relations. If the unpublished poem known as 'The Ruined Cottage' is a transformation of the tradition of moral sentiment, the second unpublished poem, which Jonathon Wordsworth calls 'The Pedlar', points to a more philosophical implication within this. For Wordsworth's reworking of moral sentiment is a way of reaching beyond the ethical realm altogether. Rousseau enjoyed experiences in the natural world which gave him a peculiar 'sentiment of being', but he explained this in predominantly moral or social, and at times self-justificatory, terms. Wordsworth, on the other hand, while keeping the connection with the ethical, needed also to distinguish his intuition into Being from the ethical and personal realms. A further reason for his rubbing occasions of moral sentiment against their expected ethical grain was to reveal their latently ontological, as well as ethical, character.

The sentiment of being

Gerhart Sauder points out that when Rousseau's disciple Bernadin de St Pierre contrasted his 'Je sens, donc je suis' (I feel, therefore I am) to Descartes' foundational formula, he was in fact picking up a theme of the sentiment of existence that runs back through the philosophes to Descartes himself.[16] A given quality of feeling may be the source of an ontological intuition. At the end of his story, the Pedlar does not just weigh Margaret's suffering *against* his broader sense of life but feels his own participation in that suffering as inseparable from the body of sympathetic *connections* which constitutes his world. His sympathy for Margaret has reinforced, and made suddenly conscious, the larger set of sympathies binding him to existence, thus giving him one of those moments of ineffable happiness which, in the second version of the text, has already been attributed to the Pedlar's 'sentiment of Being'.

> He was only then
> Contented, when with bliss ineffable
> He felt the sentiment of Being spread
> O'er all that moves ...
>
> (*The Pedlar*, 206–9 [cf. also *Prelude* (1850), ii, 399–402])

Margaret's story is the vehicle for a larger recognition. Wordsworth recognizes that the emotions engendered by the occasion transcend the ethical, and as the Pedlar resumes his road, he does indeed, in a sense beyond the literal one, leave Margaret behind. In so far as the Pedlar is an avatar of the man of sentiment, the phrase 'sentiment of Being' suggests that there lurked within the afflatus of the man of feeling, whose emotions always carried a moral sign, an ontological intuition which Wordsworth made properly self-conscious. The abruptness of the ending in which Margaret's distress and the narrator's happiness are at once linked and discordant encapsulates a primary ambiguity not just in Wordsworth's *oeuvre*, but in the relation between the ethical and the ontological as such.

The phrase 'sentiment of Being' opens up the level of experience within which the Pedlar finally places the tale of Margaret, and several of Wordsworth's sentimentalist occasions have a similarly ambiguous implication. Just as the Pedlar admonished the poet's 'weakness' in his response to the tale of Margaret, so the Leech-Gatherer, the Old Cumberland Beggar and the Discharged Soldier, initially seen as objects of commiseration, all prove to be figures of superior endurance in a way that transcends customary notions of moral strength. This is the most striking reversal of the sentimental model. Although the man of sentiment found in such encounters with distress or poverty a recognition of humanity both in himself and in the other, and in the abstract the same could be said of Wordsworth, the effective relation is opposite. Rather than simply a lofty withholding of compassion, such as Wordsworth is sometimes charged with, or a sentimental pity, the poet speaker finds that these figures, even as they initially seem to elicit the sentimental response, rather admonish the poet with their superior strength through which he gains an insight into Being.

A certain tact is required. Wordsworth is clearly open to the objection of projecting his own meanings onto these figures. His tact, both human and poetic, lies in trusting the reader to see the point which, if it were further spelt out, would be lost. What the poet gets from these figures is something over and above moral and social relations and to be drawn too much into that level of consideration is a damaging distraction precisely because, as with the 'Old Cumberland Beggar', it has its legitimate weight. Hence, when Wordsworth internalizes the example of these figures of solitary endurance, it is hardly as an endorsement of his own ethical character in the way the more conventional man of sentiment saw his 'complacency' as a virtue. What they endorse in him, in the first instance, is his own impersonality and solitude, while any sense of underlying human solidarity is more indirect. In the simpler case of Simon Lee, who *is* more an object of compassion, the poet is thwarted of the expected immediacy of response: as old Simon's tears 'into his eyes were brought' the poet, instead of giving the sentimental tribute of his own tears, remarks

> Alas! The gratitude of men
> Has oft'ner left me mourning.

> (*Lyrical Ballads*, 63)

It is as if the poet were mourning the whole sentimental tradition of ready compassion. But the enduring, admonishing solitaries, by disrupting its conventions, point beyond the realm of moral sentiment altogether. Wordsworth had a conscious technique, reflected in his poetry such as in the Boy of Winander or the skating episodes, of creating a moment of special responsiveness by building a pattern of expectation and then suddenly halting it. When, for example, he suddenly stops circling on the ice, he feels the hills continue to turn around him (*Prelude*, i, ll. 456–9). Wordsworth's sentimental occasions often do this to the whole tradition of sentiment. Such moments are concentrated, analytic descendants of the man of sentiment's leisured pause. By stopping the sentimental convention in its tracks, and thwarting the expected model, he enables us to intuit another level of feeling.

David Ferry long ago pointed out that Wordsworth's transfigurations of the commonplace ultimately transcend the ethical: his truest significance is as a philosopher of Being in a sense that was not fully articulated until Martin Heidegger, who himself had increasing resource to German romantic poetry to illustrate his meaning.[17] Rousseau used the same phrase, 'sentiment of Being', but did not quite have the discourse by which to give it that implication, although his Reveries on the Ile de St Pierre came close to it. By the same token, Rousseau's egoism, at once heroic and naive, was a significant precursor of Wordsworth's ontological concentration. In so far as Wordsworth represents a resolution of the Rousseauvian instabilities as analysed by Schiller, it is in the spirit of the Hölderlin quotation which Heidegger adopted as a philosophical dictum: 'Poetically man dwells upon this earth.'[18] Heidegger meditated at length on the relations of poetry and thought and this remark depends on an absolute privileging of poetry while keeping it coterminous with human being-in-the-world. That echoes Wordsworth's attempt to keep the category, or medium, of poetry both thickly evident and yet transparently absent. It is the peculiar power, vulnerability and elusiveness of Wordsworth that poetry and thought are in him so fully intermingled. I have already indicated how the underlying difficulty of sentimentalism was its struggle to overcome the dualism of feeling and reflection on which it was premised. In this respect, Schiller's account of Rousseau's difficulty in finding a truly poetic mingling of sensibility and reflection bears on the creative achievement of such poems as 'Tintern Abbey' and *The Prelude*.

Feeling and reflection

As a philosopher, Heidegger sought to maintain the viewpoint of philosophy while increasingly emphasizing how only poetry could express the nature of Being. In this respect he followed German thinkers of the romantic era, such as Schelling, and one of his suggestive formulae for the relation of poetry and thought is that they should 'neighbour' each other.[19] Wordsworth, by contrast, was not a philosopher, although his preoccupations were intrinsically philosophical, and hence his philosophical elusiveness which has troubled readers of a philosophical bent since Coleridge. Analytically, Coleridge could take apart the arguments of Wordsworth's Preface yet Wordsworth clearly has the root of the matter in him in some way that transcends the critique. To achieve the recognition of Being which is in question for Wordsworth or Heidegger it is necessary to bypass not only the ethical but the conceptual, although some context of reflection is at the same time necessary for this significance to emerge as meaning. The problem of Being, that it is at once completely transparent and completely hidden, is re-enacted at the level of language. Heidegger is aware of this to a degree which is almost painful in its combination of philosophical insight and linguistic strain. Wordsworth, on the other hand, is a curious mixture of philosophical naivety, in the ordinary marketplace sense that suggests an incapacity for the discipline, and naivety in the uniquely creative sense that Schiller saw Goethe as having achieved despite his inhabiting a culture of sentimental modernity. In Wordsworth, the first level of naivety seems, by a half unwitting cunning, to protect the more important one, and one surmises it is half unwitting because of its capacity for startling lapses.

What is at stake in practice is the relation between the intuitive moment, usually one of intense feeling, and the body of reflection from which it acquires its transposition into meaning. Once again, the various versions of 'The Ruined Cottage' theme actually enact the problem of neighbouring and separation on which this meaning depends, and they do so with relation to a central 'philosophical' issue of his *oeuvre*: the pantheistic doctrine of the 'one life'.

In 'The Ruined Cottage', the Pedlar is accorded his final 'happiness' as an unexpected gift occasioned by his immediate feeling for Margaret combined with his longer-term habits of reflection. In 'The Pedlar',

Wordsworth develops the internal history of the Pedlar so as to make clear his philosophical disposition, his capacity for 'the sentiment of Being', long before the culminating experience of the poem. We carry this body of reflection to the final experience as does the Pedlar himself. In the final and published version of the story, however, as it appears in *The Excursion*, the acceptance is explicitly attributed to religious faith. The three versions represent three degrees of conceptual explicitness amounting to different orders of meaning. Commentators have always debated the extent, duration and literalness of Wordsworth's belief in the 'one life' shared by nature and man. Is it an emotional metaphor or a formally conceptualized position? As William Ullmer has pointed out, a clear doctrinal commitment to this as a philosophical view is rather rare in the poetry and, more importantly, such a literal belief would tend to short-circuit the dramatic presentation of the world held in this emotional form.[20] John Beer has likewise emphasized the distinction between 'primary consciousness', the universal spirit, and 'primary sympathy'.[21]

Whatever his personal belief may have been, pantheistic allusions in Wordsworth's early poetry derive their power from an essentially metaphorical focusing of his emotional meditation, while the heterodox nature of pantheistic belief within his culture helped to protect it from abstraction and banality. In the latter part of his life, however, his commitment to an orthodox Christianity provided precisely the short circuit, the doctrinal foreclosure of significance, which his greatest verse had characteristically avoided. Hence, in its finally published version, 'The Ruined Cottage' story becomes religious and, in the Wanderer's conclusion, its

> ...meditative sympathies repose
> Upon the breast of Faith

> (*Excursion*, i, 954–5)

thus providing a statement of Christian theodicy rather than meditation on tragic paradox or the sentiment of Being. Wordsworth's great poetry depends on his avoidance of conceptual closure or definition. It is partly because the Pedlar's happiness grows too directly from his habit of Wordsworthian meditation that readers have found it perversely forced onto the poem as a matter of principle, and this is even more damagingly the case in *The Excursion*. It is not just the religious faith, but the very statability of the philosophical position which short-circuits his more intrinsic and fundamental intuitions.

'Tintern Abbey', as a summative expression of Wordsworthian emotional reflection, is a classic example of this principle. When the poet speaks of

> A motion and a spirit, that impels
> All thinking things, all objects of all thought,
> And rolls through all things

> (*Lyrical Ballads*, ll. 101–2)

he has already acknowledged that his 'belief' may be 'vain' (l. 50) at any level beyond his emotional experience. This is more than the locally concessive gesture it is perhaps designed to appear; it is structural and strategic. For Wordsworth goes on, compellingly, to make his emotional experience the reader's and, even while affirming its personal character, he thereby persuades us of its universality. Whereas it is usually philosophical thought that claims universality and the man of feeling, as in Werther, embodied the individual as a value in conflict with the generality of principle, the underlying project of sentimentalism was to challenge this, to give feeling the value of the universal.

A weakness in the supplementary structure of sentimentalism, from Shaftesbury onwards, was that the emotional dimension, precisely because it was supported by a structure of belief, could not discover and develop its own power. What appeared at the time to be its strength, its support of and by moral principle, was actually, by the logic of the supplement, its weakness. By contrast, as Wordsworth takes us into the central affirmation of 'Tintern Abbey', the emotionally focused experience is all we have. Although the poem does not invite us to consider the matter in quite this analytic way, if we took its central affirmation as the literal expression of a philosophical doctrine that we might accept independently of its context in the poem, the lines would go suddenly flat even in their context. The uncanny power of Wordsworth's affirmation derives from our being obliged to grasp its meaning emotionally, from the hovering uncertainty as to what these words mean, how the language is being used. His power and weakness lie in being a Deist in a world for which that must be either a poetic achievement or an anachronistic vacuity.

In that respect, Wordsworth's later religious position is a return to the old structure of sentiment as feeling governed by principled belief whereas his earlier naturalistic theodicy depends on disrupting it. His later category of 'Poems of Sentiment and Reflection' seems to hint, in its very phrasing, at such a falling apart. In the great Wordsworth poetry, by contrast, reflection is dissolved into feeling. *The Prelude*, for example, constantly modulates between specific emotional episodes and general reflection, the two elements which Schiller saw Rousseau as unable to combine poetically. The central problem of sentiment was its seeking to identify thought and feeling, to make one perform the function of the other, while keeping the distinction itself in place. The typical structure of sentiment, however, did not dissolve the distinction, and Rousseau shows how it was possible to have a secret investment in maintaining the dualism. But Wordsworth, although he uses the word 'sentiment', and his phrase 'sentiment of Being' encapsulates the important line of connection between him and the Rousseauvian structure, does not rely heavily on the terminology of sentiment. He rather uses the common terms 'thought' and 'feeling' which, by frankly acknowledging the conventional dualism, enabled him creatively to engage their problematic relations which the term 'sentiment' sought to gloss over.

The underlying intuition of eighteenth-century sentiment is that 'thought' and 'feeling', although a necessary distinction, are not separable. Even mathematical thought, which may be the strongest example of abstraction, is only thought by a particular individual with some specific motivation. The very purity of mathematics may motivate a particular human being to engage in it, as Wordsworth notes (*Prelude*, vi, ll.142–67). Whatever has value to a human being is to that extent an emotional object. Although such a recognition is far from new, even to the classical or medieval mind, some truths have constantly to be rediscovered or reformulated for new situations, and the post-Cartesian, post-Lockean world required a reworking of these terms. Just as Wordsworth's narrative poetry was a way of critically reworking, and thereby reinforcing, the situational psychology of moral sentiment, so his reflective poetry is most truly philosophical in its reworking of 'sentiment' as a mutual suffusion of 'thought' and 'feeling'. His philosophical intelligence lies in his enacting the indissolubility of thought and feeling.

Hence the structural oscillation between emotional episodes and reflective summaries is dependent on Wordsworth's characteristic concentration on a complex of key terms, such as 'image', 'motion', 'vision' and 'form', which progressively dissolve the conventional demarcations. These highly abstract, or empty, terms typically acquire an emotional significance within a vividly specific episode which is then carried over to a passage of more generalized reflection. Then the same term recurs in a further recollected episode along with its gathered freight of meanings. He uses such abstract terms precisely for their emptiness, their capacity to be filled and to be almost infinitely adapted. The word 'motion' was chosen by Bentham to exemplify the dangerous element of the 'fictional' in all thought and discourse. Bentham sought, if not to obviate such fictional entities altogether, then at least to mitigate their delusory effect by a critical self-consciousness. They were for him specifically the empty vessels through which a subjectivizing 'sentiment' sneaked into the language and, in this respect, Bentham's dualistically based critique is the analytic guide to Wordsworth's dissolution of dualism. Wordsworth, that is to say, is not the victim of an unconscious process, as Bentham's critique suggests, but uses these terms to explore the interpenetration of feeling and reflection and, by the same token, the interplay of inner and outer worlds. The episode of the skating is a concrete emblem of this process. His own suddenly arrested motion causes the impression of a whirling motion on the part of the surrounding hills, yet that very impression is in turn aware of itself as an internalizing of the outer world. Only within the subjective condition does this motion occur. The process has more subtly psychological rather than physical versions as, for example, at the end of the woodcock-stealing episode, he feels

> Low breathings coming after [him], and sounds
> Of undistinguishable motion, steps
> Almost as silent as the steps they trod.

> (*Prelude*, i, 323–5)

The dramatic conviction of a motion outside himself is created by its very indistinguishability. So, too, in the subsequent episode of the stolen boat, the crag which reared before him

> seemed, with purpose of its own
> And measured motion like a living thing …

> (ibid., 383–4)

The subjectivity of feeling is explicit within the dramatic objectivity of the narrative. Yet when he moves to his next passage of reflection, which is not explicitly linked to these episodes, he declares:

> Thou Soul that art the eternity of thought,
> That givest to forms and images a breath
> And everlasting motion …

> (ibid., 402–4)

As he now attributes this motion 'objectively' to the world, we recognize the degree to which it reflects both his emotional participation, as in the preceding episodes, and the longer-term emotional formation which these exemplify. He has been formed

> Not with the mean and vulgar works of man,
> But with high objects, with enduring things – ,
> With life and nature, purifying thus
> The elements of feeling and of thought…

(ibid., 408–11)

'Feeling' and 'thought' are distinguished yet side by side. They are neither confused nor separable. As in Heidegger's metaphor of 'neighbouring', feeling and thought are aspects of a whole world and, throughout the poem, Wordsworth's sonorous blank verse holds the inner and outer realms in a continuum of reflective feeling. Every aspect of syntax, diction, rhythm and image enacts this interfusion.

What this means for the nature of 'argument' emerges in a revealing confusion between two critics. Building on Donald Davie's account of Wordsworth's romantic syntax, David Perkins notes how a relatively simple idea provides the armature for long sentence structures of emotionally pregnant parenthesis and apposition whereby the 'idea' becomes a dramatically achieved recognition enacted with the reader.[22] He then draws on this to contest a remark, ascribed to F. R. Leavis, that Wordsworth gives only the 'illusion' of argument. But Leavis's comment is a compliment in the spirit of Perkins's reading by ironically endorsing Matthew Arnold's statement that Wordsworth's 'philosophy' is an illusion. Wordsworth is aware that no one arrives at a view on fundamental life questions simply by processes of reason, and this is not merely a matter of the 'emotional' element in rhetoric, the persuasion of others. It is rather to do with the nature of conviction, and the calling up of experience and associations in the communing with the self. *The Prelude*, of course, is addressed to a single trusted friend and preserves the fictional standpoint of explanation to one already convinced rather than persuasion of a hostile or neutral audience. The force of Leavis's remark is that, while there has to be a propositional armature, the larger process of thought cannot be encapsulated *as* argument. Wordsworth's 'illusion' of philosophy is not deceptive, therefore, but unusually self-aware about the relations of 'thought' and 'feeling'.

By the same token, when divorced from this wholeness of emotional being, 'thought' becomes a chaos of undecidable possibilities, which is what Wordsworth records happening to himself when he falls into intellectual confusion after the French Revolution. For this interfusion of thought and feeling was to be put under an unexpected pressure, and to be invested with an urgent political significance, at this crucial moment in his life. Like Mary Wollstonecraft, he found the categories of reason and sensibility sharply, and mythically, polarized in the 1790s although this gave him a less holistic insight than hers into the nature of ideology. In the later books of *The Prelude*, Wordsworth describes the period of disappointment following the first progressive hopes of the French Revolution and sees himself as having been eventually bewildered into despondency and despair at the level of reasoned argument. Like many of his contemporaries, he accepted the dualistic opposition, perhaps with a measure of collusion in that it justified his anti-ideological stand. Strictly speaking, however, it is not 'reason' that bewilders him but the fall into dualism as he seems to acknowledge when he affirms that what saved him from this condition was the joint influence of his sister Dorothy and of Nature:

> Nature's self,
> By all varieties of human love
> Assisted, led me back through opening day
> To those sweet counsels between head and heart
> Whence grew that genuine knowledge, fraught with peace,
> Which, through the later sinkings of this cause,
> Hath still upheld me...

> (*Prelude*, xi, 350–6)

As Wordsworth thematized these questions in the latter part of *The Prelude*, however, he had little further light to throw on them other than to refer back to the best intuitions of the earlier books in which the meaning of phrases such as 'solemn thought' (ibid., iv, 190) and 'pensive feeling' (ibid., iv, 241) had been made richly substantial.

Modern critical debate re-enacts a split which opened not just in Wordsworth but in his culture. It is both a necessary and an irresolvable argument. The political polarization of 'Reason' and 'Sensibility' was compounded by the split between ways of conceiving the individual, on the one hand, and the political or social whole, on the other. Individual feeling and social principle, the elements which the term sentiment had sought to combine, had become irrecoverably separate. Although not separate in reality, that is to say, a gap had opened in the modes of understanding them. The mode of emotional meditation just described in *The Prelude* clearly does not lend itself to properly political thought although political thought uninformed by such reflection is likewise impoverished. This was the historical juncture when the Enlightenment hope of creating a universally moral and humane social order suffered a violent shock, increasing incredulity and a recognition of the difficulties in principle as well as in practice. Sentimentalism was always in part a process of privatization of feeling, the creation of a domestic realm and of the modern individual. But at this point it became evident that the culture of moral feeling, even while it significantly informed individuals' conduct as citizens, provided no compelling or universalizable model for the social whole. It was privatized perforce and any attempt to apply an imperative of feeling too directly to the whole society would henceforth court the charge of sentimentality in its modern sense of false feeling. The achievement of Wordsworth and Schiller was to recognize how crucially yet obliquely feeling works in the moral life. By the same token, it can only work in an even more oblique way in the life of society, and their mutual turn from progressive politics was a reflection of the modern condition.

5
Victorian Sentimentality: the Dialectic of Sentiment and Truth *of* Feeling

If the eighteenth century is remembered as the age of sentiment and sensibility, the Victorian period is usually considered the peak, or trough, of sentimentality. Victorian sentimentality is a byword for indulgent and lachrymose excess, and the reaction against it, as encapsulated in Oscar Wilde's remark that it would take a heart of stone to read the death of Little Nell without laughing, was crucial to many writers of the modernist generation. It may be that literary criticism is not the best mode for considering the significance of this cultural phenomenon. A popular culture of tears may serve an intuitively therapeutic purpose requiring simple triggers rather than artistically complex occasions. Nonetheless, literary texts, and contemporary ways of understanding them, are an especially significant part of the Victorian culture of feeling and in recent years Victorian sentiment has been seen with greater sympathy, and internal discrimination, while the modernist response now seems an overreaction. But this critical turn in favour of sentiment still largely misses the process of transformation. Victorian sentimentalism grappled, creatively and self-critically, with the inherited problems of ethical sentiment and its great achievements are just as sentimentalist in their deeper derivation as the moments of excess. The implicit criterion of true feeling which developed within the tradition of sentiment cannot be fully disentangled from sentimentality in the pejorative sense. In the realm of feeling, the true and the false define each other in a process of constant discrimination; true and false feeling have a dialectical relation.

The recent sympathetic interest in nineteenth-century sentimental literature, therefore, requires some further discrimination. It can arise simply from a confusion of terminology as if one could negate the modern meaning of the word by deciding to approve, rather than disapprove, of the sentimental. But merely to praise a work for being sentimental conflates the original and modern senses and to that extent simply reflects the larger confusion about the sentimental in modern culture. Fred Kaplan's *Sacred Tears: Sentimentality in Victorian Literature* (1987), for example, attempts to vindicate Victorian sentimentality by exhuming eighteenth-century sentimental theory as its rationale without seeing that a specific and contemporary critical case would need to be made for each work.[1] Conversely, several essays in Winfried Herget's *Sentimentality in Modern Literature and Popular Culture* (1991) make such critical cases while the volume remains uncertain in its collective claim.[2] Kaplan, however, provides the important negative clue by revealing the anachronism of an eighteenth-century rationale for the conditions of nineteenth-century society, and for the novel form in which it was most characteristically encompassed. In contrast, Philip Fisher and Jane Tompkins have both shown the cultural work done by sentimental classics of nineteenth-century America.[3] Sentiment is historicized. Tompkins traces the process by which certain works, typically written by women and devoted to female experience, have been comparatively forgotten or regarded as artistically inferior, while others, such as Hawthorne's novels, although they were initially reviewed in rather similar terms, were gradually made into canonical classics. She challenges the critical charge against her popular classics while Fisher broadly accepts the lesser artistic value of the works he discusses, but both argue that these works performed an important cultural function precisely through the characteristics which have made them critically vulnerable.

For present purposes, the question is not so much the artistic quality of such works, which may well be lesser, but the degree to which they explore the problems of sentiment. It was pre-eminently Anglo-American tradition which kept faith with the underlying impulse of moral sentimentalism. The German man of feeling, Werther, although most immediately modelled on Rousseau, had sported English attire, while English self-consciousness is encapsulated in Mr Knightley's distinction, in *Emma*, that Frank Churchill is *aimable*, in the French sense, but not truly 'amiable'.[4] He has a polished social manner but lacks a sincere regard for others. Jane Austen's consummate and integral art in *Emma* is a culminating resolution of the conflict of individual feeling and social principle in the tradition of sentiment. But by the same token her achievement is deeply conservative and has a conscious note of the idyllic in its comedic control. The historical conflicts of sentiment had still to be lived out in later nineteenth-century fiction.

The continuing transformation of sentiment was inseparable from both the strengths and the strains of the Victorian novel, and particularly with respect to its aspiration to social totality. As the major novelists of the time repeatedly affirm, the sphere of personal feeling and domestic life is not separable from the wider processes of society and politics. Each encompasses the other. Yet the two scales proved to be increasingly incommensurable. Even the best understanding of social and economic process does not tell you what you need to know about the lives and moral qualities of individuals, and nor can the larger process be understood simply as an imaginary moral aggregate. The classic models of eighteenth-century sentiment assumed a fixed, hierarchical society within which personal benevolence could ameliorate the lives of the unfortunate. By the end of the eighteenth century the modern science of economics, and experiments with new social constitutions in America and France, meant that the social order could no longer be taken as given, and the personal benevolence of individuals was no answer to structural evils. Once the social order comes to be seen as a complex impersonal process changeable only by collective political will, then any appeal to individual feeling begins to seem necessarily, structurally, sentimental. As has been seen in Wordsworth and Wollstonecraft, the problematic relation of reflection and feeling was reinforced by the rupture between the individual and social scales. At its worst Victorian sentiment merely reflected the structural falsity of confronting social evil with no more than a vicarious emotional investment in personal benevolence. But at its best it recognized the question of feeling as vital and unavoidable while seeking to find an appropriate object for it. Accordingly, this chapter traces three major transformations of the sentimental tradition: in the political sphere, in the personal moral life, and leading from these, in its relation to the emergent category of the unconscious.

The 'real presence' of Uncle Tom

The most famous and efficacious instance of sentimental fiction in the political sphere is *Uncle Tom's Cabin* (1852). At one level, the novel is a political weepy which happened to catch a public mood at a moment of profound and necessary cultural change. But the political case rests precisely on the role and value of feeling in the public realm, and the thematizing of this question within the text gives it an implicit toughness and an elusive complexity of impact. Despite the transparency of the narrative, the precise object of the feeling is not always so obvious.

The characteristic method of *Uncle Tom's Cabin* is epitomized in the sudden appearance of the runaway slave, Eliza, with her child in arms, at the home of Senator Thomas Bird. He has supported the Runaway Slave

Act of 1850 requiring the capture of escaped slaves in the non-slave-owning states, and had 'scouted all sentimental weakness of those who would put the welfare of a few miserable fugitives before great state interests', but when Eliza and her child come to his door he succumbs to the 'magic of the real presence of distress'.[5] The phrase 'real presence' could hardly be more transparent, even naive, in its nudging of the reader's response, yet it focuses, in an implicitly meta-fictional way, both the narrative strategy of the novel and the effect that it had on many of its readers. Like its ancestor, *Clarissa*, the book continually focuses the question of response and achieves a more complex effect than one would confidently attribute to a conscious artistic design. In the light of the previous tradition of sentiment the phrase 'real presence' yields several layers of implication.

The immediate impact of Eliza's 'real presence' on the Senator suggests a continuity with the affective verisimilitude of eighteenth-century senti-mental fiction and several moments in the novel could have been written at the unselfcritical height of the age of sensibility:

> 'Lor, now, Missis, don't – don't' said Aunt Chloe, bursting out in her turn; and for a few moments they all wept in company. And in those tears they all shed together, the high and the lowly, melted away all the heart-burnings and anger of the oppressed. O ye who visit the distressed, do ye know that everything your money can buy, given with a cold, averted face, is not worth one honest tear shed in real sympathy.
>
> (*Uncle Tom*, 103)

Objective differences in social destiny are washed away in tears. Yet the novel as a whole does not just appeal to feeling in this simple way, it argues a demonstrative case for seeing feeling as of the essence with respect to the slavery question. Senator Bird is one of several characters in the book who, like Rousseau's account of Mme de Warens, go wrong in the head rather than in the heart. And where the heart is not in the right place arguments about slavery conducted in terms of a supposed rationality are not only empty and ineffective, they are obscenely inappropriate. Senator Bird initially voices to his wife the perennial view that principle is universal and therefore must take preference over feeling which is intrinsically private:

> ... we musn't suffer our feelings to run away with our judgement; you must consider it's not a matter of private feeling, – there are great public

interests involved, – there is such a state of public agitation rising, that
we must put apart our private feelings.

(ibid., 85)

What the book shows in contrast is that feeling is not only the more
fundamental but the more truly universal element. Even the supposedly
universal truths of the Declaration of Independence and the Constitution
are limited or vacuous until linked to a genuine universality of feeling, a
sense of common humanity. Hence, as is well-known, Stowe's narrative
strategy is to present her black characters through the values most dear,
and 'natural', to her assumed white readers: family, home and religion.
Yet the appeal to feeling is constantly problematized and mere kindness is
no solution. For the kindness of individuals within the world of chattel
slavery is not only defeated by the workings of the system, humane slave-
owners give a specious moral cover for its evils. Their personal kindness is
socially harmful. As Mrs Shelby laments:

> 'I was a fool to think I could make anything good out of such a deadly
> evil. It is a sin to hold a slave under laws like ours, – I always felt it was, –
> I always thought it was so when I was a girl, – I thought so still more
> after I joined the church; but I thought I could gild it over, – I thought
> by kindness, and care, and instruction, I could make the condition of
> mine better than freedom – fool that I was.'

(ibid., 39)

The recognition that benevolence is not enough gives a different
inflection to the book's own sentimental appeal, an appeal which was
to have a controversial bearing on black self-perception long after
abolition. Indeed, the book thematizes some of the principles by which
it has itself been criticized right down to the present. The controversy
partly arises from assumptions about the mode of identification with the
characters, from the enduringly sentimental belief that simple identification is what is in question and that we can readily identify its object. But
what exactly do we respond to in *Uncle Tom's Cabin*?

It is here that the phrase 'real presence' begins to shimmer and gives the
mode of affective verisimilitude a new inflection. For although Eliza is
unquestionably real to Senator Bird, in so far as the reader shares his
response it is strictly to a fiction, or what Kames called an '*ideal* presence'.
At one level 'real presence' here is Kames's 'ideal presence' with the
emphasis reversed: where he stressed the emotional impact of fiction *per se*
Stowe privileges the 'reality' effect within her fiction. But Eliza's way of

representing 'reality' is more specific. As she appears at the Senator's home, the legislator and politician's viewpoint into which she steps lends her individual distress a typical, even a statistical, force. Stowe's later 'Key' to *Uncle Tom's Cabin* is devoted to arguing the typicality of the cruelties suffered by the slaves, and that these are a natural outcome of chattel slavery rather than extreme and isolated instances.[6] On the one hand the statistical spirit is the enemy, blinding even the fundamentally humane Senator with its abstraction, so that it has to be countered by the individual presence of Eliza, and yet her very presence, in order to be effective, has itself to take on the force of the abstraction, the moral weight of typicality.

Her significance as a living statistic changes the basis of her appeal to sentiment. Kames argued the value of the fictive element *per se* in affective verisimilitude. Because it aroused an excess of feeling, or feeling focused on an unreal object, it created a kind of felt vacuum, or deficit in reality, which the morally moved reader was therefore motivated to fill. The literalistic model of immediate response to occasions of distress was reinforced by a psychological reaction depending on its very status as fiction. Both would lead to benevolent action. By the mid-nineteenth century, however, when the systemic, and politically removable, nature of much social evil was overwhelmingly evident, this characteristic of sentimental fiction acquired a new value and point. Social legislation can only arise from a general change of heart, a surge of public feeling, and has to focus on a general object. Legislation cannot directly address individuals. Hence the free-floating exercise of feeling that characterized the earlier tradition now finds a legitimate location in an object not just randomly individual, or religiously cosmic, but meaningfully typical. In this way Kames's definition of fiction as 'ideal presence' takes on a sharper meaning as Stowe's elision of the real and the fictional refers to a social category, or a statistical truth, which partakes of both modes of being at once. That is not to say that statistics are fictions, although they may of course be lies. Indeed, if they were fictions they would not count as lies. But what is at stake in the response to Eliza, even as Stowe stresses her individual reality against abstract generalities, is her ideality. In the new world of the nineteenth century, or of modernity, moral feeling has to focus on strictly *ideal* objects. Curiously enough, the outmoded sentimental model has become newly appropriate in its very idealism. Idealization has acquired an ontological point.

The principal focus of sentimental idealization, however, is Uncle Tom in whom the expression 'real presence' also takes on its richest implications. He is conceived in a spirit of pious literalism, as a moral and religious example, yet because he is a fiction he has a more complex tactical impact on the reader. Frederick Douglass objected at the time to the example of Uncle Tom and retold, as a counter-model, the story of the successful uprising led by the young black, Madison Washington, on the slave ship, the *Creole* in 1841. Douglass's *The Heroic Slave* (1853), however, although based on fact, is narrated in the manner of an eighteenth-century sentimental tale complete with gothic atmosphere and unlikely coincidences. More importantly, his intended counter-example to Uncle Tom shows his literalistic reading, his assumption that Tom can be lifted out of his fictional context, as in the modern pejorative use of the term 'Uncle Tom', without loss of meaning. Athough this usage is fully understandable, detaching the figure from the book loses his effect within it. Within the fiction, his very idealization gives him a particular impact.

Uncle Tom, like many other nineteenth-century fictional characters, is a man of sentiment in a new context. In himself he is an unironic centre of humane value yet his relation to the world in which he lives has overtones of a David Simple or a Parson Adams who, although their hearts are in the right place, are absurdly out of touch with common social reality. In Tom's case, however, this is not under the sign of irony. Indeed, rather than being corrected by experience he has precisely to resist it, and his moral purity, his likeness even to Christ, is recognized as extraordinary by other characters. His imperviousness is a 'moral miracle' (*Uncle Tom*, 220). Tom is not just idealized, he consciously lives up to a difficult ideal. His refusal to kill Legree, when Cassy has him at their joint mercy, seems Quixotic, yet it is a specifically Christian challenge which has been prepared for, and given a historical as well as religious grounding, by the earlier introduction of the Quakers whose refusal to take life is treated with respect. We are made to recognize that, however hard it may be to stomach within the momentum of the narrative, this is actually no more than what the Christian religion strictly enjoins in its command to 'turn the other cheek'.

In this way, Stowe's use of Tom's strong-minded gentleness is challenging. Such a passive hero throws the responsibility completely onto the white world while offering as the centre of feeling a pure expression of Christian principle which her assumed readers cannot repudiate. Elizabeth Ammons has persuasively argued that his character is not just Christian but female: 'Far from being the least admirable of Stowe's creations, [he] is the ultimate heroine of *Uncle Tom's Cabin*.'[7] On this argument, he is the man of sentiment taking on the positive female force, rather than the weakness of the feminized male, noted by Janet Todd. The book is an emotional trap in that, while Madison Washington may provide a more practical example for blacks in the real world, in the fictional world Tom represents a more inwardly disturbing shock to white feelings. We now know that, in the right circumstances, complete non-violence has its own moral power and can prove the more radical challenge. Mahatma Ghandi has since shown the power, as well as the vulnerability, of such a stance as a mode of political action. Tom explicitly does not have the political vision of Ghandi or Martin Luther King, but he is the means of generating a comparable power within the feelings of the reader, not despite, but because of, his fictional status. As a simple example of Christian passivity he helped to make the book less overtly threatening, but in the dynamics of response that is effectively a feint giving an acceptable moral sign to the actual emotional impact. Tom's simplicity is the focus for complex, if not always self-conscious, responses.

The emotional cunning of the book lies in its simplicity and, without meta-fictional pretension, the question of reading is also focused in Tom. His recourse to the Bible is an object lesson in reading reinforced by overtones of Quixotry. Having learned to read with difficulty and comparatively late in life, his reading is especially slow and responsive but he develops an opposite dependence to Don Quixote's. Like Don Quixote, he takes a moral code from a book as a completely literal guide to his own conduct, but the Bible is the one narrative for which such a response is actually enjoined. More significantly, Tom finds the Bible 'so evidently true and divine that the possibility of a question never entered his simple head. It must be true; for, if not true, how could he live?' (*Uncle Tom*, 150–1). His life is such that only an absolute faith in a just hereafter could make it bearable and so, whereas Don Quixote mistakes his world for a romance, Tom's faith enforces the separateness between the world of the book and the world of life. Likewise, the death of the significantly named Evangeline suggests a clear-sighted recognition of the incompat-ibility of the gospel values and the given social world. She has neither her father's ironic lightness nor Tom's simple Quixotry. After her death, her father begins to read the Bible under Tom's influence '. . . often pausing to wrestle down feelings which were roused by the pathos of the story' (ibid., 311). Tom, by contrast, reads with feeling and his biblical reading is a hint to ours which must likewise absorb the emotional weight of the story as the key to its significance. Emotional Quixotry is elicited on the basis of the most distinguished example.

The centrality of the Bible to Tom's life, and his own enactment of Christ's suffering, suggests a further possibility which Stowe does not exploit in the phrase 'real presence' but which neatly encapsulates the relation between her religious faith and the broader secular impact of her book. Ironically, in its appeal to Anglo-American Protestant conscience, the book uses the very phrase which signifies, in the Catholic Eucharist, the literal presence of Christ within the 'accidents', or external appearances, of bread and wine. The historical relation between protestantism and the movement of sentiment has long been recognized and an accident of phrasing enforces what has been said about the ontological significance of modern secular sentiment.[8] Although Tom himself believes literally in the hereafter, if he is an embodiment of Christ for a wider modern readership, it is through an intensity of feeling engendered by an act of reading.

Uncle Tom's Cabin, then, transforms the earlier novel of sensibility into a focus of politically self-conscious feeling and thematizes the importance of feeling in the new understanding of society. The book contains historical layers of sentimentalist tradition. Its popular appeal is of the essence and the point here is not to claim a greater artistic achievement but rather to see why other writers, like George Eliot, who were themselves capable of a more ambitious art, regarded Stowe with appreciation.[9] The attempt of nineteenth-century novelists to grasp the social whole is a tonal as well as a substantive matter and, although sentiment was largely aristocratic and bourgeois in its historical origins, its claim of human solidarity came increasingly to be realized by its gradual downward shift as a lower-class form. Hence the curious doubleness in the nineteenth-century appreciation of popular sentiment epitomized in Alfred de Musset's declaration 'Vive le mélodrame òu Margot a pleuré' which celebrates a popular form only on condition of clearly recognizing it as such.[10] This double relation is reflected in the broader narrative structures, and the shifting rhetorical registers, of much Victorian fiction in which episodes of popular sentiment are interwoven with complex studies of moral and emotional development. Such structures attempt to hold together, in feeling, a total vision of society. But they tread a fine line between inclusion and condescension which is why the deeper implication of Dickens's command of the demotic was often lost on middle-class writers who fell under his influence. Nonetheless, the great Victorian novels, while typically reversing Stowe's directly political emphasis, submit the tradition of sentiment to a searching internal transformation expressing in its very structure the dialectical relation of sentimentalism and true feeling.

The dialectic of sentiment

The two greatest Victorian novelists who sought a summative vision of the whole society, Charles Dickens and George Eliot, privileged the individual as an end in itself and only through that as a source of social change. The larger order is changed for the better through the moral growth and emotional education of individuals. At the same time, their conception of the ethical life principally as the overcoming of egoism meant that true personal growth was inseparable from a responsible awareness of the wider social world as in Dorothea Casaubon's morning vision of 'the manifold wakings of men to labour and endurance' before she goes on her unselfish visit to Rosamund Lydgate in *Middlemarch*.[11] Yet there is a difference in emphasis reflected in Dickens's more overt recourse to the earlier tradition of sentiment while Eliot shows its transformation into modernity.

Dickens was steeped in the novels of Fielding, Sterne and Smollett. He frankly enjoyed the humour, the picaresque momentum and the ready appeal to sentiment in the period. He was in some ways even anachronistic in his own narrative methods. But his strength lay in giving apparently outdated forms a contemporary force and this applies pre-eminently to his use of sentiment. Along with many other nineteenth-century writers, he gave a new meaning to the man and woman of sentiment. The three eighteenth-century novelists just mentioned already suggest the problematic nature of the inheritance. Sterne and Smollett had a mutual dislike turning largely on the question of sensibility, with which Sterne was popularly identified and which Smollett distrusted. And both were different from Fielding's more Shaftesburyan celebration of moral and social order. In other words, the nineteenth century inherited sentiment as both an outdated fashion and an unresolved problematic. The two aspects proved to have a fruitful relation. Wolfgang Herrlinger has shown how, across a wide range of Victorian fiction, the inheritance of sentiment was a continuing struggle between sentimentalism and anti-sentimentalism but in a crucially different form.[12] The opposed camps of reason and sensibility became a necessary mutuality. And this perception was enabled by a complementary shift in the ontology of sentiment. Rather than being entangled in literalistic views of moral psychology, as was the case with the initial understanding of sentiment, nineteenth-century writers could see its forms and rhetoric not just as an outdated but as a largely literary fashion, or more precisely as a set of emotional tropes ambiguously placed between psychological mechanisms and literary conventions. Hence, without necessarily resolving the intrinsic anti-nomies of moral sentimentalism, they could see it with a different kind of detachment and turn its now familiar tropes into an analytic means of insight into the elusiveness of moral feeling. Above all, Dickens's quite overt sense of fiction, and his play of humour, highlight the unwittingly fictive and rhetorical nature of sentiment itself.

While the original movement of sentiment involved what can now be seen as a fruitful internal struggle between sentiment and its critics, for its participants this was not perceived as a productive dialectic but as a stultifying opposition fraught with dreadful moral and social consequences. The gap between principle and feeling was an abyss focused dramatically around conflicts of conscious sincerity and hypocrisy while the more subtle suggestions were embodied in the dramatic subtexts. But if the less conscious aspects of emotional life are intuited through the very inadequacy of discourse, then the word 'through' takes on a double sense: even as we have to get behind the discourse of sentiment to intuit the true feeling, our understanding is nonetheless focused by it. Only as we learn to read 'through' it in this way does its value as a lens rather than as the object itself become clear. By the nineteenth century, perhaps as result of the sheer outmodedness of sentiment, a new dialectic grew up between the present and the past in which the original forms could be intuitively understood in this double way. The rhetorical tropes of sentiment are almost automatically bracketed, seen as humorous excesses, but in a way that now reflects the elusiveness of feeling as such. The conventionalized expressions became an indirect means of *reading* feeling rather than the *feeling* itself. Seen in this way, the critique of sentiment, and the very instability of sentiment, came to be appreciated as a reflection of, and therefore a means of understanding, the otherwise opaque and deceptive dynamic of feeling in the moral life. As a literary and social fashion not just analytically exposed but now socially outmoded, the man or woman of sentiment could represent certain emotional proclivities, complacencies and self-deceptions in a diagnostic spirit. The discourse of sentiment became a way of representing psychological formations which had no other name. In short, rather than sentimentalism merely reflecting the weakness of a mistaken culture of feeling, it becomes a crucial mode of self-critique in a culture for which feeling is a vital premise. Two important aspects of this we might call 'sentiment as trope' and 'sentiment as symptom'. Reading each author with some partiality, the tropes of sentiment can be seen with especial clarity in Dickens and its symptomatic significance in George Eliot.

Charles Dickens: sentiment as trope

Dickens is still commonly associated with the indulgent excesses of sentiment and indeed it was not until the latter half of the twentieth century that his true power as a major English novelist emerged through his reputation as a popular entertainer and social reformer dependent on a sentimental appeal. Most significantly for the present theme, he developed in the middle of his novelistic career, around 1850, a highly organized thematic structure which was inseparable from an internal transformation of sentiment. The Dickensian novel form effectively enacts the internal dialectic whereby the tropes of sentiment became the means of expressing, or discovering, true feeling.

His early novels, *The Pickwick Papers* (1837), *Oliver Twist* (1838) and *Nicholas Nickleby* (1839), draw on the value of good-heartedness in characters and readers. The predominant structural principle is picaresque with individual benevolence as the typical means of moral resolution. Even so, both *The Pickwick Papers* and *Nicholas Nickelby* are already aware, however affectionately, of certain absurdities in their sentimental heroes. *Pickwick* is an especially revealing case given the suddenness with which the young Dickens found himself writing it. One can see him seizing on usable elements to turn to entertaining account as in the brief appearance of a lawyer's clerk:

> Here Mr. Jackson smiled once more upon the company, and, applying his left thumb to the tip of his nose, worked a visionary coffee-mill with his right hand: thereby performing a very graceful piece of pantomine (then much in vogue, but now, unhappily, almost obsolete) which was familiarly denominated 'taking a grinder.'[13]

Although the mature Dickens might give such a detail a greater thematic resonance, this suggests the elements from which his more complex narrative structures would be formed and shows in microcosm the method of *Pickwick*. The vivid presentness of the action within the narrative is set off by the awareness of its being outmoded at the time of the narration. Similarly, Pickwick is a man of benevolent sentiment seen in the light of eccentric, but not unselfconscious, anachronism. The whole tradition of sentiment has become self-conscious in a different way as in Sam Weller's response to receiving a subpoena and a shilling:

> 'And it's uncommon handsome o' Dodson and Fogg, as knows so little of me, to come down vith a present,' said Sam. 'I feel it as a wery high compliment, sir; it's a wery hon'rable thing to them, as they knows how to reward merit werever they meets it. Besides wich, it's affectin' to one's feelin's.'
> As Mr Weller said this, he inflicted a little friction on his right eye-lid, with the sleeve of his coat, after the most approved manner of actors when they are in domestic pathetics.
>
> (*Pickwick*, 422)

The tropes of sentiment have become a demotic possession in a spirit of irony but not cynicism. The many comically false tears in the book set off the moments of genuine feeling as in the late exchange between Sam Weller and Job Trotter, whose forename recalls earlier models of distress:

> 'There is no deception now, Mr Weller. Tears,' said Job, with a look of momentary slyness, 'tears are not the only proofs of distress, nor the best ones.'
>
> (*Pickwick*, 733)

And as he goes on to speak of Pickwick's charity to himself and Winkle, Job speaks 'with real tears in his eyes' (ibid., 642).

Whereas *Pickwick* makes very broad use of sentimental tropes to discriminate true feeling, *Nicholas Nickleby* develops a more complex set of mutually echoing narratives expressing different degrees of theatricality and falseness. As Nicholas seeks to understand his own true feelings, he encounters the acting theme blown up to comic proportions in the Crummles travelling theatrical company while Mr Mantolini shows a more subtle kind of exploitative performance in domestic and social life. In the mid-century sequence, however, of *David Copperfield* (1850) and *Bleak House* (1852), Micawber, Uriah Heep and Harold Skimpole express a darkening view of the manipulative insincerities and self-deceptions in the rhetoric and self-image of the man of sentiment. Just as significantly, this sequence of novels enacts a tightening of picaresque form into complex thematic structure. For example, Wilkins Micawber, David Copperfield's absurd yet much beloved *alter ego*, has the traits of the man of sentiment which David eventually comes to recognize critically in himself. Skimpole is another version of the man of sentiment now seen in a more sinister light. But these characters acquire their significance through their place in a thematic structure by which Dickens presents a nuanced and searching moral psychology through a seemingly two-dimensional and popular means. These books, while apparently using an external method, are secretly and radically internalized.

Sterne's 'Story of Le Fever' combined the comic and the sentimental to achieve a complex emotional discrimination by an apparently transparent and non-analytic method. He pulled on the heartstrings even while revealing the puppetry of sentiment. In doing so, he showed that an awareness of fiction does not necessarily break the spell of sentiment and can give it a critical self-awareness. Dickens's mixture of humour and sentiment was a more highly developed version of this possibility. His novels organized apparently simple elements into the psychological equivalent of an engineer's 'exploded' diagram. Just as the assembly of a complex machine can be indicated in a picture which holds all the parts in their proper places but with explanatory gaps between them, so Dickens's moral theme is expressed by a series of comically fixed minor characters radiating out from the central narrative. In this way, these simple characters express collectively a complex psychological structure. So, for example, in *Bleak House* the question of a truly loving authority, or responsibility, is expressed by the variations on this theme in several families who may seem at first to have little function but extraneous comedy. Indeed, it gives the effect of sheer imaginative profusion which is the first impact of the Dickensian novel. These comic or grotesque characters seem *sui generis* and transparent while giving the dramatic impression of a dense and varied outer world. But once the thematic thread is seen, the imaginative variations seem like the strict working out of psychological possibilities. They collectively form an animated diagram of the psyche. So, for example, in the military family of the Bagnets, whenever important decisions are to be made, an elaborate ritual of paternal authority both disguises and acknowledges that Mrs Bagnet is the true source of judgement. In the less benign Smallweed family, the young son is the streetwise guardian of parents who, rather than retiring into revered old age, are like grotesque dolls reminiscent of Beckett's Nag and Nell. Most famously, the Jellyby family life is effectively destroyed by Mrs Jellyby's sacrificing everything to her charitable cause in Africa. The larger social theme of responsible authority as invested in the law, and as experienced by the fatherless wards of court, is thereby played through a series of comic, sinister and grotesque variations. To see the range of these possibilities, in which the very two-dimensionality throws their individual psychological mechanisms into relief, is to gain a sense of insight and power within the domain that they collectively represent. As in psychiatric therapy, there is no simple point of illumination which resolves lifelong problems, but there is an insight into what the problems are, and a practice in living with them. A comic victory is emotionally liberating.

At one level, then, Dickens's method is anachronistic. It derives from a world antedating modern internalization, a development, perhaps, of the Shakespearean subplot. But it has assimilated the affective individualism of eighteenth-century sentiment and the resulting effect points elusively inwards and outwards at the same time. It dramatizes the individual psyche as a social form and treats the social presentation as a psychological unity. This elusiveness may be part of the point as the opacity of individual feeling mirrors that of modern social relations.

Compared, for example, to *Tom Jones*, the responsible self is now much more internalized, opaque and quirky so that even as Dickens preserves something of Fielding's sense of social proportion, his effect of ultimate transparency is gone. The ramifying system of secret thematic connections presents both the individual and the social domains as a felt mystery. It is not just that characters do not always understand themselves or their motives but that there is an intrinsic opacity to self-reflection. This awareness is a Kantian revolution in the domain of feeling. An earlier, simpler scepticism is assimilated as the necessary condition of another form of knowledge. When it is recognized that the ultimate, noumenal truth of feeling cannot be directly known, the phenomenal play of emotion and language is understood in a different light. The rhetoric of sentiment stands in a knowingly indirect relation to truth of feeling.

The Dickensian novel, with its roots in the past and its intimations of modernity, is an extraordinary balancing act. It preserves the sense of overall social vision and clear moral direction of Fielding yet it carries the potentiality of both the vertiginous introspective regress which Dostoevsky developed out of it and the despairing enigma of Kafka. In contrast to Stowe, its social vision is internalized and exacerbated by the mystery of the self while the uncertainties and self-deceptions of the personal life are echoed in the opacity of social process. Dickens as a novelist showed a certain tact in refraining from social omniscience and from the more simple mobilizations of social feeling which it encouraged. He had a mythopoeic, rather than a directly political, impact, holding the social whole within a unity of feeling and suggesting its partial porousness to benevolent feeling.

The mythopoeic unity of the Dickensian novel is one of the century's last great attempts to hold the individual and the social whole in a meaningful relation. He typified a broader Victorian outlook in that he saw the *fate* of the modern individual as inescapably social, although this did not encompass the *meaning* of an individual life. Truth of feeling had inevitably to be centred in the individual. Responsibility can lie nowhere else. At the same time, the inevitable embeddedness of the individual in larger social process gives rise to new forms of false feeling. Mrs Jellyby's error lies in her collapsing of these spheres. It is not her social cause *per se* that is satirized so much as her using this as an alibi for abnegation of responsibility in the personal and domestic realms. In that respect, the satiric portrait of Mrs Jellyby is the emblem of a specifically modern transformation of sentimentality and in this broader context it is at once telling and troubling. For the public sphere is peculiarly susceptible to falsity in the projection of individual emotional motives yet, by Dickens's own example, it is only through feeling on this scale that the social whole remains human. She therefore represents a warning which is at once pertinent and yet unfocused. To what extent is Dickens satirizing an extreme or the underlying principle? What is the real presence of a social cause?

The Dickensian novel epitomizes the dialectical nature of the Victorian transformation of sentiment. The apparently straightforward appeal to popular sentiment is underwritten, in his mature fiction, by the serious critique of individual feeling to which it contributes. Grotesque images of the false are a mode of insight into emotional truth. Sentiment is no longer a philosophical generality but a local and symptomatic falsity of feeling. Of course, Dickens himself was also capable of sentimentality, particularly in relation to some of his female characters. The Dickensian structure was problematic and was held together by Dickens's personal genius and the genuine range of his social sympathies. Not surprisingly, therefore, his typical impact on subsequent novelists has been as much mischievous as creative: for later novelists to slip into the 'Dickensian' mode is usually a symptom of some falsity or uncertainty of social feeling on their part. This can be seen even in George Eliot who is the other great instance of the transformation of sentiment in the nineteenth-century novel.

George Eliot: sentiment as symptom

George Eliot inherited the Wordsworthian tradition of educating the emotional life through natural and communal pieties.[14] Yet the sustaining sense of community in *Adam Bede* and *Silas Marner* contrasts with the increasing sense of moral isolation in the later fiction. By the time of *Daniel Deronda* the life of feeling had taken on a self-questioning complexity and a separation from communal support that overlaps with the world of Henry James. Within this development Eliot maintains the sentimentalist commitment to feeling and, like Dickens, alludes to the earlier tradition of sentiment in a way that signals its contemporary transformation. In her own way, she too shows the internal dialectic by which 'sentimental' became a diagnostic term and she also reveals more significantly perhaps than Dickens how the charge of sentimentality can bear not just on the characters but on the author. Her own moments of sentimentality stand out against the power of examined feeling in her narrative.

Readerly awareness of this was sharpened after the modernist turn against sentiment and, in this respect, F. R. Leavis's reading of both

Dickens and Eliot in *The Great Tradition* is epochally representative. He rejects the earlier view that Eliot's fiction suffers from too much moral reflection and argues that her weakness lies in her tendency to emotional fervour and identification. Yet the question especially concerns him because, unlike others of the modernist generation, he was himself squarely within the tradition of true feeling and therefore subjected all his reading to a searching examination by this criterion. Hence, his remark on Eliot, 'How closely her weakness attends upon her strength', is a central clue to the whole inheritance of sentiment.[15] There is a knife-edge relation between sentimentality and true feeling and the one is only definable, or knowable, in terms of the other.

The double inheritance also appears in the way 'sentimental' is the most damaging item in early twentieth-century critical vocabulary while 'sensibility' is one of the most indispensible. Whereas late eighteenth-century 'sensibility' represented a lurch from the mid-century ideal of socially responsible 'sentiment' into an indulgent extreme, in the early twentieth century 'sensibility' came to represent the totality of responsive being against which sentimental falseness could be diagnostically recognized. T. S. Eliot's 'dissociation of sensibility' epitomized the cultural diagnosis of several modernist writers and critics seeing the eighteenth century, the age of sentiment, as the period in which the gradual falling apart of thought and feeling in post-Renaissance culture had become evident and disastrous. Yet the use of the term 'sensibility' to make this very point suggests the less conscious counter-process by which the underlying problematic of sentiment was working to provide these modernist writers with a language, and the implicit criteria, by which to engage the question.

Leavis's notoriously unacknowledged shift from near dismissal to approval of Dickens also reflects the ambivalence of sentiment and its epochal transformations.[16] Unfortunately, he tended to leap absolutely from one side to the other of the dialectic of sentiment by simply rejecting the sentimental. The same desire to preserve the true achievement from contamination by sentimentality is reflected in his other notorious exclusion: his proposal to abstract the Gwendolen Harleth story from *Daniel Deronda* and to cut out what he saw as the embarrassing failure of the Deronda portion of the book.[17] Although in his case the internal discrimination became a wholesale rejection, these exclusions were generated by his unusually intense commitment to the act of reading within the dialectic of sentiment and, despite the demurrals of successive critics, the main thrust of the case seems to have been silently accepted. David Carroll is a sharp example of defending the unity of the novel against Leavis's critique but misses the point that Leavis was questioning not the thematic relations but the artistic quality.[18] Deirdre David, however, assimilates a similar critique into a more explanatory and diagnostic account.[19] Whereas Leavis treated the shifts in the emotional quality of the narrative as direct reflections on the author, she explores their symptomatic value in Eliot's struggle with her material. David's reading precisely exemplifies the positive critical inheritance of senti-ment: she does not just diagnose sentimentality but reads sentimentality diagnostically.

The transformations of sentiment are partly thematized within the book. An important link between the two parallel narratives is that both the idealistic Deronda and Gwendolen's heartless husband, Grandcourt, are avatars of the 'man of sentiment'. The opening chapter of Book III, which traces Deronda's first stirrings of sympathy for the Jewish people after his rescuing of the young Jewess, Mirah, from attempted suicide, begins with an epigraph from Sterne's *A Sentimental Journey*: 'I pity the man who can travel from Dan to Beersheba, and say, 'Tis all barren;' and so it is: and so is all the world to him who will not cultivate the fruits it offers.'[20] The quotation is a touchstone, as are allusions to Richardson and Schiller elsewhere in the novel, but it stands outside the narrative and the other allusions have a note of worthy anachronism about them: eighteenth-century moral sentiment is invoked in the novel with a view to testing its present application. In the present instance, for example, it highlights precisely Deronda's unusual ability to find objects of nobly sentimental response in the prosaic world of Victorian modernity. Deronda is an uprooted Sir Charles Grandison in search of a context of social authority like that in which Sir Charles's personal qualities have their significance and efficacy. One way of looking at the weaker aspect of the Deronda story is that Eliot carries the tradition of sentiment into her own time with an insufficient updating. The fact that *Sir Charles Grandison* is still current reading in the Rector's family in which Gwendolen lives before her marriage suggests an equivocal blend of moral touchstone and outdated fiction (*Deronda*, 261). It reflects the persistence of an earlier sentimentalism both in the world of the novel and in its creation.

Yet the strength of Deronda's characterization is a transformation of the same tradition. Until he makes his commitment to Zionism, he lives in a condition of indecisive potentiality which echoes the neutrality of the aesthetic state in Schiller's definition. The difference is that what Schiller proposes as a momentary, and even notional, condition within an active moral life has become in Daniel, because of his lack of a fitting social context, a chronic condition. But the echo of Schiller's model here usefully focuses the fact that Daniel even now is not a 'moral *aesthete*', in the usual pejorative sense, so much as a '*moral* aesthete':

> ... the very vividness of his impressions ... had contributed to an apparent indefiniteness in his sentiments. His early-awakened sensibility and reflectiveness had developed into a many-sided sympathy, which threatened to hinder any persistent course of action ... and he was gliding farther and farther from that life of practically energetic sentiment which he would have proclaimed ... for himself the only life worth living. He wanted some way of keeping emotion and its progeny of sentiments – which make the savours of life – substantial and strong in the face of a reflectiveness that threatened to nullify differences.
>
> (*Deronda*, 307–8)

There is a strong affinity here with late nineteenth-century, Paterian aestheticism except that the condition of maximal sensitivity in Daniel is not an end in itself so much as a condition to be overcome. Later aestheticism is not a logical outcome but a reversal of Schiller and permeating the account of Daniel, therefore, is a potential critique of his condition. He turns to the public cause of Zionism as a resolution of his personal condition and for that purpose Zionism itself is, strictly speaking, an algebraical x in the emotional equation, although it is not, of course, an arbitrary choice. The cause commands all Eliot's idealism and generosity which, as Leavis pointed out, is precisely what causes the creative problem. Her fervently uncritical presentation misses the opportunity, latent in Deronda's sentimental derivation, of seeing his espousal of the Zionist cause with a measure of diagnostic ambivalence. Just as popular sentimental fiction can espouse a political cause, as in *Uncle Tom's Cabin*, so a political commitment can be an avatar of sentiment. But Daniel is no Mrs Jellyby and his narrative, with its Schillerian overtones, is a remarkable and persuasive insight into the forming of a serious political dedication in which his being unusual is a necessary part of the package.

Unfortunately, this element of the Deronda story involves an aspect of Victorian culture which the modernist generation were to regard with a suspicion which still lingers. Carlyle's *Heroes and Hero Worship* (1841) and Lytton Strachey's *Eminent Victorians* (1918) epitomize a shift towards suspicion not just of heroes and causes but of the public sphere as an arena of personal fulfilment. In the book itself, however, a more radical difficulty lies in the nature of the political cause, Zionism. Deidre David sees the Jewish question, very persuasively, as the central clue to the novel's areas of sentimental weakness. As far as Deronda is concerned the artistic difficulty lies in his adopting a cause and a culture perceived as lying outside the domain of English society in which Gwendolen is trapped and which Grandcourt epitomizes. It therefore lacks the critically testing context which is otherwise the source of Eliot's characteristic power.

If the presentation of Deronda in the early part of the novel has a critical potential which is not followed through, this applies even more strikingly to Mordecai, Mirah's brother, whom Deronda meets as the Cohen's lodger, and from whom Daniel acquires his awareness of the Zionist cause. At one point, the Cohen's child, Jacob, is terrified by Mordecai's intensity:

> ... the patient, indulgent companion had turned into something unknown and terrific: the sunken dark eyes and hoarse accents close to him, the thin grappling fingers, shook Jacob's little frame into awe, and while Mordecai was speaking he stood trembling with a sense that the house was tumbling in and they were not going to have dinner any more.
>
> (ibid., 410)

But Mordecai immediately checks himself and the disturbing potential of this moment proves to be authorially pre-emptive. The sudden reduction to the child's perception in the last phrases undercuts the significance and heads off any critical response. Yet the Dickensian echo in these final lines only reinforces the critical point: in Dickens the comically exaggerated perception of the child would precisely linger as a significant insight, giving an ambivalent depth rather than obfuscation. It is a curiously undeveloped flash of critical insight. Whereas Dickens's Mrs Jellyby is something of an overreaction to a critical possibility of modern political life, so Eliot's moral idealism seems rather to repress it.

Likewise, Deidre David argues that Eliot's working-class Jews are an idealized model for the working class at large still living within a traditionary and communitarian culture. Just as the pawnbroker, Cohen's, family is reminiscent of Dickens, so the exemplary female household of the Meyricks is like *Little Women*. In true Victorian style, Eliot seeks to incorporate a popular, sentimental note but rather than acting as part of the Dickensian dialectic of sentiment, a testing light thrown on the main character, it reinforces the note of fervour in his conception. In short, the Deronda story attempts to bring the tradition of sentiment into the contemporary world but is partly ensnared in its own sentimentality. The Gwendolen and Grandcourt narrative, on the other hand, conducts a rigorous examination of true and false feeling stemming from the same tradition.

Deronda's espousing the Zionist cause as a 'remedy' links his condition to Grandcourt's. His interest in Judaism 'is an effectual remedy for *ennui*, which cannot be secured on a physician's prescription ...' (ibid., 306–7). 'Ennui' is pre-eminently Grandcourt's condition too although for opposite reasons, just as Schiller noted the apparent similarity in the neutrality, the even weighing of the scales, in states of both emptiness and fullness (*AEM*, 145–7). In Schiller's definition of the 'sentimental', feelings are attached to moral ideas rather than objects and he notes the dangers of this. Given Deronda's Schillerian idealism, it is appropriate that his adoptive family, the Meyricks, are readers of Schiller. But Schiller also warned that where a genuine moral sensibility and philosophical reflection are lacking there will be, in the era of sensibility, merely an empty *Schwärmerei* and, in the backwash from that afflatus, the lack of an object leaves a complete emptiness such as Grandcourt exemplifies. In a Dostoevsky novel, Deronda and Grandcourt would be secret doubles rather than moral opposites. Indeed, Dostoevsky is himself a striking instance of the nineteenth century's internalization of sensibility into psychological analysis, a development in which he was directly influenced by Dickens.[21]

Eliot, however, is not Dostoevsky. The difference can be seen in the Tolstoyan contrast of her double narrative rather than psychological doubling. The difference also shows in their uses of gambling, the theme with which Eliot opens her novel. In Dostoevsky, whatever psychological complexity it involves, the obsession with gambling and risk is given a predominantly metaphysical focus: it is a secular equivalent of Pascal's wager on the existence of God. Dostoevsky might indeed echo, with an opposite implication, Schiller's dictum that 'Man is only fully a human being when he plays.' In Eliot, by contrast, such metaphysical implications are minimized and Deronda's disapproval of gambling on the grounds that life is already too much of a gamble is rather a way of heading off this possibility. Eliot's focus is emotional. Where characters are unable to find the direction of their lives in their own feelings, and hence make the necessary external decisions, they throw themselves instead on a random externality. This can happen equally through *ennui* or through the chaos of strong feeling seen in Gwendolen. In Gwendolen's case it arises from her having a strong belief in the efficacy of her own will while having avoided, or escaped, the life occasions by which her will could be more truly tested and formed. She has a strong will, and the lucid consciousness with which she agrees to marry Grandcourt despite her knowledge of his character is premised on her belief that she will, in marriage, continue to exert her dominance on him as she has previously done in her family. Unfortunately, the marriage is a bad gamble too and other possibilities, such as the public cause espoused by Daniel, are pretty much closed to her as a woman, as the unhappy history of Deronda's actress mother suggests. Yet although she is self-regarding and immature, Gwendolen is not frivolous. She has strong feeling and would wish to live in honest accordance with it. Eliot has an underlying epochal link, therefore, with Dostoevsky through the disintegration of the sentimentalist structure. Feeling is no longer contained by a social morality yet retains the claim to being the source of guidance and fulfilment. Where Dostoevsky explores the vertiginous sense of metaphysical freedom to which this gives rise, Eliot wishes to give it a moral containment. In the overall structure of the novel, as Gwendolen is morally chastened and Daniel finds a moral purpose for his life, the partly unreconstructed sentimentalism of the Deronda narrative encloses the bleak and dangerous modernity of Gwendolen's.

The bleakness of her story, however, relates to another contemporary possibility that Eliot does not pursue. Gwendolen's failure to find emotional fulfilment points to larger transformations of sentiment in the period which Eliot can only accommodate with difficulty and, once again, a note of sentimentality is one of the symptoms of her swerve against it. Several of George Eliot's male characters, such as Stephen Guest and Will Lladislaw, have repeatedly been found dramatically weak and there is something more radical at stake here than a local failure of tone. Apart from the emotional softening that has been objected to in Eliot's over-identification with her more soulful heroines, in seeking to describe what they find attractive in a man her terms are not fully adequate. Her pursuit of emotional fulfilment within a fundamentally ethical concern gives rise to an occasional sentimentality. This is symptomatic of a larger shift for which Jane Austen provides the useful contrast.

Emma is the triumphant imaginative reconciliation of the rival strains of 'sense' and 'sensibility', of 'principle' and 'feeling', in eighteenth-century culture. In its fictional world, the heroine's feelings are fully objectified in the moral quality of the socially defined male figure with whom she is finally united and, because we accept the large element of literary convention in this, we are not bothered by its ideal relation to experience. The element of artifice and social comedy sharpens rather than weakens the moral implication. It lends a note of conscious fragility to the social order. But over the course of the nineteenth century the significance of individual desire came to be conceived in way that could not be contained within such a convention. Indeed, something was at stake in sexual love which might on occasion actively require the breaking of such conventions, both in their literary and their social manifestations. This is not a matter of setting the abstract 'individual' above the abstract 'social', nor of valorizing romantic passion over the social realm. It is rather the humbly familiar fact that love and desire, although they significantly include the ethical, cannot be explained in simply ethical terms. Individual 'rightness' of emotional choice cannot be fully accommodated in the tradition of which Austen is the magnificent summary. In her fictional world at least, love is moral and feeling is principled without remainder. The seismic implications of this shift for moral and emotional culture are reflected in the form of the novel. A new phase of modernity is another transformation of the tradition of sentiment in which, once again, the discourse can be crucially at odds with the substance which is why, although the story is familiar in its general outlines, its meaning is far from clear even now.

The two major Brontë sisters herald this shift mythopoeically rather than explicitly. *Wuthering Heights* and *Jane Eyre* are intensely moral books which place the ethical realm itself under a testing strain since the counter-term is not just romantic passion but a passional morality. This is more evident in *Wuthering Heights* but *Jane Eyre* also expresses the rightful demand of passionate fulfilment by the evident strains in its narrative containment. The ambivalent power of the ethical can be seen in the fact that Jane's most serious temptation is not her love for Rochester but St John Rivers's offer of self-abnegation. The gradual shift in the emotional centre of gravity is often subtextual rather than a matter of overt principle as can be seen in Elizabeth Gaskell's *North and South* (1855).

Gaskell does not pretend either to Dickens's moral mythopoeia or to Eliot's philosophical resonance, yet in some respects she had a clearer perception of contemporary social life. *North and South* is an admirable work of social conscience as the genteel heroine, Margaret Hale, in newly straightened circumstances, is obliged to settle in the northern industrial town of Milton where, after an initial reaction of social distaste, she comes to appreciate the working people and falls in love with the industrialist, John Thornton. Much of the strength of the novel lies in Margaret's emotional growth, to such an extent that the social theme apparently indicated in the title is internally transformed into a metaphorical geography of Margaret's emotional development. The 'south' is effectively her youth and the 'north' her maturity. By the same token, the larger social geography is illuminated by the personal story since she grows, not just into a traditionary moral maturity, but into the appreciation of a specifically modern world. At both levels there is a move into the new or unknown requiring some shift in the form of the novel.

The story of her growth depends on a close understanding of her family relations. Over the course of the novel, Margaret, her mother, her father and her exiled brother, Frederick, if largely by his absence, all play shifting familial roles in relation to each other. All are 'parents' and 'children' at different moments, sometimes because of personal inadequacy and sometimes as a matter of mature response to the needs of others. As with many nineteenth-century heroines, Margaret's initially most vital relationship is with her father, although her eventual choice, in John Thornton, is someone very unlike him and the relationship with Thornton is developed partly through his doubling and comparison with her father and brother. Gaskell supplements this, however, with a rival suitor, the ambitious young lawyer, Henry Lennox, who acts as a running contrast to Thornton. When Margaret's father resigns his living as an Anglican clergyman on conscientious grounds, she is relieved not to have to endure the displeasure she assumes Lennox would have felt at his prospective father-in-law and, much later in the novel, he does indeed express such an attitude.[22] The later episode seems retrospectively to blacken Lennox and justify Margaret's judgement as if the shell of the Austen form survives around an action which is developing a different internal significance.

Lennox is incidental to the relationship of Margaret and Thornton, but in George Eliot the problem typically concerns the heroine's actual partner. The potentiality of feeling discovered indirectly by Dorothea's reaction to Rome on her honeymoon trip with Casaubon has a strikingly inadequate counterpart in the moment of mutual declaration with Lladislaw to the accompaniment of a storm (*Middlemarch*, 592–4).In leaving the mode of Jane Austen, Eliot comes at this moment dangerously close to that of the novelette. This aspect of Eliot would need D. H. Lawrence for its proper development after he had digested, not only Eliot herself, but Hardy and the great American and continental novelists. It accompanied the recognition that emotional fulfilment could not be simply contained within ethical and social terms. Or more strongly, the ethical itself begins to rest on a quality of emotional being and at this point the whole problematic of moral sentiment as inherited from the eighteenth century, the preoccupation with living up to an external social principle, begins to dissolve. In practice this is focused in a shift, or a new internal discrimination, within the notion of egotism. To act upon the legitimate demands of the ego is a characteristic modern form of responsibility. The damage of not doing so is reflected in the modern rise of psychotherapy although, here too, the widely noted vices often obscure responsible practice.

Where the dominant moral concern of classic high Victorian fiction, including Eliot's, was the overcoming of egoism, Meredith's *The Egoist* (1879) strikes a more modern note in recognizing that Clara Middleton, the woman who defeats Sir Willoughby Patterne, the egoist of the title, does so through the assertion of her own vital ego. Ego*ism* is still reprehensible but it is less readily identifiable without recourse to another, more primordial, category such as life. The book, however, adopts a self-conscious mode of social comedy that for many readers jars with its thematic modernity. Its ponderous formal anachronism, rather than leading into the future, suggests the difficulty of finding an appropriate form and discourse. Over the course of the nineteenth century the downward movement from moral sentiment to sensibility, which had characterized the late eighteenth century, was re-enacted in a different key. It is not just that the ego asserts itself as a vital value in tension with social principle but that ego itself dissolves into psychological opacities. The attempt to live up to truth of feeling has increasingly to accommodate the possibility that this is not available to introspection, that the imperatives of feeling may come in large measure from unconscious sources. On the face of it, this represents the end of the discourse of sentiment as the eighteenth century had conceived it: the definable questions of hypocrisy or sincerity gave way to more elusive possibilites of self-deception. Yet it was a further, even more radical, transformation of the underlying sentimentalist impulse to base the moral life on feeling and the true problem once again, as in the eighteenth-century phase, was a lag between the new intuition and the discourse for understanding it. Contemporary discourse could still fail to capture the nature of feeling, particularly when seeking to acknowledge the unconscious.

Feelings and the unconscious

The attempt to overcome the related dualisms of 'personal versus social' and 'feeling versus analysis' in the period was approached from the non-sentimental side by John Stuart Mill and Thomas Carlyle, both of whom are premonitory of a continuing difficulty. According to his *Autobiography*, having been brought up by his father to disregard the sphere of personal feeling or to see it only from the point of view of a social reason, Mill suddenly found himself in a crisis of apparent emotional impoverishment. The emotional crisis which shook his absolute conviction of Utilitarian principles, and his Benthamite suspicion of sentiment, presented itself as a posing of the questions lurking implictly in Dicken's novel form. If all the social evils which his

Benthamite convictions had persuaded him were removable were indeed removed, would he be happy in his personal life? The realization that he would not be so eventually opened up for him, as he recovered from the initial paralysing shock, a whole new interest in literature and in the 'internal culture', as he put it, 'of the individual'.[23] The 'cultivation of the feelings became one of the cardinal points in [his] ethical and philosophical creed', especially as exemplified in the poetry of Wordsworth. Yet his very way of expressing this preserves the assumed dualism of thought and feeling which is the root of the problem. The 'internal culture of the individual' is added to, rather than truly part of, his social rationality, so that even as he turned to a new acknowledgement of feeling, it is not clear how far he overcame the dualism as such.

This can be seen in his own language. The elder Mill had passed on to his son the classic rationalist error of imagining himself to be rational so that, in so far as he recognizes feeling at all, he is impelled to suppress it. But a conviction placed at the centre of a life is more than a rational matter and J. S. Mill's account of his first reading of Bentham catches, it is hard to say how wittingly, the paradox of this:

> Yet in the first pages of Bentham it burst upon me with all the force of novelty. What thus impressed me was the chapter in which Bentham passed judgement on the common modes of reasoning in morals and legislation, deduced from phrases like 'law of nature,' 'right reason,' 'the moral sense,' 'natural rectitude,' and the like, and characterized them as dogmatism in disguise imposing its sentiments upon others under cover of sounding expressions which convey no reason for the sentiment, but set up the sentiment as its own reason. It had not struck me before, that Bentham's principle put an end to all this. The feeling rushed upon me, that all previous moralists were superseded, and that here indeed was the commencement of a new era in thought.
>
> (*Autobiography*, 67)

Like Lydgate's reading of Bichat in *Middlemarch*, or Rousseau's inspiration for his first prize essay, this is a classic expression of intellectual passion.[24] But in so far as this passion is an intellectual hostility to the tradition of sentiment it provides a vivid emblem of the whole fate of sentiment. In the very act of denying the value of sentiment the prose communicates the power of feeling which is actually involved. Setting up 'sentiment as its own reason' is no bad summary of the word's history during the cult of sentiment, while the completely natural, apparently unconscious, transition to 'the feeling rushed upon me' suggests the living complexity which Bentham's dualism denied. The denial survives in Mill's own language even as he narrates his conversion to the importance of feeling. As an Enlightenment philosopher, David Hume had seen that the word 'reason' often denotes a more tranquil phase of feeling, while a romantic, or revolutionary, sensibility could experience it as intensity, but in neither case is it actually separate from, or somehow opposed to feeling. What we call 'reason' is, on such occasions, the sharp edge of passion, or as Blake put it, 'Reason is the bound, or outward circumference, of energy'.[25]

Seen in this light, Mill's early education, as he describes it from his later standpoint, is an inverse image of Émile's:

> My father ... was the last person to whom, in such a case as this, I looked for help. Everything convinced me that he had no knowledge of any such mental state as I was suffering from, and that even if he could be made to understand it, he was not the physician who could heal it. My education, which was wholly his work, had been conducted without any regard to the possibility of its ending in this result; and I saw no use in giving him the pain of thinking that his plans had failed, when the failure was probably irremediable, and at all events, beyond the power of *his* remedies.
>
> (*Autobiography*, 139–41)

The big difference from *Émile* is that the educational process is now seen from the pupil's standpoint rather than the preceptor's, and with this shift the externality of the process in both cases is exposed. A more subtle difference is that although Rousseau's system of coercive freedom, his identification of feeling with principle, was based on an absolute conviction which alone could provide its internal justification, Rousseau did not despise or discount the realm of feeling. On the contrary, his coercion arose from his optimistic belief that it could be identified with reason itself. At the same time, his genuine commitment to feeling, and his recognition of its frequent arbitrariness within his own personal development, gave him an underlying insight into the likely resistance of feeling to such a regime and, in that respect, he could foresee the kind of crisis undergone by Mill even without knowing quite what to do with it. Rousseau imagined the possible failure of his system when, in the uncompleted fictional continuation of the original treatise, Émile and Sophie fail to withstand the corruptions of a sojourn in Paris. Is their failure emotional or intellectual? They know, and sincerely believe, what they have been taught yet under pressure this knowledge is revealed to be not truly their own.

What has been said earlier concerning Rousseau's coercive identification of principle and feeling suggests that James Mill's most essential
'mistake' lay in seeking to impart his mature convictions, the results of his
own individual development, too directly to his pupil. For although
J. S. Mill has come to recognize a serious limitation in his father's outlook,
the problem lies not in the convictions themselves, which he still finds
persuasive, but in the need for them to be felt. By a reversal of the
Augustinian conversion experience, in which feeling followed intellectual
persuasion, at Mill's moment of crisis, his convictions, while remaining
objectively compelling, lost their emotional significance. And since all his
feeling is habitually in the grip of principle, there is no form in which his
depressive evacuation can be thought. He finds restoration, however, like
Augustine, in an emotional reading, in his case the *Memoirs* of Marmontel
whose relation to his father was an inverse image of Mill's (ibid., 145).

If Mill's story of his conversion is emblematic of the history of
sentiment, his reference to Wordsworth gives this a sharper edge. When
Mill saw his habits of analysis as having 'a tendency to wear away the
feelings' he was echoing Wordsworth's thought that 'we murder to
dissect', and it is not surprising that Wordsworth became the crucial
example for Mill, just as Leslie Stephen saw Wordsworth was the only poet
from whom emotional sustenance could be drawn in times of ultimate
distress.[26] Mill partly attributed the impact of Wordsworth on himself to
his own condition, and acknowledged that there were greater poets even
in his own time. Mill even refers to Wordsworth as the poet of 'unpoetical
natures' as if to bracket the emotional importance he found in him. Yet
Wordsworth has emerged for posterity as the crucial English poet of the
period, and Mill's phrase suggests the apparently unassuming power of
Wordsworth's poetry. It has a peculiar transparency whereby one often
feels to be reading not for the poetry but for the experience of which it
tells. And hence the difficulty of containing the experience afterwards as
being merely 'in' the poem. From reading Wordsworth we rather acquire
half-subliminally, are naturalized into, a whole way of feeling and
thought. By contrast, Mill had initially turned to Byron, 'whose peculiar
department was supposed to be that of the intenser feelings', and had
found in him only a reflection of the emotional emptiness he was seeking
to overcome (ibid., 149).

In so far as Byron's Harold and Manfred, in whom Mill found reflections
of his own world-weary state, are descendants of the eighteenth-century
man of feeling raised to a further level of ironic consciousness, Mill's
response echoes the transformation of sentiment seen in Dickens. Where
the man of feeling continued in a recognizable form he gave no

sustenance and seemed something of a pose, as Dickens indicated through such characters in his fiction, but where the tradition had been transposed to reflect the underlying recognition that 'feeling' and 'thought' are reifications, and that the life of feeling is life itself, then its manifestations ceased to be thought of as part of the sentimentalist tradition and it was able, in this subliminal form, to exercise its true power. Moral sentimentalism as a conscious project lives off the reified dualism of thought and feeling even as its underlying impulse is to dissolve this. By the same token, its deeper purpose is its own extinction as a conscious project and this was indeed its true success. Yet precisely as the conscious project of sentiment dissolves, the category of sentimentality or false feeling survives as an important part of the dialectic of true feeling. Mill's dissatisfaction with Byron enables him to recognize what is at stake in Wordsworth.

If the wrong kind of self-consciousness about feeling is part of the problem, the notion of the unconscious might present a possible solution and J. S. Mill notes that in his recovery from his crisis he was led to 'adopt a theory of life . . . having very much in common with what at that time [he] . . . had never heard of, the anti-self-consciousness theory of Carlyle' (ibid., 145). Once again the language is revealing and, if he did not speak of himself as following a 'theory of life', one might suspect him of some irony at Carlyle's expense in referring oxymoronically to the 'anti-self-consciousness *theory*'. For Mill means simply that, while happiness is the end of human endeavour, it cannot be an overt and conscious one without frustrating its own purpose. In practice, happiness is achieved through pursuing goals and activities for their own sakes. Carlyle had something more radical and pervasive in mind by way of a critique of modern culture and sensibility which he defines as the damaging legacy of sentimentalism. Echoing Schiller's critique of fashionable sensibility, and the whole analytic structure of 'naive' and 'sentimental' poetry, he concentrates on the inappropriate self-consciousness encapsulated, for example, in his term 'view-hunting':

> In our elder writers, there are no paintings of scenery for its own sake; no euphuistic gallantries with Nature, but a constant heartlove for her, a constant dwelling in communion with her. View-hunting, with so much else that is kin to it, first came decisively into action through the *Sorrows of Werter*; which wonderful performance, indeed, may in many senses be regarded as the progenitor of all that has since become popular in Literature; whereof, in so far as concerns spirit and tendency, it still offers the most instructive image; for nowhere, except

in its own country, above all in the mind of its illustrious Author, has it yet fallen wholly obsolete.[27]

Carlyle has an important point, and has noted earlier in the essay the crucial relation between sentimentality and true feeling: '... when the genuine Affections have become well-nigh paralytic, we have the reign of sentimentality' (*Miscellanies*, 9). Yet even while enjoying the historical perspective that enables him to define the genuine by its discrimination from the false, he himself strikes a false note. Whereas Schiller saw the excesses of sensibility as the vice of something genuine, the reductiveness of Carlyle's dismissal of the sentimental is evident in the quality of his prose. His attack on sentiment illuminates a representative and continuing formation. He anticipates a genre of modern commentary lamenting popular sentimentality with little consciousness of what its own repressive condescension reveals.[28] His lay sermon argues that

> ... the fever of Scepticism must needs burn itself out, and burn out thereby the Impurities that caused it; then again will there be clearness, health. The principle of life, which now struggles painfully, in the outer, thin and barren domain of the Conscious or Mechanical, may then withdraw into its inner sanctuaries, its abysses of mystery and miracle; withdraw deeper than ever into that domain of the Unconscious, by nature infinite and inexhaustible; and creatively work there.
>
> (*Miscellanies*, 40)

Like some Victorian architecture, the prose overlays its functional element of idea with anachronistically baroque or gothic ornamentation designed to give weight and stature but with the effect of monolothic insistence. The religiose language of 'sanctuaries', the personification of 'life', the alliteration of 'mystery and miracle', are rhetorical elaboration rather than argument. Instead of acquiring internal subtlety, therefore, the central intuition becomes bluster and the prose embodies the very condition it seeks to criticize. A nostalgia for a pre-modern sensibility, and for a less self-conscious state, is enacted in a language of extreme rhetorical deliberation. The effect is directed outwards onto the reader in a way that the reader is likely to resist since, while it is driven by passionate conviction, 'driven' is indeed too much the word, for this prose does not suggest that the writer has ready, or comfortable, access to his own feelings, still less to the unconscious.

What the prose actually registers is not the internal dialectic that distinguishes sentimentality from true feeling but a repressive attack on the whole domain of feeling. Carlyle's attack on a capitalized Sentimentalism is, by his own definition, sentimental in its essential structure and his 'Unconscious' is likewise too much of a conscious idea excogitated in a context of meditation on general cultural conditions to which it is then applied with the force of a political solution:

> Again, under another aspect, if Utilitarianism, or Radicalism, or the Mechanical Philosophy, or by whatever name it is called, has still its long task to do; nevertheless we can now see through it and beyond it: in the better heads, even among us English, it has become obsolete; as in other countries it has been, in such heads, for some forty or fifty years. What sound mind among the French, for example, now fancies that men can be governed by 'Constitutions'; by the never so cunning mechanising of Self-interests, and all conceivable adjustments of checking and balancing . . .
>
> (ibid., 41)

As Carlyle dismisses the realm of political thought here for a political unconscious, a potential point is lost in monolithic rhetoric. While the individual may well need to escape excessive self-consciousness and make contact with the inner life of feeling, it is not clear that this model can be applied in the same way to the modern political sphere.

An important achievement of nineteenth-century culture was its gradual recognition of an unconscious domain to be articulated by Freud at the end of the century. Victorian writers such as George Eliot and the Brontës developed inferential means of presenting emotions whose meanings were unconscious to the characters. Eliot's description of Dorothea's reaction to her honeymoon in Rome communicates, without overtly sexual reference, not only the shock of emotional disappointment, but the confused awakening of Dorothea's passional and sensuous nature. The growing recognition that emotional life may run underground, and may even present overt manifestations directly counter to its true meaning, added a whole new dimension to its unreliability yet by the same token it threw an increased burden on getting the feelings right.

The modern era, therefore, inherited a multiple tradition of sentiment, each stream of which was fraught with possible dangers. The public sphere needed a collective education, or emotional recognition, focused on social evils which were now recognized as open to amelioration through socio-economic structures and legislation. Huge changes in sensibility concerning general categories such as animals, children, women, industrial workers, other races and so on have been effected, with fiction often providing the necessary focus of feeling. But this is not a recipe for great art and can lack a sense of the waywardness and proneness to evil within the self which is otherwise projected onto villains or seen simply as an aspect of the social process. Meanwhile on the individual plane the excessive self-consciousness in the tradition of sentiment had come to be recognized as its major weakness even as its underlying impulse was being more subtly assimilated. Above all, the recognition that the life of feeling may be intrinsically unavailable to introspection, yet can be known indirectly through its manifestations in consciousness and its objectification in art, gave a whole new force to the diagnostic reading of sentimentality as the means of discriminating true feeling. Before seeing the fruit of this recognition in the twentieth century, however, it is necessary briefly to summarize an opposite conception: the view of emotion as illusion, with its largely French provenance, was another important influence on modern literature.

6
Feeling as Illusion: Rousseau to Proust

If some Victorian writers show a growing recognition of something at stake in sexual love which cannot be defined in purely ethical terms this is distinct from the continental myth of romantic passion as illusory and in conflict with social being. It is a passional ethic and is therefore different from other forms of romantic myth which incorporated the impact of eighteenth-century sentiment. Where the English tradition pre-eminently transposes sentimentalist instability into a dramatic means of understanding feeling, the French tradition typically treats emotion with suspicion and exploits the fictive as an emblem of its illusory nature. Rousseau's Julie re-enacts the decision of Lafayette's Princess of Cleves a century earlier. She rejects her lover, Saint-Preux, for the commitment to social reason enshrined in her marriage to Wolmar. If Rousseau's internal conflicts and external impact arise partly from the epochal literalism of his emotional psychology, it may be that if he had sought mainly literary, poetic expression for his strongest emotions and commitments, as Schiller suggested, it might have muffled some of his most significant impact. Instead, his desire to find practical realization in the external world helped to force the issues, and this in turn revealed how much his own emotions were in themselves an inner world. His own account of the composition of *La Nouvelle Héloïse* acknowledges its partial origin in compensatory fantasy arising from his triangular relationship with Mme d'Houdetot and her accepted lover, Saint-Lambert.[1] His greatest literary success was conceived partly as an emotional indulgence or desperate overflow.

In his last years, following a period alone on the Ile de St Pierre in Lake Bienne near Geneva, he produced his *Rêveries du promeneur solitaire* in which his analysis of certain beatific experiences, although they were not themselves fictional, was to provide one of his most enduring legacies for literature. In the fifth promenade he recounts almost Proustian moments of irrational happiness. In these unusual circumstances, he experiences the pure sentiment of his own being unmixed with the myriad everyday, and social, considerations by which it is normally overlaid. Sitting by the lake shore, he achieves, passively and accidentally, a momentary balance in his relation to the natural world. The regular sound of the waters occupies and lulls his senses, and connects him to the outside world without intruding on his inner calm and absorption. The background awareness of the water recalls the effect Wordsworth attributed to poetic metre in lulling without deadening the emotional consciousness. But the underlying precondition is his social isolation; only his outcast state has made this experience and its accompanying insights available to him, and he sharpens this recognition by suggesting that he could achieve this state even in a prison cell or the Bastille, since the features which normally make the cell a punishment are precisely those which make it favourable.

> This kind of reverie can be enjoyed everywhere one can be tranquil, and I have often thought that in the Bastille, and even in a cell where no object could be seen, I could still have dreamed agreeably.[2]

The prison image arises partly from his now chronic desire to imagine himself persecuted and to turn the tables rhetorically on his persecutors. This leads him to play down the value of the external world in favour of his inner one:

> Without doubt, the situation was fine for a dreamer who, knowing how to nourish himself on pleasant chimeras in the middle of the most unpleasant objects, could gather himself at his ease in making consonant everything which struck his senses in reality. Coming out of a long, sweet reverie, seeing myself surrounded by greenery, flowers, birds, and letting my eyes wander at a distance over the romantic shores bordering the vast expanse of clear and crystalline water, I absorbed into my fictions all those delightful objects and, finding myself gradually brought back to myself and my surroundings, I could not tell the point of separation between the fictions and realities since everything equally combined to make precious to me the retired and solitary life I lived during that beautiful sojourn.
>
> (*Rêveries*, 73–4; *Reveries*, 90–1)

Rousseau sees the world as absorbed into his internal 'fiction', rather than the more Wordsworthian movement of finding his inner state objectified in the outer world, and he thinks of his solitude in external and social terms, defined largely by the conditions he has escaped. Wordsworth, by contrast, absorbs the outer world into his inner state in a way that allows the internal to be known in an outer form. The difference is reflected in their relations to time. Rousseau is a secular Augustine in lamenting the transitoriness of earthly happiness, and finding the beatific in an escape from time. For Wordsworth, on the other hand, the emotional wealth of his inner experience arises from an emotional accumulation in time.

> I gazed – and gazed – but little thought
> What wealth the show to me had brought:[3]

His past is an inexhaustible well. It is true that such moments are also seen by Rousseau as a source of inner wealth in that he can now recover them in reverie even more pleasurably than when he enjoyed them in reality, which was Wordsworth's claim about the recurrent memory of the daffodils. But Rousseau defines the original experience as a fiction. Wordsworth, while recognizing the constitutive role of imagination in his moments of blessedness, would not think of them as fictions either originally or in recollection. Rousseau's definition of his experience as fictional may arise from a desire to sharpen the defiant edge of his chosen isolation, but it also acknowledges an ontological unease at possible illusion and self-deception.

Given his naturalistic explanation of his beatific moments, his invoking of the category of fiction at all seems an unnecessary rhetorical supplement and one might wonder how much critical weight it really bears. Yet however casually Rousseau invokes the term fiction here, it provides a benchmark for subsequent French writers within this tradition who placed an increasingly substantive emphasis on fiction to define the ontological status of their supreme moments. Rousseau's disciple Senancour, in *Oberman* (1804), presents the hero's romantic transcendence within the fictive convention of a set of letters. The consciousness of fiction is minimal here and the first-person letters rather represent a strong element of autobiographical emotion. In that respect, *Oberman* is in the sentimentalist tradition of affective verisimilitude. At the same time, however, Senancour is readier than Rousseau to accept the privacy or illusoriness of his feelings and therefore to present them in a form which, although in its day it had an emotionally compelling verisimilitude, nonetheless protects them within a fictive frame. There is a certain softening of the real-life challenge as compared to Rousseau's discomforting literalism.

Stendhal, a generation later, sharpens the contrast internally to the fiction. Following Rousseau's claim that he could find happiness in the

Bastille, the young heroes of *Le Rouge et le Noir* (1830) and *La Chartreuse de Parme* (1839) discover their longed-for romantic experiences in the enclosure of a monastic or prison cell. Once the hero has realized the internal contradiction of romantic passion, that it is the projection of a value which disappears on possession of the object, then the only place in which he can experience the passion to which he is nonetheless committed is the antechamber to eternity represented by the cell. Moreover, the sober historical realism of Stendhal's narratives further intensifies the recognition of social reality itself as such a prison while a pervasive sense of farce subjects the historical world in the novel to a parodic subversion and further endorses not just the emotional, but the ontological, commitment of the Stendhalian hero. For him, the world inside the cell has more reality than the everyday world outside. In Flaubert, this double-edged presentation becomes more evident, and more polar. His meticulous realism is a way of excluding reality, of elevating the artistry of the treatment so much over the value of the external world that the book itself becomes the equivalent of the condemned cell. The only fitting location for the romantic longing is the realm of the aesthetic understood now as representing a mode of contemplation explicitly opposed to life. In this tradition, the romantic emotion constantly acknowledges its illusory status in the self-consciousness of the fiction as fiction.

Proust implicitly summarizes much of this tradition, but with a new inflection. His admiration for Mme de Sevigné suggests a base in seventeenth-century *moralistes* and, much as the narrator describes the little church of St Hilaire at Combray as including in its structure 'each successive epoch from which the whole building had emerged trium-phantly', so the architecture of Proust's *roman fleuve* incorporates several epochal models of sentiment, moral analysis and reflection on the nature of fiction.[4] At the same time, following the emphasis on emotional response in the tradition of sentiment, Proust's celebration and analysis of feeling is inseparable, not so much from fiction, as from his sustained meditation on the act of reading. He concentrates on the emotional ingestion, rather than the ontological category, of fiction as a step towards dissolving the fiction/reality dualism. He was well-read in English literature with its more positive commitment to sentiment as such and as it was entwined in the response to fiction. The Wordsworthian mode reached him partly through Ruskin and, in effect, he created an equivalent of the 'English' paradigm through 'French' means, which of course means that it is not in fact the same thing. It is a complex culmination of the 'French' myth of feeling.

In this regard, the most teasing relationship, or non-relationship, in European literature is that between Proust and Sterne. Given Proust's knowledge of English literature and the European impact of Sterne in the era of sensibility, followed by his impact as humorist on the German romantics and then as self-conscious fictionist on modern authors, it is extremely unlikely that Proust had not read him although there appears to be no direct evidence of this.[5] The important aspect of Sterne here, however, is not the sensibility on which his continental reputation was initially based but the underlying structure of *Tristram Shandy* as an eighteenth-century *À la recherche du temps perdu*.[6] Both works are meditations on the human significance of time, privileging its subjective emotional meaning against an objective, public process, just as the public world of military and political history takes on a shadowy and miniaturized status in the domestic or personal foreground of the narrative. Both are first person narratives, proceeding with an apparently random, associative method which disguises a deeper logic of connections. Each narrator seeks to understand himself as formed by a family psyche, and as reflected in his telling the stories of others. Indeed, the narrators' self-analyses are conducted largely by the imaginative effort of under-standing others through presenting them as 'characters' and fondly enjoying their eccentricities. Although understanding others is the crucial terrain, the principal comedy of both narratives turns on the mutual misreadings arising from the individual obsessions, or hobby-horses, of a cast of quaint personalities. Hence the common focus on language as the sphere in which private associations become a source of both mutual confusion and emotional enrichment. So too, the defects of language go with an emphasis on the body as the *de facto* mode in which individuals frequently express themselves, both consciously and unwittingly. Body 'language' is a powerful metaphor in each. And finally, behind the seemingly endless distractions of the narrative pyrotechnics, the humour, the essayistic discourses, etc., each author creates a model of human kindness appreciated, in context, with a radiant simplicity. The narrator's grandmother with her obsessive idiosyncrasies, or his bed-ridden Aunt Leonie, are female versions of Uncle Toby. Indeed, this shift in gender points to one of the significant differences. Against the male humour of Sterne, the tutelary geniuses forming the best side of Marcel's character are a notably female succession: his mother, his grandmother and his aunt. Lisa Appignanesi has noted the important association of femininity and creativity in a number of modernist writers, including Proust and James, and sees Proust's thematized homosexuality as a third term detaching this creative matrix from both biological sex and social gender.[7] One could add to her list Joyce's kindly hero of *Ulysses*, the 'womanly' Bloom, and given the historical gendering of sentiment and the often programmatic critique of sentimentalism in modern writers, it is notable that the best of the male modernists are often those who assimilate, rather than reject, the female. A dissolution of several such conventional dualisms is central to the sentimental education of the Proustian narrator.

His emotional quest begins most consciously with the episode of the madeleine in which he finds himself suddenly in an inexplicable state of bliss so entire and overwhelming that it removes the fear of mortality. The subsequent volumes are devoted to the attempt to recover, and to understand, this experience. It may initially escape notice, however, in the apparently random, associative method of the narration, that the immediately preceding episode is the first of many in which the narrator meditates on the act of reading. His mother's reading of George Sand's *François le champi* is just as foundational as the moment that gives rise to the overt quest.

He is initially in the grip of a forbidden feeling. Having been sent to bed, he hides on the stairs hoping to see his mother at the end of the parents' dinner party. When she comes up, he seizes her before his father arrives. The father follows and surprises them but, rather than angrily sending the boy to bed, he tells the mother to stay with him for the night. The boy cannot risk what his father would see as the 'sentimentality' (*sensibleries*) of thanking him but when alone with his mother he gives vent to the sobs he had suppressed in his father's presence (*Du Coté*, 36; *Swann's Way*, 28). His mother, trying to be firm but finding his sobs contagious, proposes reading a book as a comfort and a distraction whereupon the situation is essentially similar to that of Charlotte and Werther in *Werther*: the childish male figure, overwhelmed by a feeling he knows to be wrong, obliges the woman, who feels the emotional infection despite her loyalty to the husband figure and her sense of duty, to suggest a reading. The similar situations, however, illuminate an epochal shift: where Goethe critiqued sentiment against the fashion of his time, Proust is recovering it in a new way. In *Werther* the sentimental reading only increases the emotional contagion to the point where Werther makes the embrace which obliges Lotte to reject him and thereby leads to his suicide. Whatever our dramatic sympathies, the diagnostic impact of Goethe's episode is clear. In Proust, on the other hand, it is much harder to distinguish the elements of possible critique of sentimental response, if indeed critique is really in question. For Proust finds a value in the sentimental aspects of the reading as distinguished from the properly aesthetic.

As the mature narrator records the episode, he distinguishes its emotional meaning within his childish relation to his mother from the literary-critical demands he would now make on the work. But precisely in recognizing retrospectively 'the everyday incidents, the commonplace topics and hackneyed words' of the story, he distinguishes something intuited behind them: 'an intonation, a strange rhythm' (*Du Coté*, 41–2; *Swann's Way*, 54). As in 'The Story of le Fever', he distinguishes while combining the human and artistic aspects of his response. He feels a moral relation in the reading which is not explicable from the text itself. Proust's use of Sand echoes a point made by Coleridge about the player's speech in *Hamlet* which some commentators had seen as a parody of earlier Elizabethan dramatic rhetoric. Coleridge points out that any note of parody would undermine the scene since Hamlet appreciates the speech, although it has to be distinct from the style of the play since the player's tears are remarkable only because they arise within a dramatic fiction.[8] Shakespeare's subtlety lies in creating a poetic artificiality without parody or condescension, and that is closer to the spirit of Proust's use of Sand. The point is reinforced by the preceding account of Marcel's grandmother buying the book as his birthday present. She had originally bought some romantic reading and 'a volume of Rousseau' but when the father pointed out the unsuitablity of her choice for so young a reader she returned to town to purchase instead the four pastoral novels of George Sand, explaining to the mother 'I could not bring myself to give the child anything that was badly written' (*Du Coté*, 39; *Swann's Way*, 31). As she reads, the child responds less to the story than to his mother's reading

> ... in which she found the note of true feeling; an admirable reader in the respectful simplicity of her interpretation, in the beauty and gentleness of her voice. Even in life, when human beings, not works of art, aroused her tenderness or admiration, it was touching to see her deference in avoiding by her tone, or gesture, or a change of subject, the outburst of gaiety which might have hurt a mother who had lost her child; the recollection of a feast, or birthday, which might remind an old man of his great age; or a domestic theme which might seem trivial to a young scholar. Likewise, when she read the prose of George Sand, which always breathes a goodness, a moral distinction, which she had learned from my grandmother to place above everything else in life, and which I was not to teach her till much later to refrain from placing equally above all other qualities in literature, careful to banish from her voice all weakness or affectation which might impede the reception of that powerful current, she supplied all the natural

tenderness, all the rich sweetness, which they demanded to sentences which seemed to be written for her voice, and were, so to speak, entirely within the range of her sensibility. She approached them, as they required, with the heartfelt tone which pre-existed them, and dictated them, but which is not contained in the words themselves; and in this way she smoothed away in passing any roughness in the tenses of the verbs, giving the imperfect and the simple past all the sweetness of the good, and all the melancholy of tenderness, leading the sentence that was finishing towards the one about to start, now hastening, now slowing, the pace of the syllables, bringing them, despite their different quantities, into a uniform rhythm, and breathing into this commonplace prose a kind of life, continuous and full of feeling.

(Du Coté, 42–3: Swann's Way, 55–6)

The passage affirms the 'generosity and moral distinction' of George Sand herself even while recognizing her 'ordinary prose'. Only as read and listened to in the right spirit does the prose become the vehicle for the quality which the mature narrator's own sentence enacts. He now expresses artistically an equivalent for the feeling which his mother's reading imparted into George Sand's prose.

But the literary quality or otherwise of George Sand, and the interweaving of her text with the mother's reading, are significant because, just as Hamlet gets the players to enact a version of the story of *Hamlet* and thereby creates the most famous instance of the play within the play, so *François le champi* is an inverted miniature of Proust's *roman fleuve*. The boy does get to read Rousseau, his grandmother's original choice, albeit transposed into a different and specifically fictional form. For, like most Europeans, he imbibes Rousseau at second-hand and unawares through Rousseau's radical and pervasive influence on other writers and thinkers, in this instance through the medium of George Sand. This influence is reflected in his own life as retold in the larger narrative. Proust's whole novel is a final appreciation of the meaning of Rousseau's beatific state, and by incorporating the apparently simple kernel of *François le champi* it irradiates both narratives.

Given the unwitting significances of the reading it is appropriate that the boy listens with some emotional mystification, but there is a more specific reason since his mother discreetly omits all the sexual references. These actually prefigure his own emotional quest for *François le champi* concerns a foundling who, having been adopted at the age of about seven by an 18-year-old woman married to a rather rough miller, grows up to marry her himself. The mother's editing out of the sexual references echoes the narrative she is reading since the action turns on the slow stages by which the two characters become aware of the nature of their love for each other. The maternal is only gradually replaced by a marital feeling, which is itself only gradually recognized as such. Since they are not biologically related, the *champi* can enact the Rousseauvian idyll of marrying his mother and, although the story is in certain respects quite realistic, as in its treatment of the rural economy of the mill, it has a consciously idyllic remove throughout. All this gives the story, despite its risky theme, the 'generosity and moral distinction' to which the narrator rightly refers.

These qualities make the story an inverted, and simpler, miniature of Proust's own novel. The blend of idyllicism and realism is echoed in Proust's complex mixture of realism and aestheticism. The Edenic return to the mother is the underlying structure of the Proustian emotion too, and the grandmother's initial choice of a volume of Rousseau suggests its deeper historical root. Rousseau called Mme de Warens, who was his first great love and somewhat reminiscent of the *champi* relation, 'Maman'. The *Confessions* and the *Rêveries* record his literalistic pursuit of his emotional idyll with a nascent hint at its fictional or imaginative nature. Proust's overall narrative, by contrast, recognizes the impossibility of literally recovering the lost paradise, and that the beatific feeling is occasionally vouchsafed only from an imaginative source for which fiction is the analogue. So too, the narrator's idyll stands in contrast to the historical world depicted in the novel. The genuine triumph of goodness and love in George Sand's story is precisely what is missing in the snobbery, heartlessness and self-deception of Marcel's social world. In this sense, the fictional world of *François le champi* suggests the missing centre, or the inaccessible axis, around which Proust's vast narrative slowly turns.

The embedded reading of George Sand, therefore, suggests a more positive understanding of the narrator's ambivalence towards her. At first glance it seems that the story is appropriate only for a child and, although sanctified by the relation with the mother, is viewed ironically by the mature narrator. But the underlying reason for this is that it expresses an abiding moral centre to which neither the older narrator nor the novelist any longer enjoys such simple access, and hence the emphasis on the mother's act of reading, the infusion of something beyond the text itself. Proust's narrative demonstrates what was noted earlier in Janice Radway's analysis of popular romance: what we think of dismissively as sentimental may not be just the failed or inadequate case of reading, or fiction, so much as its secret archetype. Of course, this is not to say there are no naive or indulgent instances, no failures of tact or taste, to which the term 'sentimental' properly applies. It is only to say that the sentimentalist assumption of emotional continuity between the living reader and the fictional object lies at the heart rather than the periphery of the response to fiction. Proust's whole novel works, at every level, to dissolve the boundaries of life and fiction with respect to feeling. In this regard his Rousseauvian myth of paradisal feeling is worked out with a Diderotian awareness of the vertiginous regress into which these categories collapse under pressure. For the same reason, his elaborate construction of his emotional idyll as a non-fiction within a fiction differs from the sentimentalism of the great Victorian novelists. As opposed to their dominantly ethical concern he preserves the ontological critique seen throughout the French tradition. The structural reflection of this is that, whereas Dickens and Eliot surrounded their more complex thematic centres with popular sentiment, so that it has felt to some readers as if it could be edited out, Proust has no such discrete areas of sentimentality. The idyllic simplicity lies at the heart of his sophisticated aestheticism.

Hence, when Proust's narrator defines as a universal truth of the emotional life that 'the only true paradises are the paradises we have lost' he brings to a subtle climax the aesthetic use of fiction and the consciousness of emotional illusion in the French novel.[9] His tale within the tale, in true modernist style, is a meditation on tradition. On the one hand, he dissolves the fictional or aesthetic remove so that the emotion which Flaubert hoards for aesthetic use is offered as the model of feeling in life. That is his 'English' aspect. Yet it is still from the viewpoint of a specific emotional myth, and the sexually passionate love of the mother, if not a matter of Oedipal taboo, is an image of impossibility and Proust's aestheticism still signals the irredeemably illusory character of feeling. In contrast to this, several writers in the Anglo-Saxon tradition provide transformations of sentiment into a conception of true feeling within the conditions of modernity. But it remains briefly to consider the modernist rejection of sentiment which still distorts the appreciation of them.

7
Modernism and the Attack on Sentiment

Early twentieth-century modernism was an apparently decisive break with the eighteenth-century tradition of sentiment. An attack on sentimentality was one of the few threads uniting the internal variety of modernisms and even now it takes an exercise in historical sympathy to appreciate the sentimentalist tradition. Yet the modernist generation also continued the transformation of sentiment into an implicit criterion of true feeling, a development which even now largely escapes recognition whether in the common language of feeling or in the specialist practice of literary criticism. This failure of recognition also has its origin in modernism since, in some cases, the vehemence of the hostility to sentiment, often tinged with snobbery and implicitly gendered, tended to throw the baby of feeling out with the bathwater of sentimentality and projected sentimentalism onto others rather than acknowledging its internal dialectic. Bertolt Brecht, approached through James Joyce, illuminates the consequences of this.

Impersonality and alienation: James Joyce and Bertolt Brecht

In any informed poll to determine the most influential novelist and dramatist of the twentieth century, Joyce and Brecht would be near the top. They had a decisive impact both through creative example and by their conceptions of narrative and theatre respectively. Each saw sentimentalism as a major evil in every area of culture and attacked it within his own genre by appealing to the model of the other: Joyce sought a 'dramatic' impersonality as Brecht devised an 'epic', or narrative, theatre. Yet the very power of their techniques, and their self-conscious investment in technique, promoted a blind spot with respect to feeling, if not in themselves, then in their wider influence.

The version of 'impersonality' expounded by Stephen Dedalus in *A Portrait of the Artist as a Young Man* (1916) envisages an evolutionary development from the lyric cry of the poet, through the epic middle distance of the narrator, to the disappearance of the author altogether in drama.[1] This is, of course, to speak metaphorically. A lyric poem is only art at all to the extent that the emotion is treated dramatically. And likewise, a theatrical piece may express the personal emotions of an author with naive directness. Nonetheless, the metaphor of theatre exerted a strong and wholesome influence, and provided technical clues for a narrative author such as Joyce for whom literally theatrical writing was not a forte. Joyce's apprenticeship was consciously Flaubertian, seeking the detached accuracy that Pound admired in the stories of *Dubliners*:

> Mr. Joyce writes a clear hard prose. He deals with subjective things, but he presents them with such clarity of outline that he might be dealing with locomotives or with builders' specifications.[2]

But as Joyce's art matured he was able to encompass the popular and even the sentimental in a manner that was appreciatively, rather than fastidiously, ironic. The techniques of *Ulysses* are devoted to this double irony. The successive episodes are a series of microcosms of the whole book, different highlightings of the book's overall implication. The 'Nausicaa' episode, the first half of which is made up of the young Gertie MacDowell's dreamy imaginings of Leopold Bloom through a haze of subliterary, sentimentally novelettish prose is a case in point. The effect is not, in the end, merely satiric at Gertie's expense. The sheer enjoyment of the parody not only transcends its immediate object but invests it with a wistful charm. If Gertie's longings are echoed in another key, this applies more pervasively and centrally to Leopold Bloom. Joyce places as near as one can imagine to the moral centre of the book Bloom's commitment to love as the central value in life, a commitment echoed in Gertie's more sentimental vision. High modernism constantly includes a nostalgia for the popular and Joyce's ironic appreciation of sentiment is a way of reconciling this conflict.

Joyce's overt thematizing of impersonality in *Ulysses* allowed him to encompass, rather than fall victim to, its potential dangers. He also historicizes the question as Shakespeare's impersonality, the thematic heart of the book, lies half-way, culturally speaking, between Homer and modernity. The massive achievement of this early modern author points to the increasing difficulty of emotional impersonality in the conditions of a later modernity. By developing narrative techniques of increasingly overt and parodic impersonality, Joyce incorporates the techniques within the theme. They escape being merely applied to it and maintain a self-conscious, jocular lucidity. But modernist impersonality was not always so clear-sighted. In other instances the very self-consciousness of the commitment to impersonality throws it into question. When T. S. Eliot, for example, said that 'poetry is not a turning loose of emotion, it is an escape from emotion', his phrasing revealed an emotional subtext, a fear or condescension towards feeling, underlying the general literary principle.[3] In a succinct formula: the most self-conscious and technical concern for impersonality is likely to be the most symptomatic. At the other end of the scale from Eliot would be D. H. Lawrence whose primary concern, in both his successes and his failures, was to achieve an emotional honesty. Hence, where Joyce thematized technique itself, Lawrence, in *The Rainbow* particularly, presented what he called an 'impersonal' level of feeling in his characters.[4] This, of course, required an artistic impersonality on his part, and a corresponding sense of narrative language and method, as Lawrence explained in several remarkable letters to Edward Garnett, but he did not self-consciously thematize his technique within the book.[5] Both Joyce and Lawrence effected important critiques of sentimentality but between them lies a variety of mixed cases, such as Eliot, who may seem, with regard to this theme, to be protesting too much and this is the light in which Brecht might be reconsidered. For his investment in anti-sentimental technique still has an exemplary implication for the practice of literary criticism.

Brecht attacked the bourgeois theatre of his day for its emotional identification with the characters, and developed his 'alienation' technique whereby the actor was understood as demonstrating a role rather than becoming the character. The assumption of emotional identification goes back to the sentimental bourgeois drama of the imaginary 'fourth wall' and the absorbed spectator which Diderot had developed and theorized in the eighteenth century. Ironically enough, Brecht records in a notebook that the idea of the 'alienation effect' came to him while reading Diderot's *Jacques le fataliste*.[6] As a writer of fiction, Diderot questioned the very techniques of affective verisimilitude he promoted in his drama. The eighteenth-century tendency to see theatre in terms of compelling illusion was a theoretically projected conception running counter to the inescapable artificiality of theatrical performance. Brecht was part of the early twentieth-century movement by which the artifice of theatre was newly privileged. Sentimentalism for him was strongly associated with the bourgeois class and was to be understood not just as excessive, indulgent, lachrymose feeling, occurring as a lapse of taste or from inadequate culture, but more structurally and diagnostically as a way of avoiding a recognition of socio-economic relations. In his use of the alienation effect, therefore, Brecht sought to expose ideological viewpoints and it is the internal workings of this latter endeavour which needs closer attention.

Brecht's term 'epic' theatre meant not heroic but narrative. In *The Caucasian Chalk Circle* (1949) a narrator sits on stage and frames the action as a play within the play. The primary effect of this is to enforce a critical detachment from the action although it is important to note that emotion is not thereby suppressed in the audience's response overall. Indeed, as Brecht remarks:

> It is not true ... that epic theatre ... proclaims the slogan: 'Reason this side, Emotion that.' It by no means renounces emotion, least of all the sense of justice, the urge to freedom, and righteous anger; it is so far from renouncing these that it does not even assume their presence, but tries to arouse or to reinforce them. The 'attitude of criticism' which it tries to awaken in its audience cannot be passionate enough for it.[7]

Furthermore, with Brecht one must be especially careful not to equate the work with the theory. Brecht was well aware of this danger, which is why his theorizing had always a mixture of pugnacity and reluctance. It was necessary for directors and actors to understand what effect he was after, yet as soon as the general principles are stated in the abstract they tend to become a straitjacket or an end in themselves. The theory tends to be intellectual, hard in outline and, despite the caustic wit, rather solemnly improving but, as Brecht remarked:

> It is to be hoped that the present notes, which set out some of the various explanations and devices that are necessary to a play's performance, do not give an impression of forced solemnity. It isn't easy always to make an analysis of this sort convey the lightness and insouciance which are essential to the theatre.
>
> (*Brecht on Theatre*, 221–2)

As might be inferred from an early play like *Baal* (1922), the underlying condition of his greatest drama is an amoral, carnival energy. As well as the physical appetites of such characters as Galileo, the ensemble work often has an aspect of circus. In this respect, MacHeath's nostrum 'Erst kommt das Fressen, dann kommt die Moral' (First comes eating, then morality) suggests a creative as well as an economic priority.[8] Good productions of Brecht are carried by a collective energy which excites before it explains.

But if his theory is not simply coterminous with the creative achievement, it provides an analytic lens for understanding the impact of the plays which represent not so much an attack on sentiment as another transformation of it. The attack on sentiment was for the sake of a truer, and historically specific, emotion:

> It is only the opponents of the new drama, the champions of the 'eternal laws of theatre', who suppose that in renouncing the empathy process the modern theatre is renouncing the emotions. All the modern theatre is doing is to discard an outworn, decrepit, subjective sphere of emotions and pave the way for the new, manifold, socially productive emotions of a new age.
>
> (*Brecht on Theatre*, 161)

The same historical awareness went into his perception of the past for he appreciated Diderot and Schiller even as he sought to uproot their dramatic heritage. In disagreeing with Schiller, for example, he says not that Schiller was wrong but that his 'distinction is no longer valid' (ibid., 194).

By the same token, however, Brecht himself has to be looked at historically. As long as the principal thrust was critical of conventional expectations it was both effective and justified, but there lurks a longer-term equivocation in the contrast between the old 'subjective sphere of emotions' and the 'socially productive emotions of a new age'. The theatre is to make self-conscious and problematic the audience's habitual assumptions. Yet, as Brecht readily acknowledges, however much the play may wish to privilege the problematic dimensions of its subject, it always has a viewpoint; it has an ideological *parti pris*. Indeed, the breaking of illusionistic identification with characters is for the sake of a more radical emotional involvement in the viewpoint of the play and it is not clear that the transfer of the emotional focus from the level of character to that of ideology stops it being a matter of 'hazily defined sentimental moods'. It may just change the sign of the sentimentality, the unexamined righteousnes of feeling, from conservative to progressive, from resigned to indignant. Furthermore, this conception necessitates a relative thinness of characterization, a running recognition that the stage figures are ideological constructs, so that they do not in themselves put up a resistance to the ideologically defined emotion. As emotional identification is transferred to an ideological viewpoint, therefore, its tendency to self-righteousness will have even less internal resistance. The danger is that emotion narrows into an even more self-fulfilling and righteous intensity as it acquires a sense of intellectual justification. Harriet Beecher Stowe, in *Uncle Tom's Cabin*, knew, as a committed writer, that she was being sentimental whereas the Brechtian model, read against its intended grain, suggests a characteristically modern form of unacknowledged sentimentality.

Brecht at his artistic best largely escapes such simplicity. The plays are greater than the theory and express the collective emotion which necessarily underlies concerted political action. Even the theoretical finessing of detachment and commitment at the level of theory reflects the deeper creative matrix of amoral carnival and moral purpose. But taken in conjunction with the theory, his theatre also shows how ideological righteousness can become dogmatic and self-fulfilling in a way that has become more common since Brecht's time. A younger German writer, Günter Grass, turned from Brechtian drama to the novel with a view to smoking out complacency from whatever ideological quarter. His consciously epochal novel, *The Tin Drum* (1959), developed extraordinary narrative means for disturbing all emotional consensus including, perhaps above all, the ideologically correct ones. His central figure and principal narrator, Oskar Matzerath, is born with a fully developed adult intellect but with, one might say, the undeveloped emotions, and therefore the absolute ego, of a three-year-old child. The result is a monster with whom we must identify. If Oskar's name makes him partly a critique of an aestheticist conception of art, the internal mismatch between intellect and feeling is suggestive for Brecht's case too. Brecht is something of a monster and his equivocation on intellect and emotion points to a characteristic late twentieth-century blend of quasi-scientific, detached ideological critique and passionate self-righteousness. The progressive edge of modern thought slips with fatal ease into ideological bullying with little internal space for self-critique. Once again, the attack on sentiment is deceptive. Remembering that the original meaning of sentiment was not simply feeling, but feeling justified by a moral idea, then modern ideological passion is actually the truest avatar of moral sentimentalism, and with all its ambivalence.

This criticism bears not so much on Joyce and Brecht themselves as on the attitudes to sentiment to which they have helped give currency. Joyce has been taken as underwriting the common critical view emerging from modernism that the solution to false feeling could somehow be a matter of technique, and Brecht has added to the emphasis on technique the belief that it is a matter of ideological analysis. Although technique and ideology are undoubtedly relevant they are fatally deceptive if allowed to become the causes or guarantors. There are no such short cuts and what escapes here is a responsible confrontation with the life of feeling. Lionel Trilling's critical analysis of modern 'authenticity' shrewdly picks up the vulnerable side of this development, and catches the elements of mystification and bravado in the claim to follow such an internal principle. Self-conscious authenticity is almost bound to be false. But his analysis is so governed by this emphasis that the correlative struggle to define or acknowledge true feeling remains invisible. The upshot is to imply that this dimension has been covered by the term 'authenticity' when it is rather the silent criterion of true feeling, within his own critique, which gives the problems of authenticity their tangible meaning for the reader. Likewise, Alasdair MacIntyre, in dismissing the criterion of 'emotivism' as propounded within the analytic tradition, allows this term to encompass the whole question of feeling. In *After Virtue*, he brings everything to a choice between Aristotle and Nietzsche and, in so far as he speaks as a moral philosopher, this is unexceptionable but, in so far as he also draws on literature to expose the weakness of the philosophical tradition in the ethical sphere, such a choice leaves out a large dimension of the subject.[9]

Undoubtedly, the modern shift from sincerity to authenticity is best represented discursively in Nietzsche. The eighteenth-century model of sentiment was preoccupied with sincerity since what was at stake was the identity of personal feeling with professed principle. In contrast, the revisionary reaction of the nineteenth-century effected a downward transposition of feeling into the unconscious. Self-consciousness was now seen as almost intrinsically insincere and, since there can be no access to unconscious feeling, it is rather a matter of avoiding what Nietzsche called 'the evil eye' of excessive or misplaced self-consciousness.[10] But whatever the difficulties of emotional self-knowledge, it matters increasingly to get the feelings right because, in post-Nietzschean modernity, this is the constitutive form for the conduct of life. It is not, in other words, that there is something separable, called 'feeling', which acts as the criterion for everything else but that there is nothing untouched by feeling. In his summative formula, 'God is dead', Nietzsche meant that there are no metaphysical sanctions or grounding for ethical existence.[11] It is the human which brings value into the world. Yet he did not offer this with the tragic resignation of a Victorian agnostic for whom God, in Nietzsche's sense, continued to exist as a regulative notion or as the absent centre of value. Nietzsche thought through the question of value in intrinsic or naturalistic terms. He was, in some sense, a vitalist but this, like all the other terms which ascribe to him a general attitude or position, is almost worse than useless. For 'life' is too basic and indiscriminate a value in itself: everything hinges on the quality of it, which is why his 'vitalism' can only be understood as combined with his 'aestheticism', and vice versa. Where Schiller had assumed a continuity between the life of feeling and the aesthetic state, Nietzsche had to recover this connection in post-aestheticist terms.

In his thinking about the relations of the 'vital', the 'ethical' and the 'aesthetic', Nietzsche defined himself against Rousseau, and partly through the intermediary of Schiller, but his immediate point of departure was Schopenhauer whose pessimistic philosophy of the 'Will', in *The World as Will and Idea* (1818), had provided both a theoretical under-writing for the nineteenth-century's separatist transformation of the aesthetic and a powerful premonition of the Unconscious. Schopenhauer saw human consciousness as merely serving the blind 'purposes' of nature, or the 'Will', so that all higher values and motivations were essentially illusory. The only dignified posture for the mind which recognized this was a contemplative remove such as he saw in some Eastern religions or in the aesthetic state. On this model, art is an escape from the illusory purposiveness of life. Nietzsche was initially influenced by Schopenhauer and shared his privileging of the aesthetic, but he increasingly modified Schopenhauer's meaning until he inverted it. His aphoristic declaration in the early *The Birth of Tragedy* that 'Only as an *aesthetic phenomenon* are human existence and the world eternally *justified*' set a theme which his subsequent *oeuvre* would increasingly expound.[12] For him, the 'purposiveness without purpose' by which Kant had defined the aesthetic became the model for life itself. That is to say, just as art serves no external purpose yet is a highly concentrated organization of values which are thereby understood with a peculiar intensity for their own sake, so Nietzsche would use the model of the aesthetic to acknowledge the ultimate purposelessness of life while appreciating and affirming values as human creations. By the same logic, the aesthetic model enforced an intense sense of responsibility in life. Nietzsche's aesthetic conception would bring to bear on all aspects of life the searching quality of judgement we bring to bear on aesthetic objects. In aesthetic criticism judgements of value are of the essence not just despite, but precisely because, they have no simple external criterion.

Nietzsche's 'aestheticism', therefore, opposes the common late nine-teenth-century understanding of the term as 'art for art's sake'. It also opposes the eighteenth-century model of moral sentiment as an external social principle to be lived up to. For him, the ethical is rather an effect than a goal.[13] Only a responsible quality of feeling can be an authenticating motive to action and the term 'authenticity', if it is to be used at all, has to be understood in a specifically judgemental, rather than a generic or descriptive, sense. Just as the word 'poem' can be a neutral classification, including subliterary doggerel, but derives its significance from being a judgement of quality, so the word 'authenticity' has to be understood in this latter sense. It is not an inert category but an achievement. The standard objection here is to ask, in a tone of triumphant irony, but who is to say what is authentic? But the aesthetic analogy helps to show why this rhetorical question is emptily so. Clearly no one is in an absolute position to say; it is a matter of constant responsible judgement, and the question rather reveals its own presupposition that somehow all this is a matter of choice, or that life must be assumed to present some structure of moral objectivity that could be known and followed. But if the earlier preoccupation with sincerity, or the authenticity of ethics, has been replaced by what Charles Taylor refers to as an 'ethics of authenticity', this is not to argue for such a thing as being desirable so much as simply to recognize that it is the case.[14] Of course, there are traditionary and communal horizons of value within which all individuals live, just as works of art occur within their traditions. No one has a moral life independent of others, and it is only a moral life because it relates to others. Nonetheless, the modern individual shares responsibility for what is arbitrary or questionable in the communal tradition and cannot regard it as a pure objectivity.

In all this, Nietzsche was both an inversion and a consummation of Rousseau since he was carrying out the commitment to feeling for which Rousseau is the mythical representative in European thought. In fact, the common view of Rousseau as a simple proponent of feeling reflects the reductive view of feeling in our culture while Nietzsche's hostility to Rousseau epitomizes the characteristic relation of modernism to sentiment. He spoke witheringly of Rousseau's 'femaleness' and *ressentiment*, a term which inflects 'sentiment' towards the spirit of the underdog, projecting its own unhappiness into a political arena.[15] This was the aspect Nietzsche most abhorred in post-Rousseauvian culture yet Rousseau's work is replete with 'Nietzschean' insights and, if Nietzsche effectively closes the era of Rousseau, it is because he is himself the Rousseau of a later phase of modernity.[16] In the same way, few modern observers escape the Rousseauvian heritage even when criticizing it, and this ambivalence lurks even in Trilling's critique of authenticity. The implicit criterion which exposes the weakness of authenticity can no longer be the social reason of the eighteenth century and, whatever it is, it must remain conceptually elusive, rather a background of thought, a form of life, than an idea. Nonetheless, as the eighteenth-century conception of 'sincerity' ceased to carry its former significance, much cultural work was being done to make genuineness of feeling meaningful, although those doing the work would not rely too much on the word 'authenticity' precisely because of the vulnerability which Trilling rightly detects in it. Truth to feeling is difficult to judge positively. It only exists in its specific, momentary, necessarily tentative, assessments but that does not make it less important, and that is where the term 'sentimentality' acquires its irreplaceable force. The charge of sentimentality invokes an unstated criterion of true or authentic feeling, and implies a significant step towards its recognition. This truly important modern transformation of sentiment can be seen in two modern authors who, although opposed in almost every other way, equally exemplify the struggle to live a life governed by truth to feeling.

8
Henry James and D. H. Lawrence: 'Felt Life' and Truth *to* Feeling

As a discursive thinker, Nietzsche is fraught with difficulty. His expression is as much assertive as argumentative and often switches to an opposite mode of thought experiment. As a body of ideas, his thought is elusive, unsystematic and consciously self-contradictory. His philosophical activity was inextricable from his functions as psychologist and cultural critic and his favoured form of the aphorism gave rise to apparently absolute statements on women, Jews and the nature of power, for example, which have seemed only the more unacceptable in the light of twentieth-century history. His legacy, therefore, is multiply controversial: commentators disagree both on the substance of his 'philosophy' and on whether its underlying tendency is healthy or dangerous. He might, therefore, seem an unfruitful resource for explicating the present theme. But he was acutely responsive to changes in the culture which were difficult to render in discursive terms and his value for a reading of James and Lawrence is not as an influence but as a frame of reference against which to see the significance of their achievements. They developed the relevant awareness from their own inheritance as novelists and brought to different consummations the emergent shift already seen in the Victorian novel. The concern for truth *of* feeling, still part of the overt dialectic of sentiment, gave way to a truth *to* feeling in which the link to sentiment seemed to be dissolved. The struggle for emotional truth, that is to say, was focused less on acquiring moral and social maturity, or living up to an externally statable criterion, and more on the need to discover and live out one's own emotional commitments. The difference is not always evident since the one in many circumstances encompasses the other. What matters is the shift in motivation or grounding. As Nietzsche recognized, the truly 'moral' might be rather the *effect* of a 'good' life than its *goal* or *cause*. The difference, therefore, is crucial, if not always immediately visible, and it places a different, perhaps even a greater, burden on emotional self-knowledge. That is why the inheritance of sentiment, not now as a positive ideal but as a way of diagnosing false feeling, remains crucial.

Both authors have a crucial link with the tradition of sentiment and conceive their art as having a merged yet distinctive relation to the life of feeling. The complex way in which Nietzsche privileges the concept of the aesthetic while also collapsing it back into a life term has a homely and practical equivalent in them since their highly sophisticated reflection on their art is predominantly subtextual in their creative work. Their mutual difference in this respect from earlier fiction is reflected in the nature of the following discussion. Some of the eighteenth-century works discussed above invoked philosophical questions overtly, and with formal self-consciousness, while others sought the didactic impact of affective verisimilitude. Over the course of the nineteenth century the significance of feeling increasingly disappeared into the texture of the narrative even where the whole work is sustained by a loquacious Victorian narrator. In the following works of James and Lawrence the question of feeling is, if possible, even more holistically integral to the narrative and the appropriate critical discourse is a close reading. At the same time, they both find ways, without overt formal self-consciousness, of highlighting their internal significances, of teaching the reader how to read the emotions of the text. In this regard, their epochal features are focused by an unobtrusive thematizing of their relations to the earlier tradition of sentiment, above all by their parallel analyses of the sentimental virtue of kindness.

Henry James and kindness: *The Golden Bowl*

Henry James's nephew, Billy, remembered him saying 'three things in life, are important. The first is to be kind. The second is to be kind. And the third is to be kind.'[1] Yet he doubtless saw problems in the practice of kindness. Furthermore, although kindness now seems the most unquestionable of virtues it never made it into the big seven of the morally confident Christian conception. And Charity, as one of the three theological virtues, is strictly speaking the love of God before the love of man. Against this background, mere kindness has something of a fallback status, a diminished ambition suitable to a confused and secular age. As Charlotte Stant remarks in James's *The Golden Bowl*, 'one can always, for safety, be kind.'[2]

Nor can we assume that this virtue was in any simple way central to James's personal life, not because he lacked it but because of the competing pressures of other important criteria, such as truthfulness, which would be especially intense for an artist. By the latter decades of the century the mid-Victorian moral critique of ego had been complicated by an increasing recognition of its legitimate claims and this had a further adumbration in the production of art. A great work of art requires an immense concentration of powers and an egoistic commitment to, or on behalf of, the work so that it is notorious that many highly improving artists were not comfortable or considerate companions in daily life. James's remark, therefore, rather than offering a simple clue to the life values enacted in his work, points to a significant nerve centre of difficulty and conflict in his fiction, and in the culture that fiction reflected.

The transformation of sentiment in Jamesian art is suggested in his declaration of ...

> the perfect dependence of the 'moral' sense of a work of art on the amount of felt life concerned in producing it. The question comes back thus, obviously, to the kind and degree of the artist's prime sensibility, which is the soil out of which his subject springs.[3]

James's 'moral sense', 'feeling' and 'sensibility' embody the transformative assimilation of sentiment: while constituting a dense field of sentimental vocabulary, they are so altered as to hardly reveal this. Partly this is because of the curious interweaving whereby each term rests on the whole network with no obvious primacy accorded to any one of them. 'Moral' goes into quotation marks as it now depends on the more primary term 'life'. Yet this term is itself conditioned by feeling. Meanwhile if feeling is primary, it is only as the preterite and adjectival 'felt'. As in Wordsworth, the feeling is no longer the immediate response to a present occasion, but emotional experience filtered through reflective memory or surviving as an emotional formation. Likewise, the word 'sense', as in 'moral sense', is now detached from the ethical response of the individual to become an impersonal function of the work itself. A notion of 'moral sense', in some ultimate continuity with Hutcheson and Shaftesbury, is still alive here but its locus of significance has shifted from the feeling subject to the dramatic object. Most strikingly, the artist's 'sensibility' is now linked to the impersonal function of the work and even this is not as part of the art object but as the soil from which it grows. This last image stresses the largely unconscious aspects of artistic creation.

James's network of interdependent meanings here stretches between the realm of the ethical and an organic, biological process. The relation between the ethical and the natural has been the central problematic of sentiment from the mid-eighteenth-century. Whereas the ideology of sentiment sought to identify them while retaining their separable meanings, James invokes them as a continuous web of aspects in which the abstractly distinguishable realms have no separable existence. In this respect, James's revisionary relation to the tradition of sentiment can be focused in his use of the term 'kind' in *The Golden Bowl*. The word 'kind' spans the ethical and the biological and when examined more closely it is like the piece of crystal from which the golden bowl of the title has been formed. While being valued as a natural whole it contains a secret split made good by art. Furthermore, whatever its provenance and authenticity, kindness is a virtue especially prized in the English culture in which James had settled. I recollect a conversation between a group of international students, mainly female, on the question of which quality you would most wish to be thought to possess. The French mainly wanted to be thought of as intelligent, the Americans as sincere and the English as kind. This highly unscientific impression corresponds to something which can be traced in the literature of these cultures and is to be seen in the international cast of *The Golden Bowl*.

Perhaps the most famous pun in English literature turns on the doubleness of the word 'kind' when Hamlet describes Claudius as being 'a little more than kin, and less than kind', and he gives a now proverbial expression to our sense of the possible difficulties of being kind in his later remark to Gertrude: 'I must be cruel only to be kind.'[4] It would seem that the primary meaning of the word as 'species' has engendered a secondary implication of 'benevolence': that we would naturally be kind to our own kind. Although this secondary moral, or emotional, significance developed early in the history of the word, and Shakespeare clearly had it in mind, it is not the primary impact of Hamlet's remark. I would surmise that many modern listeners take him to mean that Claudius is 'more than kin' in being now his stepfather as well as his uncle but does not treat him well, that is kindly. Yet there is no reason to believe that Claudius initially treats Hamlet badly, and Hamlet's point is a more radical one: that despite their kinship they are not of the same moral species. So too, Lady Macbeth's contemptuous reference to her irresolute husband as 'too full o' th' milk of human kindness' is now frequently used, as a free-floating proverbial phrase, in a positive sense.[5] But once again, her point is stiffened in context by the primary sense: it is not so much that Macbeth is soft-hearted as that he acknowledges the demands of human commonality. And that is indeed the meaning which his tragedy eventually brings home: he cannot kill others without killing humanity within himself. Lady Macbeth, on the other hand, represents another powerful view within our culture, and one to which modern history gives much plausibility, that the human species is predatory in its fundamental nature. The word 'kind', therefore, links two meanings which are at once interdependent and yet frequently opposed. On the one view our belonging to a common species gives rise to mutual benevolence, so that the one meaning is a natural outgrowth of the other, while on the other view the true nature of our kind is anything but kind. The word focuses the central debate of sentimentalism: to what extent is it in the nature of man to be well disposed to other members of his species?

The cultural shift between Shakespeare's time and our own is encapsulated in the likely modern readings of these phrases. In responding more to the emotional than to the biological thrust of the word 'kind' the modern listener is, in a historically precise and positive sense, sentimentalizing these phrases. In other words, without needing to be personally soft-headed such a reader has absorbed the impact of eighteenth-century sentiment. And that was the period in which the word 'kind' assumed the force and centrality exemplified in Henry James's moral advice. Historically midway between Shakespeare and James, sentimental kindness is classically embodied in the figure of Sterne's Uncle Toby, the old soldier who is so gentle he literally cannot hurt a fly. But this virtue is subjected to a more relevant questioning in the Yorick of *A Sentimental Journey*.

Parson Yorick, the narrating persona, has several sentimental dalliances with women. One is a *fille de chambre* who visits him in his hotel room to thank him for his previous gift of a crown coin, and to show him the snug little purse she has made to contain it. They somehow find themselves sitting on the bed together in a way that becomes increasingly titillating for Yorick, and the reader, until she shows him a broken buckle on her shoe which he fixes for her, whereupon the movement of raising her feet tips her on to her back. The chapter breaks off abruptly to lead into the next one called 'The Conquest'. But this proves to be another of Sterne's titillating games with the reader. For the conquest in question is not his sexual possession of the *fille de chambre* but his victory over his own sexual impulse and his sublimation of it, as we might now say, into a charitable action in giving her a parting gift. This leads him to a general reflection on the mixed nature of kindness.

> If nature has so wove her web of kindness, that some threads of love and desire are entangled with the piece – must the whole web be rent with drawing them out? Whip me such stoics, great governor of nature! said I to myself – Wherever thy providence shall place me for the trials

of my virtue – whatever is my danger – whatever is my situation – let me feel the movements which rise out of it and which belong to me as a man – and if I govern them as a good one – I will trust the issues to thy justice, for thou hast made us – and not we ourselves.[6]

Sterne presents the two meanings of kindness, the biological and the ethical, as the warp and weft of the fabric of life. He affirms the need to be virtuous while acknowledging the predatory impulse underlying his relationship with the *fille de chambre*. Without arguing the goodness of natural feeling as such, he finds a positive value in it as a motivating force in human relations. At the same time, he is able to make this affirmation because he has denied or sublimated the predatory impulse.

The ambivalence of the passage encapsulates the double impact of the cult of sentiment. On the one hand it changed sensibility for what most of us would consider the better. Few would argue now for the public torture described in the earlier passage from Thomas Nashe. Yet on the other hand, the excesses and absurdities of sensibility exposed its own more naive optimism and over the nineteenth century it was the other possibility of the word 'kind', the predatory survival instinct, which seemed to receive more and more endorsement, as Darwinian theory was given social and moral applications. Likewise, after the attempt to combine them, the two meanings of 'kind' drifted further apart but with, of course, a greater anxiety now that, in an increasingly post-religious world, their identity seemed the more crucial. If it is not in our nature to be virtuous, what other motivation is there for the moral life? This was the tension within the notion of kindness as it was inherited by Henry James and treated most summatively perhaps in *The Golden Bowl*. But the summative nature of this novel encompasses a further level in the relativity of kindness. For the novel involves American, English and continental characters who embody different cultural assumptions, or different myths of feeling, between which the virtue of kindness is ambiguously located.

It is hardly accidental that in Sterne, as in *Hamlet*, the tensions of kindness are focused by the pressure of sexual feeling since English culture, as has been noted earlier, developed a different myth of sexual passion from much of continental Europe. Whereas Denis de Rougement's *Passion and Society* defines the widespread continental myth whereby the deepest and most intense expression of sexual passion is incompatible with the stable social order represented by marriage, C. S. Lewis's *The Allegory of Love* traces through Chaucer, Spenser, Shakespeare and Milton the assimilation of the courtly structures of feeling to marriage.[7] Passion is assimilated to the moral order and Jean Hagstrum's

Sex and Sensibility traces the subsequent development of a domestic ideal of sexual love through the Enlightenment following the frequent model of Milton's Adam and Eve. Hence, the English novel was more deeply and positively affected by sentiment and the values of the domestic, but sometimes, as in the case of Sterne, with hints of sexual abnegation. Uncle Toby, Sterne's benevolent old soldier, has retired from the army with a wound to the groin which leaves his physical manhood in question and points to the more substantial issue of his emotional innocence. The values of sentimental benevolence, or kindness, often imply either a lack, or a suppression, of sexual passion. Or conversely, as Stendhal frankly puts it: 'True passion is a selfish thing.'[8] If kindness is a central virtue for English moral culture, therefore, it is often at a cost.

That Henry James should have settled on the south coast of England, as near as can be to France and on the same shore from which the *Mayflower* sailed to America, is emblematic of his literary affiliations. While remaining a deeply American writer, he assimilated the tradition of the English novel and those of continental Europe, especially the French. Although he understood the French tradition sympathetically, he viewed it with a critical distance from the English side of the channel and the cosmopolitan cast of *The Golden Bowl* represents these competing myths about the relations of passion and marriage reflected very largely in the different pressures they exert on the motive of kindness.

The Golden Bowl is perhaps the most controversial work of James's already controversial late phase. It is exquisitely painful in bringing together a close group of characters who like and respect each other but have conflicting desires. Maggie, the daughter of Adam Verver, a wealthy American widower and art collector settled in London, marries an impecunious Italian prince, Amerigo. Her father then marries her old schoolfriend, Charlotte Stant. Maggie detects the flaw in the apparently happy arrangements of the two couples when she realizes that Amerigo and Charlotte have had an earlier relationship which they have now revived. The latter half of the novel is taken up with Maggie's successful attempt to recover her husband without direct accusation, which she could not prove, and without revealing her suspicion to her father. She avoids direct statement in order to maintain what she calls the 'equilibrium' of their mutual relations in a way that preserves her husband's dignity and her father's marriage (*GB*, ii, 97–8). She therefore cannot know for sure what her father knows, although we may infer his eventual recognition when he volunteers to remove Charlotte from the scene by returning with her to America. Maggie's refraining from direct statement also reflects the quality of the trust she is still offering to

Amerigo. She does not demand that he admit a sexual affair but rather that he take cognizance of her knowledge and cease to have any special relationship with Charlotte in conflict with their marriage. Perhaps the greatest trust in a relationship lies not in expecting to be told every factual truth, but in assuming that the truth is lovingly edited.

Although the action takes place almost entirely in England, Adam and Maggie have a strongly American formation as James sees it: a certain robust, rather than merely naive, innocence and a belief in the power of their own moral autonomy. Charlotte is also American, but she has been brought up in Italy and her rootless cosmopolitanism is stressed while the Prince, with his Italian aristocratic background, is puzzled by the moral solidity of Anglo-Saxon character to which he tries to adjust. The situation of the novel, therefore, involves much cross-cultural misreading and it constantly turns on the ambiguities of the word 'kind' to which these characters give different weights. Indeed their problems arise partly from an excess of kindness and the word is invoked by nearly all of them at different times. For although kindness, as in Joyce and Proust, is a dominant motive of the book, the simplicity of feeling it seems to imply is rarely attainable. When Amerigo meets Charlotte on her first visit, for example, he truly wishes her well and, being unsure of her intentions, suggests she should marry 'some good, kind, clever, rich American'. In view of his own mixed feelings about her, 'he felt it really as a lift on finding an honest and natural word rise, by license, to his lips' (*GB*, i, 57). Ironically, that advice is what she follows in marrying Adam and the tension between Amerigo's different specifications, 'good, kind, clever, rich', are the substance of the subsequent action. Even here, Amerigo's momentary directness of feeling comes only 'by license' and throughout the book we see the unhappy effects and suspicious motivations of kindness.

This is partly because of the creeping undertone of the other sense of the word since Amerigo and Charlotte always recognize themselves to be of a different 'kind' from their respective spouses. Whereas Adam and Maggie are domestically inclined and prefer to stay at home, especially after the birth of Maggie's child, Amerigo and Charlotte are effectively left to fulfil the two families' social obligations which they enjoy doing. The two meanings, therefore, come together in an early conversation between Amerigo and Charlotte about Maggie:

'She lets everything go but her own disposition to be kind to you. . . . She does everything herself. And that's terrible.'

   The Prince had listened; but, always with propriety, he didn't commit himself: 'Terrible?'

'Well, unless one is almost as good as she. It makes too easy terms for one. It takes stuff, within one, so far as one's own decency is concerned, to stand it. And nobody,' Charlotte continued in the same manner, 'is decent enough, good enough to stand it – not without help from religion, or something of that kind ...'

The Prince, obligingly, thought an instant. 'Not good enough to stand it?'

'Well, not good enough not rather to feel the strain. We happen each, I think, to be of the kind that are easily spoiled.'

(*GB*, i, 102)

Charlotte feels almost oppressed by Maggie's kindness, which makes her feel her own relative emptiness and her lack of a morally sustaining tradition, and she goes on to identify Amerigo as being, in this respect, of the same 'kind' as herself. Neither of them seems to have that 'stuff within one' which the Ververs possess apparently as a matter of course. Indeed, Amerigo, while seeking guidance in his new life from their mutual friend, Fanny Assingham, has already explained that, coming from his tradition, he lacks the Anglo-Saxon 'moral' sense, thereby invoking a phrase which takes us back to the eighteenth-century tradition of moral sentiment and its specifically English lineage (*GB*, i, 31).

Charlotte, therefore, although she has immense resources of social tact, is of the kind least likely to be genuinely kind. Yet even she knows the impulse. When Adam proposes to her, on a garden seat, she expresses her scruple about accepting him largely for his own and Maggie's sake since she cannot tell him the real problem is to know what Amerigo will make of it. She gives an involuntary start to her feet when he offers that they should immediately consult the other couple who are presently on holiday in Paris. And then, as he continues to sit in silent appeal:

Presently ... a new sense had come to her, and she covered him, kindly, with the expression of it. 'I do think, you know, you must rather "like" me'.

(*GB*, i, 225)

Even in the context of her diplomatic temporizing, her 'kindly' response is not evidently insincere and the word sits over the fathomless ambiguity of her motive and feeling, fathomless perhaps, at this point, even to herself.

Apart from Charlotte most of the other characters are positively kind in different ways. One of the reasons everyone is so pleased at Charlotte's marriage, for example, is that Adam Verver, who is too kind even to keep his servants up late when he goes to a party, has difficulty rebuffing the various female fortune-hunters by whom he is especially beset now he is no longer living in social coupledom with his daughter. Yet even Maggie and Adam come to suspect the limits of their own kindness. As the narrator remarks in an early chapter:

> They each knew that both were full of the superstition of not "hurting", but might precisely have been asking themselves .. whether that was to be .. the last word in their conscientious development.
>
> (*GB*, i, 160)

The phrase 'superstition of not "hurting"' is typical of James's open-ended irony throughout the book. Does the word 'superstition' truly undermine their habit of benevolence or rather act as a protective self-consciousness, suggesting their own pre-emptive acknowledgement of a possible criticism? Yet the kindness of the Ververs, however problematic, is evidently sincere and in that respect it differs, by several shades, from the kindness of Amerigo to Maggie.

The Prince is clearly sincere too in his desire to make a success of the marriage although he is increasingly seduced by Charlotte's beauty and passion within the collusive pressure of their situation. In his rather passive way, he treats both women with kindness. When Charlotte first arrives from America, and he is still unaware of her motive, he meets her with 'a kind, comprehending face' (*GB*, i, 52); in proposing the joint outing in search of a present for Maggie, the excursion which leads them to find the 'golden bowl', she appeals 'to his kindness' (*GB*, i, 94); and when she finally visits him for the meeting in which she makes him acknowledge their mutual feeling, his initial passivity is such that it was as if she was 'positively fitting him again with the fair face of temporising kindness' (*GB*, i, 301). Kindness is also his resource when Maggie confronts him with her suspicion about his relation with Charlotte. His sheer sexual attractiveness for Maggie is one of her temptations and when he puts his arms around her she feels her resolution slipping:

> ... he had possession of her hands and was bending towards her, ever so kindly, as if to see, to understand, more, or possibly give more – she didn't know which; and that had the effect of simply putting her, as she would have said, in his power. ... It was not till afterwards that she ... felt how the act operated with him *instead* of the words he hadn't uttered ...
>
> (*GB*, ii, 28)

Amerigo's kindness is a substitute for answering his wife's question yet it is not exactly hypocritical. Arising from a social and personal habit of concern, it is too much a social form and allows the situation to drift in bad faith. We might say that, with his continental, aristocratic background, he keeps his feelings for Charlotte and Maggie in separate compartments rather than in competition. His way of coping with the conflict of passionate and married love is to regard them as so separate as not to interfere with each other within his own mind. Only when Maggie becomes aware is the contradiction forced upon him as a choice.

In sum, the kindness of Amerigo and Charlotte is dangerously formal, a substitute for directness of feeling, while that of Adam and Maggie, although sincere, is disturbing in some of its effects particularly because it is underwritten by their immense wealth. Their kindness, even if that is not its motive, is a form of possession. Hence, rather than all these characters being kind to each other we might say that the painful comedy of the book arises from their failed attempts to be so. This does not mean, however, that no simple kindness is possible and in this respect Bob Assingham, Fanny's husband, is an illuminating figure. Bob Assingham is a retired colonel whose professional talents are administrative rather than to do with fighting and he now helps to run his London club. Similarly, within the marriage, his gift for careful economy allows the couple to live well, and remain at least on the margins of high society, despite their limited means. And these qualities carry over to the moral sphere. Bob Assingham's blunter common sense treats his wife's concern for subtle Jamesian discriminations and searchings of conscience as a luxury they cannot afford. Yet he is genuinely and straightforwardly kind, not least to his wife, and the portrayal of their genuine partnership, across great differences of personality, is one of the triumphs of the book. And it is thematically relevant in that their affectionately shared institution of marriage frames the passionate conflicts of the central couples.

If the main characters show how difficult kindness has become in their world as compared to the optimism of the movement of sentiment, Bob Assingham seems like a deliberate link to that earlier age. As the retired soldier, peacefully smoking his pipe, irritatingly indifferent to the obsessions of those around him and yet an unfailing source of benevolent feeling, he echoes Sterne's Uncle Toby. He even has the minor eccentricity of using strong language to which his wife responds as follows:

> His wife had once told him, in relation to his violence of speech, that such excesses, on his part, made her think of a retired General whom she had once seen playing with toy soldiers, fighting and winning battles,

carrying on sieges and annihilating enemies with little fortresses of wood and armies of tin. Her husband's exaggerated emphasis was *his* box of toy soldiers, his military game. It harmlessly gratified in him, for his declining years, the military instinct; bad words, when sufficiently numerous and arrayed in their might, could represent battalions, squadrons, tremendous cannonades and glorious charges of cavalry.

(GB, i, 64)

If this is a discreet nod on James's part to Uncle Toby's harmless military games on the bowling green, it links and contrasts these two figures. Bob Assingham's benevolence is more tough-minded than Toby's and is based on hard-bitten experience. As James says:

He knew everything that could be known about life, which he regarded as, for the greater part, a matter of pecuniary arrangement.

(GB, i, 67)

He looks on his fellow beings with a disabused eye which acknowledges, indeed counts on, precisely that difference in human 'kind' which is so problematic to the principal characters:

The infirmities, the predicaments of men neither surprised nor shocked him, and indeed – which was perhaps his only real loss in a thrifty career – scarce even amused; he took them for granted without horror, classifying them after their kind and calculating results and chances.

(GB, i, 67)

And so 'his fondness, in domestic discussion', for strong language may well be a psychological device for holding things at a distance for we are told that

his kindness, in the oddest way, seemed to have nothing to do with his experience. He could deal with things perfectly, for all his needs, without getting near them.

(GB, i, 67)

While he is in this respect the opposite of the eighteenth-century man of feeling, whose benevolence arose from fellow feeling and ready identification with the unfortunate, any echo of Uncle Toby in Bob Assingham is more of an updating than an opposition. Bob is an Uncle Toby for a later world.

A revisionary glance at the earlier tradition of sentiment gives a richer historical value to Bob's being a sympathetic Jamesian portrait of an un-Jamesian personality. He resists his wife's finely spun Jamesian discriminations although, by the logic of his own kindness, he is increasingly drawn in to her concern for the other characters and for her own relation to them. While Fanny's partial involvement in their lives helps James to focus the moral dilemmas of the principal characters, her husband represents a more ordinary world. Indeed, he represents the world of the common, or non-Jamesian, reader. For James's late novels are notoriously specialized in their elaboration of style, their super-fineness of moral discrimination, and above all for the leisured and wealthy lives of their major characters. Many readers of the late fiction have felt precisely the urge that Bob Assingham has towards his wife in forcing her to live within their joint means not just financially but psychologically and verbally:

> He edited, for their general economy, the play of her mind, just as he edited, savingly, with the stump of a pencil, her redundant telegrams.
>
> (*GB*, i, 67)

The charge of fine-spun circumlocution and obliquity commonly made against the late James is not merely one of personal taste. For F. R. Leavis, these late novels lose the wood for the trees: the fineness of the method has made James seriously misappreciate what he is actually doing. He loses a sense of human proportion, and fails to see the proper force of passion in Charlotte and Amerigo or the sinister possessiveness of Adam and Maggie.

> It is as if his interest in his material had been too specialized, too much concentrated on certain kinds of possible development, and as if in the technical elaboration of expressing this specialized interest he had lost his full sense of life and let his moral taste slip into abeyance.
>
> (*Great Tradition*, 161)

I find this criticism has considerable force, and yet James also persuades me of his dark vision to the extent that I wonder whether Leavis, and other readers, are not so much finding a critical purchase on the book as flinching away from James's sombre view of human life. As in the early reading of Dickens, and with *Daniel Deronda*, the abruptness of Leavis's rejection arises from the intensity of his involvement in the dialectic of true feeling, and his vocabulary here is entirely at one with James's formulation quoted earlier in its association of 'full sense of life' and 'moral taste'. It is a family quarrel, yet Leavis resists James's full vision of modernity. By contrast, Bob Assingham is like the initially unsympathetic reader who, precisely through his own more straightforward kindliness, is increasingly drawn into the Jamesian world against his natural disposition and conscious will. It is as if James was aware of the apparently over-specialized interest he was now demanding and wished us to recognize its necessity. He would, perhaps, dearly like to find Bob Assingham's kind, and his kindness, adequate to all the challenges of life but the kindly instincts the novelist shares with Assingham require for him a more arduous expression.

Just as Maggie tries to preserve the 'equilibrium' of the relationships between the two couples, so James seeks an evaluative equilibrium between the different worlds of value focused in the rival implications of kindness, which is why the book has aroused very different reactions as readers have sought to identify the key causes of its painful situation. As you turn *The Golden Bowl* around for contemplation it constantly reveals different aspects so as to resist any simple apportioning of blame. All of the major characters are at fault in incommensurate ways which make definitive comparison impossible. Perhaps most difficult of all, is the fact that the domestic and the passionate values are given nearly equal weight. We understand how the adulterers, for example, are put under pressure by the unnatural closeness of the father/daughter relationship of Adam and Maggie. Yet on the other hand, as they themselves both recognize, theirs is not ultimately a passion on which to base a mutual life and it does not, therefore, constitute any simple alternative criterion such as Leavis desiderates. Furthermore, other James novels tend to distinguish between those characters whose sympathetic feeling for others leads them to resign their own passional impulses and those who attempt to live out their passionate ego. Kindness and passion typically present themselves as a choice, which is why kindness is often associated with melancholy as when Bob Assingham is described as the 'kind, melancholy colonel' (*GB*, i. 161). Of course, no character would be of sustained interest who was purely either of these, and in other James novels there is typically a character in the middle, such as Merton Densher in *The Wings of the Dove* who is caught between Kate Croy's passionate demand and Milly Theale's saintly benevolence. But *The Golden Bowl* is unusual in its more even distribution of these qualities within the individual characters.

Furthermore, the values embodied in characters are constantly adumbrated in the stance of the novelist. The habit of passionate abnegation, strongly linked to kindliness, is also part of the characteristic posture of the Jamesian novelist. Lambert Strether, for example, in *The Ambassadors*, or Ralph Touchett in *The Portrait of a Lady*, are kindly, self-abnegating figures who live in a large measure vicariously through the passions of others, much as the novelist does with his characters. But these characters offer no definitive moral example either. Strether movingly advises the young man, Little Bilham, not to follow his own self-abnegating path and Ralph's kindness in leaving Isabel Archer his fortune, partly with a novelist's curiosity of seeing what she would do with it, is the origin of her tragedy.[9]

The novelist of *The Golden Bowl* requires a more capacious and tough-minded view such as we find perhaps in the Maggie of the latter half of the story and James seems to strain the fabric of the narrative to suggest this analogy. There is a peculiar moment at the country house party at Fawns. When Maggie begins to exercise power over the other characters to restore her marriage and banish Charlotte she feels as if she has passed momentarily onto another plane of being and images herself as an author feeling responsible for the destinies of the assembled group. James abhorred any rupture of the fictional fabric, as he showed in his critical comments on Trollope's authorial intrusions, yet he comes as close as he can here to using the image of his own art.[10] Maggie explicitly does not feel, or allow herself to feel, vulgar personal reactions of jealousy and hatred towards Charlotte, yet in her sincere high-mindedness she behaves with only the more chilling effectiveness towards her rival. Readers have always found something both admirable and appalling in her subsequent behaviour and one way of making the distinction is to say that the attitude of a novelist in disposing of individual fates is not entirely suitable for a character, for one human being in relation to another. Yet it is as if, in this late novel, James means us to brave this possibility, as if James would say that, once Charlotte has refused to accede to Maggie, Maggie's near Darwinian ruthlessness, her 'will to power', in banishing her rival is justified, or rather it falls outside the realm of justification. In that sense Maggie finally acts no longer kindly but according to her kind, and her 'moral' imperative proves as unyielding as its Kantian opposite of universalizable principle. If James effectively endorses her in this, or at least refrains from direct criticism of her, it is not because he sentimentally fails to detect the Ververs' steely will so much as because he is being very tough-minded. Maggie, if not exactly beyond good and evil, is acting on an emotional imperative which is no longer contained within the ethical. Yet at the same time she wishes to preserve the order of kindness, of sympathetic communion between those she loves, and it is only by a high level of artifice that the values of a simpler feeling can be, if not actually recovered, then honoured. The whole is preserved by artifice when the flaw is discovered.

In this regard, the linked questions of ego and artifice return us to the form of the novel itself. The central characters are, of course, unusual in their leisured existence, and in the special temptations that come to those who experience such a form of life without possessing the economic resources to sustain it. The novel mixes the two opposite means by which character can be put under revealing pressure. Characters may be placed in situations of extreme duress such as a lifeboat with insufficient provisions. That is Joseph Conrad's typical way of revealing character. Or you may imagine a character with all the benefits and securities of life, a situation of ideal freedom, and then see what she does with it as Jane Austen does in *Emma*. *The Golden Bowl* combines both of these to explore the tensions of egoistic passion and domestic kindness in the artificially concentrated conditions of the Jamesian novel. And there lies the hint as to the symbolic character of the golden bowl itself. For there is, on the face of it, a rather laboured symbolism about James's use of the bowl, unless we are to recognize precisely a certain measure of artifice in the whole and that his novel has the special concentration of art as well as being a depiction of contemporary life. The novel, that is to say, explores tensions which the confusing conditions of most everyday lives serve only to obscure rather than to remove so that what is revealed in these characters is true for more of us although only in them is it so starkly or discriminatingly revealed. By the same token, their specialized existence provides an alibi for those who would flinch away from what James presents. One wants to cut the Gordian entanglement of the situation with an overriding judgement but Maggie's ordeal arises from the refusal to do so and, in so far as she is seen on the analogy with the novelist, the implication is hardly upbeat. Her ordeal is partly one of extreme loneliness for which the isolation of the aesthetic object is a fitting symbol. Despite the humour with which James makes it palatable, it is a peculiarly comfortless book.

The symbolism of the bowl as a figure of artistic self-consciousness also concludes the theme of kindness. The most banal significance of the golden bowl as an emblem of the marriage is that, despite its apparent beauty and perfection, it has a flaw. But the subtler suggestion for Maggie's new life is the opposite: although it is constructed of crystal with a natural flaw, artistry has produced an object which seems flawless. Having destroyed the bowl, Maggie's supreme effort of imagination, will and delicate feeling gives form to her marriage despite its natural imperfections. Seen in that light, the bowl is an image not of falsity, but of responsibly creative consciousness and will. At the same time, the aestheticizing imagery reflects the fragility and loneliness of her achievement. James likewise sees the flaws in the simpler view of natural kindness optimistically propounded by the eighteenth-century movement of sentiment but he seeks to keep faith, through a labour of consciousness and artistry, with its underlying impulse. As Maggie affirms her passionate will, the principle of kindness, in its full range of meanings, still provides the guiding, if now highly qualified, motive. Eighteenth-century sentiment has been turned inside out. The natural material is flawed while culture creates the semblance of integrity. Yet even as the fissure in natural kindness is made good by art the categories start to shimmer. The bowl as art object is destroyed and Maggie's art serves her natural desire. 'The art itself is nature', and James's fine-spun artistry affirms a tragic, comic, ultimately sustaining vision of a young woman's truth to her feelings.[11]

D. H. Lawrence and the language of feeling

The most troubling aspect of *The Golden Bowl*, whether in its relationships or in its narrative, is its indirection. So much hinges on what is not said. Maggie's reasons for conducting herself in this way are clear. It is at once protective of others, a necessary self-protection, and ultimately a form of power. But there is a voice in most readers which says it would be healthier for her to express her suspicions to Amerigo directly and, without becoming the figure of passionate vindictiveness which she explicitly refuses, she could either create a new relationship with him or recognize that the present one is finished. Hence, even for readers who acknowledge the force of James's vision, the moral and dramatic premises remain questionable and, since D. H. Lawrence is in this, as in most respects, the antipodean extreme from James, it is illuminating to see how far they are nonetheless at one on the theme of truth to feeling.

Even more explicitly than James, or the modernist writers discussed earlier, Lawrence placed sentimentalism at the heart of his critique of modernity yet he constantly courted the charge himself both in his subject-matter and in his manner. And of course he continues to be read sentimentally. One reason for this is that, despite his hostility to sentimentalism, and his struggle to overcome it in himself in his early years, he had no fear of or condescension towards it. He never set out to be programmatically, ironically, anti-sentimental as a matter of literary technique, or as if the problem belonged to someone else. His poem 'Piano' or his late essay on 'Hymns in Man's Life', express the power of potentially sentimental feeling without being sentimental and his critique of sentimentalism, or rather perhaps his continuing struggle with truth of feeling, was from the inside.[12]

In literary-historical terms, Lawrence was aware of his own romantic formation and understood its dialectic with sentimentalism, for romanticism is not only historically speaking a transformation of sentimentalism, wherever it lives on it has continually to enact that transformation as part of its inner nature. Yet the dialectic of sentimentality and true feeling is different in successive generations. In his own time, he saw feeling as having become mentalized; it was not just a matter, in his own phrase, of 'sex in the head', but of all feeling becoming an alienated object in the mind.[13] Speaking of Dostoevsky's Prince Myshkin in the essay 'The Crown', written alongside the wartime composition of *Women in Love*, Lawrence remarks:

> And of course, all this reducing is draped in alluring sentimentalism. The most evil things in the world, today, are to be found in the chiffon folds of sentimentalism. Sentimentality is the garment of our vice. It covers viciousness as inevitably as greenness covers a bog.
>
> (*PII*, 395)

Despite the imagery of clothing and covering, sentimentalism is not just the cover but the process itself. Myshkin's childlike state represents for Lawrence a more general process of 'sentimentalized disintegration'. It is the obverse moment from Schiller's in that Schiller sought to raise feeling to a level of responsible self-consciousness defined in the epochal terms as 'sentimental', a state for which the aesthetic condition represents a supreme achievement. Schiller's was a necessary turn from the literalism, and the underlying coercion, of the earlier models of sentiment and sensibility. By Lawrence's time, however, the notion of the aesthetic had been transposed into its modern separatist implication.

> This achieved self, which we are, is absolute and universal. There is nothing beyond. All that remains is to state this self, and the reaction upon this self, perfectly. And the perfect statement presumes to be art. It is aestheticism.
>
> At this crisis there is a great cry of loneliness. Every man conceives himself as a complete unit surrounded by nullity. And he cannot bear it. Yet his pride is in this also. The greatest conceit of all is the cry of loneliness.
>
> (*PII*, 391)

The link between loneliness and aestheticism echoes Maggie Verver's lonely exercise of quasi-authorial power within the world of James's highly aestheticized fiction, and Lawrence goes on to note a continuing relation of the aesthetic to sentimentalism:

> At this crisis, emotion turns to sentiment, and sentimentalism takes the place of feeling. The ego has no feeling, it has only sentiments. And the myriad egos sway in tides of sentimentalism
>
> (ibid.)

where Schiller had sought to overcome the unstable dualism of feeling and reflection at the heart of sentiment, Lawrence now sees sentimentalism as the very means of disintegration. In *Women in Love*, the novel which seeks most fully and directly to represent this condition, Loerke and Gudrun conclude an artistic theme begun in *The Rainbow*. Towards the end of the novel, they play, in what would now be called a postmodern way, at historical charades returning above all to the period of sentiment:

> It was a sentimental delight to reconstruct the world of Goethe at Weimar, or of Schiller and poverty and faithful love, or to see again Jean Jacques in his quakings...
>
> (*Women in Love*, 453)

Given the extreme distance of these two modern artists from vulgar sentimentality, the phrase 'sentimental delight' seems to encompass both the modern and the eighteenth-century meanings in a curious trans-historical amalgam of self-conscious play. Yet their game is now far from the spirit of Schiller's dictum that 'man is only fully a human being when he plays', and there is a fine irony in the way the great figures of the Enlightenment are reduced to marionettes by a debasement of the tradition they inaugurated.

Not surprisingly, when Lawrence thinks of the topic in general, his emphasis falls on the damaging aspect of the historical transformation effected by sentiment:

> To the Restoration dramatist sex is, on the whole, a dirty business, but they [sic] more or less glory in the dirt. Fielding tries in vain to defend the Old Adam. Richardson with his calico purity and underclothing excitement sweeps all before him. Swift goes mad with sex and excrement revulsion. Sterne flings a bit of the same excrement humorously around. And the physical consciousness gives a last song in Burns, then is dead. Wordsworth, Shelley, the Brontës are all post-mortem poets. The essential instinctive-intuitive body is dead, and

worshipped in death – all very unhealthy. Till Swinburne and Oscar Wilde try to start a revivial from the mental field. Swinburne's 'white thighs' are purely mental.

(*Phoenix*, 552)

Lawrence's cultural history is sweeping here because he is using shorthand images. In truth, he 'adored' *Tristram Shandy*, and was more appreciative of the Brontës than this passage suggests.[14] Writing for an educated non-academic readership, he seized, in phrases like 'calico purity' and 'underclothing excitement', on the underlying movements of culture within which more nuanced discriminations can be made.

A more nuanced response to sentimentalism, and a parallel with James, can be seen in his reflection on kindness in the Introduction to Maurice Magnus's *Memoirs of the Foreign Legion*. Magnus was an expatriate American committed to a 'first-class' lifestyle, who borrowed money from Lawrence and others by trading quite overtly on their kindness. When his luck ran out he committed suicide leaving the manuscript of his memoir which Lawrence tried to publish to repay some of Magnus's debts to others. His acquaintance with Magnus leads him to reflect on the nature and obligations of kindness. On the one hand, Lawrence saw affection as the middle-class substitute for passionate feeling, and social kindness as a possible alibi, wittingly or otherwise, for generous feeling or real human contact. He remarked elsewhere that 'the true *pose* of the modern egoist is that of perfect suaveness and kindness . . .' (*Phoenix*, 200). and when it emerges that Magnus may have had aristocratic blood, Lawrence concludes that this blood too has 'gone white, in our spiritual era', leaving 'no bowels of deep compassion and kindliness. Only charity – a little more than kin, and less than kind' (*PII*, 360). In a later essay, on the modern male generally, Lawrence concludes by reversing Hamlet's formula: 'He knows he's not a man. Hence his creed of harmlessness . . . of relentless kindness. A little less than kin, and more than kind' (ibid. 622).

Yet if kindliness to others, including strangers, is often a subtle fake, then that implies the genuine is a true value, although being kind may be not so much a duty as a function of one's own disposition. The 'moral' is a Nietzschean effect rather than a cause. Likewise, Lawrence sees the Nietzschean power of the weak as he is manipulated, against his own clear will, by Magnus's entreaties. When asking a particularly large favour, Lawrence says, '. . .he pleaded and struggled, and tried to bully me with tears and entreaty and reproach, to do his will' (ibid., 336). After his death, Lawrence wonders 'how much warm kindness, generosity, was showered on him in the course of his forty-odd years' and the only memory of him that survives is perhaps 'that the blood still beats warm, hurt and kind in some few hearts' (*PII*, 356). It is the genuinely kind who are his victims.

Yet Lawrence's judgement is not one of simple disapproval. He admires Magnus for having had the courage to live out the consequences of his chosen principle and in doing so to 'beat out' some 'boundaries of human experience' for 'It is not this that will do harm, but sloppy sentiment and cant' (ibid., 359–60). We need to know the possibilities and limits of human nature in our time, 'let the sentimentalists wiggle as they like' (ibid., 358). As an artist, Lawrence himself notoriously made 'use' of his acquaintance and remarked in another review 'You have to have something vicious in you to be a creative writer' (*Phoenix*, 373). In this respect, Magnus, although a '*human* traitor', was 'not traitor to the spirit' and was even something like an artist (*PII*, 357). For this judgement on Magnus follows a comparison with Dos Passos's lack of comparable courage in his art and when Lawrence says of Magnus: 'I admire him: a courageous isolated little devil, facing his risks, and like a good rat, *determined* not to be trapped', both the rat image, and the half-admiring judgement, are applied to his prototypically modern artist, Loerke (*Women in Love*, 428).

Emphasis on the courage needed to live out the spiritual possibilities of humanity in the present recalls Lawrence's review of Hemingway's *In Our Time* which, while appreciating Dos Passos's technique in *Manhattan Transfer*, and his truth as a witness, identifies Hemingway's superiority as a matter of honesty:

> It is really honest. And it explains a great deal of sentimentality. When a thing has gone to hell inside you, your sentimentalism tries to pretend it hasn't. But Mr. Hemingway is through with the sentimentalism.
>
> (*Phoenix*, 366)

Lawrence links Hemingway to the American pioneer experience, which he had described in a review of Edward Dahlberg's *Bottom Dogs*, as

> ... what would have been called in the old language the breaking of the heart. America was not colonized and 'civilized' until the heart was broken in the American pioneer ...
>
> By the sympathetic heart, we mean that instinctive belief which lies at the core of the human heart, that people and the universe itself are *ultimately* kind.
>
> (ibid., 268)

Lawrence saw white America as more advanced in modernity than Europe and, although Hemingway is praised for his honest and inward record of this, Lawrence is hardly approving the condition he is being honest about.

> This is a negative goal, and Mr. Hemingway is really good because he is straight about it. He is like Krebs, in that devastating Oklahoma sketch: he doesn't love anybody, and it nauseates him to have to pretend he does.
>
> (ibid., 366)

That Lawrence should praise Hemingway's honesty while deprecating his condition clarifies the inadequacy of the notion of 'authenticity' as a positive criterion. Hemingway's rejection of sentimentalism, albeit necessary, is precisely reactive; his stance takes its meaning too much from the other term. In this analysis, sentimentalism and authenticity are two mutually exacerbating extremes arising from the same disintegration. They constitute a vicious polarity rather than a dialectic of true feeling.

However far one wishes to endorse Lawrence's general analysis of American experience, about Hemingway's authenticity he is surely right. Far from being the direct inheritance of the original sentimental impulse as a privileging of feeling, such authenticity is, along with the modern term 'sentimentality', one of the twin conditions which the true inheritance, the implied criterion of true feeling, allows us diagnostically to identify. Hence, too, the limitation of both Trilling's and Nuttall's accounts of the modern transformations of sentiment. Trilling's perception of authenticity as central rather than marginal is echoed in Nuttall's concentration on Sartre as the type case and both critics, despite their admirable treatments of the question of authenticity, miss the true inheritance of the culture of feeling.

Lawrence, it may be noted, does not use the word 'authenticity', even for Hemingway, and his own positive terms, in opposition to 'disintegration', are usually 'integrity' or, more simply again, 'wholeness'. And this is closely linked to the relativity of time. In contrast to Wordsworth's emotional investment in time, Lawrence emphasizes the difficulty of living in the present.[15] Hence his sharp critique of what he saw as Wordsworth's emotional idealizing and anthropomorphizing, although he also acknowledged Wordsworth's ontological recognitions:

> The joy men had when Wordsworth . . . made a slit and saw a primrose. Till then, men had only seen a primrose dimly . . . They saw it through Wordsworth in the full gleam of chaos.[16]

It is worth pausing on what exactly distinguishes them. Their common ground is evident in Wordsworth's Lawrencean reflections in his attack on the Convention of Cintra, including the image Lawrence was to use in his essay 'The Crown' written at a moment of similar opposition in the context of a continental European war:

> The outermost and all-embracing circle of benevolence has con-centric circles which, like the spider's web, are bound together by links, and rest upon each other; making one frame, and capable of one tremor; circles narrower and narrower, closer and closer, as they lie more near to the centre of self from which they proceeded, and which sustains the whole. The order of life does not require that the sublime and disinterested feelings should have to trust long to their own unassisted power. ... The higher mode of being does not exclude, but necessarily includes, the sentient; the sentient, the animal; and the animal, the vital – to its lowest degrees. Wisdom is the hidden root which thrusts forth the stalk of prudence; these uniting feed and uphold 'the bright consummate flower' – National Happiness – the end, the conspicuous crown, and ornament of the whole.[17]

Many English novelists would subscribe to this statement of personal and social interrelation but the more radical commonality of Words-worth and Lawrence lies in an ontological vision in which Lawrence reverses Wordsworth's emphasis. Where Wordsworth's natural piety is constituted in memory, for Lawrence it is vitally important emotion-ally, if not to forget, then to let the past go when necessary. Truth of feeling, wholeness of being and access to Being are moment-by-moment achievements likely to be prevented by emotional hoarding. In defining his own 'poetry of the present', and the difficulty of truly living in the present, he says 'free verse is ... the direct utterance from the instant, whole man' (*Phoenix*, 220). This sense of truth not just to the self, but to the self in the moment, contrasts with Wordsworth. It also stands at the opposite extreme from Hemingwayesque authenticity by its acknowledgement of relatedness, and is Lawrence's central problematic. I have discussed elsewhere the ontological vision which underwrites his *oeuvre*.[18] The present emphasis is on the role of emotion not just ontologically and in personal relations, but in discursive thought, and to see what is at stake here it is helpful to consider first a creative piece.

The Daughter-in-Law and 'only saying'

Lawrence's fiction pervasively, if discreetly, thematizes the adequacy of language to express emotional being, but the complexity and scope of works like *The Rainbow* and *Women in Love* make it hard to separate this question out for discussion and for present purposes the point can be more clearly seen in a relatively minor work concentrating on this theme. His play *The Daughter-in-Law* (1912) parallels *The Golden Bowl* in being the struggle of Minnie, the young wife of a miner, Luther Gascoigne, to establish a true relationship with her husband despite his prior emotional commitment, in this case to his mother. In both works it is the wife who most fully understands the marital situation and takes responsibility for resolving it. Indeed, the play, though dramatically impersonal, uses the woman's standpoint in a way that, given the gendered history of feeling, leads us to recall both Lawrence's strongly female associations as a writer and Lisa Appignanesi's reading of the 'feminine' in James. Otherwise, of course, the two works could hardly be more different, being set at the opposite ends of the social scale and with correspondingly divergent uses of language. Where James pushes to its extreme the principle of reticent obliquity, Lawrence's characters, under the pressure of feeling, speak with a directness for which acts of physical violence, such as destroying pictures or breaking crockery, are barely an extension.

In Lawrence's fiction the limitations of speech and consciousness in characters are typically carried by symbolic and subliminal expression of unconscious feeling in the narrative whereas in the plays, although he still creates rich and shifting sub-texts, the emotional use of language in speech is more readily isolated. If Lawrence's best drama had been appreciated before Peter Gill's revelatory productions of the 1960s it might have given a different significance to the naturalist mode in theatre.[19] Compared to Lawrence, Strindberg's *Miss Julie* (1888) is stiffly programmatic. Miss Julie is enmeshed in social and biological forces which ultimately explain the outcome. The author's ideological thumb is in the scale. From that point of view, Lawrence's drama also provides a testing counterweight to Brecht's. Lawrence's characters are likewise formed by inner and outer conditions, which are given a full weight in the action and psychology of the play, yet they negotiate these in a spirit of responsible struggle implying a proportionate weight both to the conditions and to their own capacity for emotional growth. The play privileges no general principle of a social or political kind, but enacts a crucial episode in the emotional relations of a group of characters. Rather than being trapped within their conditions, the characters share a form of life which is both a resource and a difficulty. They have multiple and conflicting commitments, the most important of which are the most habitual and therefore the least conscious. Tolstoy communicates a similarly unconscious recognition in the opening of *Anna Karenina* as the Oblonsky family and household feel like a group of strangers who have met by chance in an inn. Since real strangers would precisely not feel their lack of relation to be shocking, the family's conscious feeling of estrangement vividly dramatizes their implicit sense of belonging. In a similar way, the conscious conflicts in *The Daughter-in-Law* reveal the strength of their implicit relations, both good and bad. The way the characters shift in and out of dialect speech also reflects this. Dialect can express both clannishness and community, and its positive force is nowhere better encapsulated than in the way a family member, even as he is being bitterly excoriated, will be addressed as '*our* Luther', or in the case of Lawrence himself, '*our* Bert'.

The play opens with a dialogue strongly conditioned by the naturalistic, yet resonantly jarring, stage image of a grown man, actually Luther's unmarried brother, Joe, sitting at the kitchen table with his food cut up by his mother. Although she complains at still having a baby to attend to:

> It's a rum un as I should start ha'in' babies again, an' feedin' 'em wi' spoon-meat.[20]

it rapidly becomes apparent that she has a deep investment in keeping him that way and that the remark is a half-conscious statement of this; its true meaning is the opposite of its semantic face-value. He is obliged to confess that he has broken his arm in a pit accident which, because it was caused by his own horseplay, has not entitled him to sick-pay. The dialogue enacts the mother's emotional dominance and Joe's sheepishness, even as he recounts the limited, compensatory rebelliousness he has shown in the outside world. Although a whole social and economic world is implied in the dialogue, the attention is on what the human individual makes of it. Joe feels a social anger against the manager, Hewett, whose non-dialect speech he imitates. The dialogue catches Joe's urge to rebellion, its essentially immature form underlying his class *ressentiment* and his hangdog yet defiant performance for his mother. She immediately detects that the final witty retort he claims to have made to the manager was not actually made; he has been performing for her the rebellion he did not express in the outer world. Even within what appears to be a necessary piece of opening exposition, the language is being used at a high level of subtextual gesture. In fact, Joe's accident proves to be hardly necessary to the subsequent action except by virtue of this gestural subtext which it initiates. Both sons are in some sense self-lamed and throughout the play speech is part of a larger body of gestural meaning through which speech itself has to be interpreted.

The situation of the play throws into relief the shifting emotional commitments of the characters. The initiating action is the arrival of a neighbour, Mrs Purdy, to announce that her, rather simple-minded, daughter, Bertha, is expecting a child by Luther. With some delicacy, she has come to the mother's house, which she implicitly acknowledges as still the centre of authority in the family, to make an arrangement with least damage to the new marriage. But Mrs Gascoigne refuses to discuss a financial settlement and sends Mrs. Purdy to Luther's house to face him, and his much-resented new wife, with this information. She arrives while Minnie is out on an errand arranged by Joe, and despite her intention of facing Luther with his responsibility, Mrs Purdy immediately adopts a motherly manner towards him as if he were one of her own boys. She picks up his just discarded pit-trousers to air by the fire and, when he goes on to express, with self-pitying sentimentality, his appreciation of Bertha's undemanding affection which he has not had from his wife, she takes the wife's side and explains that Minnie is just 'wriggling a place out for hersen' (*Plays*, 235). The motherly motive which has brought Mrs Purdy to protect her daughter's interest is just as present in her relation to Luther himself, and in her concern for the new family unit.

Luther's sentimental self-pity is as clearly and implicitly understood as Joe's rebelliousness, for the subtext of multiple emotional considerations, including concern for others, is no less rich than in James's novel. The central turning-point of the play is a direct accusation of Mrs. Gascoigne from Minnie about how she dominates her sons emotionally and leaves nothing over for another woman. The mother makes no reply to Minnie. Instead she turns possessively to her son and, with entirely unwitting irony, confirms Minnie's point by denying it: 'We're learning a thing or two, Luther' (*Plays*, 256). It could seem that Minnie's criticism, even when endorsed by Joe, has had no effect. Yet later on, when Joe and Luther have gone out to join a potentially dangerous strike picket, which the mother sees as the men's way of spiting their women folk, the mother comes to Minnie's house, which is in itself to acknowledge a shift in authority. And she makes this explicit by admitting the truth of Minnie's earlier charge to which Minnie replies 'I didn't mean it – I was in a rage' (*Plays*, 265), whereupon mother and daughter-in-law wait at home together in emotional solidarity. The mother's genuine strength comes over here, and it is appreciated as such by Minnie. Indeed, one might say that the mother needed someone to stand up to her both at the level of character and at the level of art for the dramatic handling of her character is in striking contrast with that of the dominant mother, Mrs Morel, in *Sons and Lovers*. In that case, Mrs Morel's genuine strength is not dramatically acknowledged in the way that Mrs Gascoigne's is. Lawrence's residual inability to criticize the figure radically enough leaves the character herself more critically vulnerable to the reader.

The essential *action* between Minnie and her mother-in-law is verbal. Bitter things are said, many of which are true and important, yet, as the situation continually shifts, these truths are relativized in a process of emotional understanding and implicit adjustment. My own initiation into what is going on here occurred at the age of three or four when an older sister, while being verbally abused by a neighbouring child during one of their periodic fallings out, remarked: 'she is only saying that.' It takes decades to appreciate the force and subtlety of this homely formula, for part of the difficulty of understanding apparently simple things is the realization that they need understanding. Things said under the heading of 'only saying' are not necessarily less sincere – indeed they are likely to be only too sincere – but their generalizable truth is not the point and often has to be in some sense bracketed. In a quite precise and significant way, it is a folk version of the adjustment we readily make to the aesthetic, that blend of continuity and difference which Schiller called a 'modulation' and, as will be seen later, it gives a pertinent clue to what Lawrence meant by his phrase 'art speech' coined for the more demanding analytic context of his *Studies in Classic American Literature*.[21]

This informal expression gets closer to the spirit of Lawrence's language than, for example, an academic invocation of Bakhtin's 'dialogism', for what is commonly at stake is less the negotiation of externally formulable truths, or of conflicting worldviews, than individuals' struggles with each other, and with themselves, for emotional recognition.[22] Mrs Gascoigne makes the point to Luther: 'Tha'rt a fool, our Luther. I ter ta'es a woman at 'er word, well, tha deserves what ta gets' (*Plays*, 252), while at the end of the play, when he says to Minnie 'I know what tha says is true', she replies, 'No, my love – it isn't – it isn't' (*Plays*, 267). Of course, as with her similar retraction with the mother-in-law, what she has said is still just as true objectively speaking, but it is no longer what needs to be said, and in that sense it is not true. Emotional truth is tied to its moment.

Within its limited compass, the play achieves an extraordinary intensity of emotional process in which the assertion of Minnie's will in breaking the hold of the mother-in-law is obviously endorsed but is hardly reducible to, or motivated by, moral terms. Comparing the role of feeling in both Maggie Verver and Minnie Gascoigne to George Eliot's heroines, the force of the development already noted in respect of nineteenth-century fiction becomes more evident. The seismic shift, which could be philosophically associated with Nietzsche, from a concern with living up to an ethically formulated ideal to an assertion of their own emotional being, is equally exemplified in these two heroines. Yet it would be impossible usefully to define the quality of emotional truth in question here in discursive terms abstracted from the whole form of life in which it is exemplified. Lawrence made his own way to this shift largely by reflecting on nineteenth-century literature, including George Eliot, and, most importantly, Thomas Hardy. He also saw at the heart of the American experience, from the settlement of the continent onwards, something new coming into being which he contrasted with the nineteenth-century Russian writers who, despite their extraordinary imaginative explorations, were ultimately trapped in old moralistic forms. He expressed his frustration with the Russians in the letter to Edward Garnett explaining the new conception of identity, and therefore of narrative method, in the work that became *The Rainbow* and *Women in Love*. Despite the extraordinariness of its characters, Russian fiction was still contained within a moral conception rather than the 'phenomenal' view Lawrence now sought to express.[23] This was the sharpest difference between Lawrence and his high Victorian forebears. They were still typically concerned with truth of feeling within an agreed moral and social order, even if the present order was itself deeply flawed, whereas he was concerned with a process of emotional exploration and recognition both for the individual and for the culture.

If one says that Lawrence's peculiar genius lay in his awareness of language, whether in his own use of it or in others, as being always an embodiment of feeling, many of his readers would be likely to agree. This may be, however, because the proposition is implicitly confined to a context of imaginative literature, such as poems, novels and plays, dealing with personal emotions but, if what is said is true, it cannot be limited simply to the world of fiction. One of Lawrence's most remarkable and still challenging qualities was that he acknowledged the aspect of 'only saying', the emotional relativity of argument, not just at the more familiar level of personal relations but at all the higher levels of intellectual and literary culture. It remains to consider, therefore, how this applies in the domain of discursive and critical thought.

Feeling and argument

Lawrence's discursive writing, like Nietzsche's, combines what seems like an absolutist dogmatism with an almost infinite capacity to shift and relativize. In his concern to break old cultural formations and open the mind to new possibilities, he constantly honours the principle of 'only saying'. To appreciate why T. S. Eliot spoke more truly than he realized in saying that Lawrence was 'incapable of what is ordinarily called thinking', it is necessary, once again, to avoid the conventional dualisms.[24] Nietzsche, for example, spoke slightingly of reason and dialectic, and privileged the aphorism as against formal argument because it depended directly on a quality of experience and intelligence in the listener. Yet he was not dismissing as such the capacity to argue in a more formal and systematic way. Such a capacity is assumed rather than despised and, similarly, Lawrence, without thematizing the question so explicitly, is as appalled as Nietzsche at simple incapacity in this domain. His review of Eric Gill's *Art Nonsense and Other Essays* begins with his irritation at Gill's incompetence in this respect:

> Still less is he a born thinker, in the reasoning and argumentative sense of the word. He is ... a crude and crass amateur ... like a tiresome uneducated workman arguing in a pub – argufying would describe it better – and banging his fist.

> *(Phoenix, 393)*

This is how Lawrence himself has been perceived by those whose criterion is the 'reasoning and argumentative sense of the word' which Lawrence's phrasing casually but firmly relativizes. 'Argumentative' capacity is necessary but not sufficient, and may in itself be deadening or repressive. Lawrence's counter-model is suggested in his comment on the narrative language of *Women in Love*:

> In point of style, fault is often found with the continual, slightly modified recognition. The only answer is that it is natural to the author: and that every natural crisis in emotion or passion or understanding comes

> *(Women in Love, 486)*

At first glance this sounds 'emotional' and self-defensive. But the statement that it is '*natural* to the author' takes on a different force, becomes indeed an ambitious claim, when the same term becomes part of 'every *natural* crisis'. His mode of expression is allied with processes of nature underlying not just 'emotion' and 'passion' but 'understanding.'

All argument in Lawrence encompasses, and is structured on, emotional realization. Most typically, saying what he thinks involves finding out what he feels in the spirit suggested by his comments on 'emotional' thought as sparked by Giovanni Verga:

> Now the emotional mind, if we may be allowed to say so, is not logical. It is a psychological fact, that when we are thinking emotionally or passionately, thinking and feeling at the same time, we do not think rationally: and therefore, and therefore, and therefore. Instead the mind makes curious swoops and circles. It touches the point of pain or interest, then sweeps away again in a cycle, coils round and approaches again the point of pain or interest. There is a curious spiral rhythm, and the mind approaches again and again the point of concern, repeats itself, goes back, destroys the time-sequence entirely, so that time ceases to exist, as the mind stoops to the quarry, then leaves it without striking, soars, hovers, turns, swoops, stops again, still does not strike, yet is nearer, nearer, reels away again, wheels off into the air, even forgets, quite forgets, yet again turns, bends, circles slowly, swoops and stoops again, until at last there is the closing in, and the clutch of a decision or a resolve.
>
> (*Phoenix*, 250)

Athough Lawrence is thinking here of an individual response to a specific emotional shock rather than more general modes of argument, the one aspect is not separable from the other. His phrase 'emotional mind' is typical of his use of oxymoron. It is sometimes taken as simply a reversal of the conventional understanding of 'mind' but its point is precisely to dissolve, or extend, these conventional categories while respecting their partial necessity. The emphasis on '*emotional* mind' implies an 'emotional *mind*' for even within this emotional process lies an intellectual or reflective one. The circling and repetitive process enacted in the language is highly purposive and the motive is to come to terms with, or to reach a decision about, an emotionally charged occasion. It is a matter of judgement which cannot be rushed and the concern, therefore, is not to exclude intellection, but to prevent it intruding on, governing, suppressing or rushing the emotional issue.

Just as an emotional decision has a conceptual element, so conceptual thought has an emotional dimension and Lawrence's discursive essays,

such as 'Pornography and Obscenity', often have an analogous movement.[25] They proceed, like much of his narrative prose, by a series of
emotional constatations and heaves, each constatation repeating much of
the former process while giving it a different twist. And as in the fiction,
this is not empty repetition or mannerism. It is a way of exposing, sharing,
consolidating the ingestion of a point of view which may be strange or
difficult for reasons largely of emotional resistance. The method, if it
should be called such, allows for an apparent simplicity or directness in
the moment-by-moment statement, like the direct touching on a sore
point, but it has the more subtle indirection too of massage. It has always
been recognized, in the art of persuasion, that an irrefragably logical
argument can fail to convince while other means may succeed. But the
point here is not a rhetorical one and Lawrence is not, in that sense, a
rhetorician. He is working through a problem rather than working on a
reader.

Of course, Lawrence's style is no model for others. It works for him
because, as he said, it is 'natural' to him. But his extreme instance
highlights a necessary element in all critical discourse. His recognition of
the aspect of feeling in thought pervades his criticism and focuses the
combined questions of true feeling and response to fiction which are the
legacy of sentiment.

Criticism and feeling.

The formal study of literature in the late twentieth century is still affected
by the attitudes of modernism. Lawrence was an acute critic of other
modernists and his academic unpopularity during the end-of-century
hegemony of ideological critique remains revealing for the relation of
ideology and feeling. His case focuses the more general cultural status of
feeling in that he is widely read by intelligent common readers around the
world yet is a byword for naivety and wrong-headedness in large sections
of the academy. Like Wordsworth, he is a litmus test for a reader's ability
to register a range of significances without which he is at best banal and at
the worst absurd. The absurdity and wrong-headedness are there, of
course, but that is what should make him an object of criticism, a
significant case for discrimination. Without developing a critical case
here, I want to highlight some relevant qualities of his own criticism. His
phrase 'sex in the head' refers to a radical and collective condition which
could be extended to areas other than sex. It requires no uncritical view of
Lawrence to suggest that he illuminates a condition of 'criticism in the
head' in the academy.

He opens his essay on John Galsworthy with the bald statement:

> Literary criticism can be no more than a reasoned account of the feeling produced upon the critic by the book he is criticizing ... The touchstone is emotion, not reason.

And he goes on to add:

> A critic must be able to *feel* the impact of a work of art in all its complexity and its force. To do so, he must be a man of force and complexity himself, which few critics are.
>
> (*Phoenix*, 538)

In almost any current academic forum this proposition would invite instant scorn yet it proves no bad description whenever anyone actually undertakes the act of criticism. Despite the qualification about quality of feeling in the critic, what many hear in this statement is a simple-minded, if not to say sentimental, privileging of feeling. Such a pre-emptive mishearing reflects a common desire to achieve the ends of criticism without its emotional responsibility. The larger cultural rejection of feeling is manifest in the very discipline for which it is of the essence.

As the essay continues, Lawrence's generalization acquires a more specific point. Falsity of feeling in Galsworthy is the burden of his critique and he circles in on it by proposing the relevant standard. A standard, by definition, carries a universalizing force, as Kant argued, although Lawrence privileges not 'taste' but truth of feeling. In doing so, he focuses initially not on the writer but on the reading and instances a number of well-known critics who are inadequate because of their relation to their own emotions, such as Macaulay who 'juggles his feelings'. Having amplified his specifications of 'honesty', as well as 'complexity and force', in the emotional realm, he goes on to assert that the purely 'social being' of the Forsytes occasions in the reader a 'refusal, an emotional refusal, to have them identified with our common humanity' (ibid., 541). His procedure is deftly appropriate. The primacy of feeling has initially to be stated, somewhat vulnerably, as a general principle even as he implicitly acknowledges the limitation of such universal principles. The necessary order of logical exposition runs counter to the actual grounding in feeling. Truth of feeling cannot be proven, but it can be given a rationale through demonstrative instances. The exposition enforces its holism while discriminating its aspects.

He then argues, in a spirit of disappointed sympathy, that Galsworthy could have produced in *The Man of Property* a truly 'great satire' if he had

had 'the courage to follow it through'. Emotional, moral and artistic courage are inseparable here as Lawrence approves 'the really consummate skill and sincere creative passion' with which Galsworthy engaged his theme. Unfortunately these qualities are lost in the treatment of 'the love affair of Irene and Bosinney, and in the sentimentalizing of old Jolyon Forsyte' (ibid., 542) Galsworthy 'put down the knife and laid on a soft, sentimental poultice, and helped to make the corruption worse' (ibid., 543). Lawrence then analyses through Galsworthy a more general condition of sentimentality:

> Sentimentalism is the working off on yourself of feelings you haven't really got. We all *want* to have certain feelings: feelings of love, of passionate sex, of kindliness, and so forth. Very few people really feel love, or sex passion, or kindliness, or anything else that goes at all deep. So the mass just fake these feelings inside themselves. Faked feelings! the world is all gummy with them. They are better than real feelings, because you can spit them out when you brush your teeth; and then tomorrow you can fake them afresh.
>
> (ibid., 545)

Likewise, both Galsworthy and his characters reveal 'an utter incapacity for anything like *true* feeling' (ibid., 549).

Lawrence's criticism always seeks emotional honesty, using the ability of the novelist in reverse by undergoing the struggle of creative recognition alongside the writer. The most sustained instance is the one volume of literary criticism published in his lifetime, *Studies in Classic American Literature* (1922). Behind its sometimes irritating informality, arising partly from its being planned as a lecture tour, this remains one of the classic studies of its topic, and its avoidance of an academic style reflects its highly personal mode of 'only saying' which it develops as a critical principle. His opening injunction 'Never trust the artist, trust the tale' is the key to his reading, and is his most substantial legacy at the level of critical principle. He saw the great American writers engaged in an internal struggle for and against emotional acknowledgement in which the most significant recognitions were, by the 'subterfuge' of 'art', achieved half against their will or despite their more conventional consciousness (*SCAL*, 2). By the same token, his warning to trust the tale rather than the artist is at the opposite extreme from the recently fashionable notion of ignoring the author.[26] On the contrary, the creative endeavour of the artist is the vital centre. Likewise, his other significant general formula in *Studies in Classic American Literature*, the phrase 'art speech', avoids the twin errors of seeing art either as separate from, or simply continuous with, human speech at large (*SCAL*, 1–2). The deceptively simple phrase keeps the two domains mutually porous without confusing them. This is the respect in which 'only saying' provides the appropriate analogy: the vital truths in question are truths of feeling and are similarly conditioned by their contexts.

Much of Lawrence's critique of Galsworthy, or of the American authors, could be made by another critic in ideological terms but the spirit and insight would be different. Lawrence is ideological in that he shows these writers to be in the grip of a system of values in the light of which he formulates his own view of how they are right or wrong, yet for all the decisiveness of his judgement he sees their work under the sign of evaluative openness and potentiality. The difference, and its pertinence for our own day, can be seen in his review of a novel, *Saïd the Fisherman* (1927), by the British orientalist writer Marmaduke Pickthall. The review, as is typical of Lawrence's criticism, consists mainly of a running account of the changing emotional impact of the story, but it once again begins with a general statement proposing some appropriate terms for the occasion. As it happens, these terms anticipate the essential thrust of a later post-colonial critique as developed by another Said.

> Since the days of Lady Hester Stanhope and her romantic pranks, down to the exploits of the Colonel T. E. Lawrence in the late war, there seems always to have been some more or less fantastic Englishman, or woman, Arabizing among the Arabs. Until we feel we know the desert and the Bedouin better than we know Wales or our next door neighbour ... In the Arab, the Englishman sees himself with the lid off.
>
> (*Phoenix*, 351)

In a deftly humorous tone, this catches the underlying insight of Edward Said's influential critique of 'Orientalism' in its romantic derivation, its unwitting self-reflection; and its illusion of knowing the other.[27] At the same time, the humour is open, sympathetically, to the generous aspect of this impulse, and its potential for a genuine exploration of both the self and the other. The question for Lawrence is what an individual does with this impulse and, of course, his own interest in various native peoples was strongly related to this. Indeed, this impulse in writers of Lawrence's generation helped to create the enlightened standpoint which postcolonial critique assumes, but tends to imagine it has invented.[28] Lawrence objects to Pickthall's novel, therefore, not in ideological principle but in practice and *ad hominem*:

> ... it's a risky thing to hold the scales for a man whose moral nature is not your own. Mr. Pickthall's moral values are utilitarian and rational: Saïd's are emotional and sensual ... the judgement ... is a white man's judgement on a dark man.
>
> (*Phoenix*, 353)

As far as Lawrence is concerned, a greater writer, and moral personality, than Pickthall might have managed to bring it off but the emphasis of Said's study, and its impact on readers, is to suggest that the orientalizing impulse is improper in principle, is ideologically incorrect. The very word 'orientalism' has changed its meaning from an academic specialism to an ideological sin. Of course, Said's work articulates a necessary feeling in furthering an important cultural work of our time. Cultural and political change, particularly in respect of racial difference, requires the solidarity of a widespread feeling. But a collective academic emphasis on ideological rightness allows the feeling itself to become conventionalized and unexamined, often as a spirit of *ressentiment* projected anachronistically on to the past. The analytic gain in ideological critique carries a danger of blunted or automatic response at the level of feeling, and that has consequences for thought and judgement. Unexamined feeling is especially damaging in an intellectual and critical clerisy.

As with the earlier discussion of Wordsworth, the point is not to deprecate ideological insight as practised by good critics. Maybe good critics are all essentially the same while bad critics are bad in their own ways. Much of the best criticism of the last decades has been under the broad heading of feminism and, although this is ideologically informed almost by definition, its critical impact has been as much a matter of moral passion. Where these two have a collusive relation, or come apart, there is either emotional indulgence or a going through the academic motions, and sometimes both at once. The point is that, while it is inconceivable that good modern criticism would not be ideologically aware, ideological perception has itself to be accompanied by emotional self-knowledge. Otherwise, ideological critique becomes the characteristic late twentieth-century form of sentimentalism: the too-ready justification of feeling by a moral idea.

Conclusion: Literature, Criticism and the Culture of Feeling

I have concluded with Lawrence because, like Wordsworth's, his case is at once representative of an important historical turn and peculiarly revealing at the level of reception. His self-conscious absorption of earlier novel tradition, and his equally self-conscious break with it, throw into sharp relief the modern transformation of the sentimental inheritance into a concern for wholeness and integrity of being. At the same time, his often losing struggle to communicate this, and the continuing blankness of his academic and journalistic reception, epitomize the cultural occlusion of feeling at large.

Likewise, the concluding concentration on academic criticism is primarily to focus a more general condition regarding the acknowledgement of feeling. The highly considered and explicit act of reading known as criticism stands in an ambiguous relation to the more implicit practice of emotional self-knowledge in the culture. In its trained explicitness, and its observance of academic protocols, a formalized discourse of literary analysis may well falsify the more practical knowledge, and may even do so with a relatively harmless seclusion from living concerns, even from those of the individual in question. To that extent the question is purely 'academic'. Professional critics may live lives of decent feeling and may express judgements and preferences in which the element of feeling is crucial without bringing the aspect of emotional commitment to the surface. But the danger here is of uncritical reinforcement of ideological postures since it is more likely that the formal mode of literary response does indeed reflect and feed underlying attitudes. The mildly repressive schizophrenia about the realm of feeling is so long-lived and habitual as to escape notice, which is why I have traced its modern aetiology and, in doing so, have sought to indicate the degree to which the same historical process has produced a largely unacknowledged cultural capacity.

In tracing the significant transformations of sentiment from the early eighteenth to the late twentieth centuries I have focused on the act of reading as an implicit form of emotional self-examination and exercise. The relations of feeling and reflection in modern criticism are only a latest manifestation of this process. The important lesson in this history is that, while there can be no direct access to 'truth' in matters of feeling, there are rich layers of cultural practice assimilated into the present capacity for understanding the life of feeling. The transformations of sentiment provide a peculiar blend of analytic means and subliminal experience which an alert criticism could acknowledge in its wholeness and thereby further the work of emotional self-knowledge.

The crucial aspect of this historico-analytic inheritance, therefore, is the learning to live with indirection. The literalistic immediacy that characterized the models of sentimental response, both to literature and in life, for the eighteenth-century novelists and theorists has modulated into an awareness of the impossibility of knowing the emotional life by direct introspection. Hence the special significance of fiction *per se*. Of course, as John Horton rightly observes in his criticism of Martha Nussbaum, it is not just imaginative literature exclusively or *per se* that does this.[1] I have sought to show how it depends on the critical encounter within whatever genre. The substance of the work and the responsibility of the reader are the important premises, even if these are never raised to a level of responsible self-consciousness. Fiction, however, has both an especially self-conscious focus on the sphere of feeling and a generic appropriateness in presenting it. The examined life of feeling is more like a lived fiction in that its object is always mediated by imagination, conditioned by context, and modified by time. Meanwhile the act of reading fiction is an exercise of 'real life' emotional discrimination in that the *discrimination* is real and, whether the given emotional object is fictive or real, the long-absorbed, implicit cultural knowledge of sentimentality as indulgence, or self-serving falsehood, is a key means of negotiating the depths and shallows of feeling.

A final emphasis for the present arises from this historical account of the transformations of sentiment: the inheritance of sentiment is not something outside us to be adopted or not, even to the extent that one might imagine accepting or rejecting a set of political principles or religious beliefs. It is something we are inescapably inside or are consituted by. At the discursive and philosophical level Alasdair MacIntyre may well be right to suggest that models of the moral life in modernity ultimately divide into a choice between Aristotelean and Nietzschean conceptions.[2] But such a choice emerges only when seeking a systematically reasoned conception. The actual practice of emotional preference is not a matter of choice between models nor, more importantly, a matter of choice at all. It takes place all the time as unavoidably as breathing, although it can be done with different qualities of awareness and discrimination. The very invoking of these philosophical names suggests, as MacIntyre intends, the difficulty of putting such broad conceptual models into practice. The Aristotelean *polis* is no longer with us while even the most constructive reading of Nietzsche is shadowed by the darker potentialities of interpretation to which he is inevitably open. But my point is a more radical one, that the very language of choice promotes the damaging slippage of imagining these questions to be open to an overall approval or rejection. In modernity, the responsibility of feeling is unavoidable. If Nietzsche and Heidegger are among the major thinkers of modernity, this lies partly in their reflecting something unavoidable about the modern condition. Much criticism of them misses the point by confusing the descriptive and the normative. The important question is not whether what they have to say is personally desirable or politically dangerous but whether it is true to our condition. Their value is descriptive, not normative, and they reflect an implicit knowledge in the culture when they insist that the ethical realm is itself conditioned respectively by quality of life and attention to Being. There is no alternative within a self-conscious modernity to the primordiality of feeling. That is why it is important to know that modern culture carries an important positive mode of self-knowledge in this domain. While the temptations of the sentimental remain infinite, our culture has a rich, if largely implicit, practice in the life, and art, of feeling.

Notes

Introduction

1. D. H. Lawrence, 'The Novel and the Feelings', in *Study of Thomas Hardy and Other Essays*, ed. Bruce Steele (Cambridge: Cambridge University Press, 1985) p. 203.
2. 'When any of these passions are calm, and cause no disorder in the soul, they are readily taken for the determinations of reason, and are suppos'd to proceed from the same faculty, with that, which judges of truth and falshood.' *A Treatise of Human Nature*, ed. L. A. Selby-Bigge, rev. by P. H. Nidditch (Oxford: Oxford University Press, 1978) p. 417.
3. Ludwig Wittgenstein, *Philosophical Investigations*, trans. G. E. M. Anscombe (Oxford: Oxford University Press, 1958) p. 88; Michael Polanyi, *The Tacit Dimension* (New York: Doubleday, 1966); Charles Taylor, *Sources of the Self* (Cambridge: Cambridge University Press, 1987).
4. Jochen Barkhausen, *Die Vernunft des Sentimentalismus* (Tübingen: Gunter Narr, 1983) p. 75.
5. Alasdair MacIntyre, *After Virtue* (London: Duckworth, 1981).
6. Kendall L. Walton, *Mimesis and Make-Believe: On the Foundations of the Representational Arts* (Cambridge, MA and London: Harvard University Press, 1990). For a reasoned summary of the debate see Margit Sutrop, 'Sympathy, Imagination, and the Reader's Emotional Response to Fiction', in *Representations of Emotions*, eds. Jürgen Schlaeger and Gesa Stedman (Tübingen: Gunter Narr, 1999) pp. 29–42.
7. For an extended discussion of this point, see Michael Bell, 'How Primordial is Narrative?', in *Narrative in Culture*, ed. Cris Nash (London and New York: Routledge, 1992) pp. 172–98.
8. Saint Augustine, *Confessions*, trans. Henry Chadwick (Oxford and New York: Oxford University Press, 1991) pp. 15–16, 35–6.

Chapter 1   'Affective Individualism' and the Cult of Sentiment

1. Lawrence Stone, *The Family, Sex and Marriage in England 1500–1800* (London: Weidenfeld & Nicolson, 1977).
2. For a relevant critique of Stone see Alan Liu, *Wordsworth: the Sense of History* (Stanford CA: Stanford, University Press, 1989) pp. 245–7, 252–7, 583, 590–4.
3. Eliot used the phrase 'dissociation of sensibility' to define the lost wholeness of early seventeenth-century 'metaphysical' poetry. He later detached himself from the phrase, without denying the underlying intuition, and he increasingly came to see Donne as expressing the process of dissociation while Dante and Medieval sensibility exemplified the pre-dissociated condition. See 'The Metaphysical Poets' and 'Lancelot Andrewes' in *Selected Essays*

(London: Faber, 1950) p. 287–8, 352, and 'Milton II' in *On Poetry and Poets* (New York: Farrar, Strauss & Giroux, 1943) p. 173.

4. Thomas Nashe, *The Unfortunate Traveller*, ed. J. B. Steane (Harmondsworth: Penguin, 1972) p. 251.

5. Henry James, 'Preface' to *The Spoils of Poynton, A London Life, The Chaperone* (New York: Scribner, 1908) pp. ix–xv.

6. David Foxon, '*Libertine Literature in England*' *1660–1745, The Book Collector*, (Spring, Summer, Autumn, Winter, 1963); see also Lynne Hunt, *The Invention of Pornography* (New York: Zone Books, 1993).

7. John Cleland, *Fanny Hill or Memoirs of a Woman of Pleasure*, ed. Peter Wagner (Harmondsworth: Penguin, 195) p. 217.

8. 'Reason being cool and disengaged, is no motive to action, and directs only the impulse received from appetite or inclination, by showing us the means of attaining happiness or avoiding misery: Taste, as it gives pleasure or pain, and thereby constitutes happiness or misery, becomes a motive to action, and is the first spring or impulse to desire or volition.' David Hume, *Enquiries Concerning Human Understanding and the Principles of Morals*, ed. L. A. Selby-Bigge, 3rd edn rev. (Oxford: Clarendon Press, 1975) p. 294.

9. Anthony Ashley Cooper, Third Earl of Shaftesbury, *Characteristics of Men, Manners, Opinions, Times*, ed. John M. Robertson (New York: Bobbs-Merrill, 1964) vol. i, p. 280.

10. Jacques Derrida, *De la grammatologie* (Paris: Editions de Minuit, 1967).

11. Henry Fielding, *The History of Amelia* (London: Hutchinson, 1904) vol. ii, p. 273.

12. Sarah Fielding, *The Adventures of David Simple*, ed. Malcolm Kelsall (New York and Oxford: Oxford University Press, 1994) p. 65.

13. Samuel Richardson, *Clarissa, or the History of a Young Lady*, ed. W. L. Phelps (London: Dent, 1932) p. 47.

14. Nancy Armstrong, *Desire and Domestic Fiction: a Political History of the Novel* (New York and Oxford: Oxford University Press, 1987).

15. Janet Todd, *Sensibility: an Introduction* (London: Methuen, 1986) pp. 101–9, 113.

16. Claudia L. Johnson, *Equivocal Beings: Politics, Gender and Sentimentality in the 1790s: Wollstonecraft, Radcliffe, Burney, Austen* (Chicago and London: Chicago University Press, 1995).

17. Hélène Cixous, 'Le rire de la Méduse', *L'Arc*, 1975, pp. 39–45, revised as 'The Laugh of the Medusa', *Signs*, Summer 1976. Reprinted in *New French Feminists,* eds. Elaine Mark and Isabelle de Courtivron (London: Harvester, 1980).

18. Jean-Jacques Rousseau, *Émile*, ed. Michel Launay (Paris: Garnier-Flammarion, 1966) pp. 119–21, *Emile*, trans. Allan Bloom (London: Penguin, 1991) pp. 98–9.

19. Diderot's play *Le fils naturel* received one performance in 1771. See Chapter 2, note 4.

20. Gerhart Sauder, *Empfindsamkeit*, vol. i, *Vorausetzungen und Elemente* (Stuttgart: Metzler, 1974) p. 75.

21. Francis Hutcheson, *An Inquiry into the Original of our Ideas of Beauty and Virtue* (1725).

22. Lawrence Lockeridge, *The Ethics of Romanticism* (Cambridge: Cambridge University Press, 1989) p. 55.

23. *The Spectator*, ed. Donald F. Bond, 5 vols (London: Oxford University Press, 1965) no. 588, vol. v, p. 11.

24. See *Spectator* papers, nos. 411–21, from 12 June to 3 July 1712. For a general treatment of this theme see James Engells, *The Creative Imagination: Enlightenment to Romanticism* (Cambridge, MA and London: Harvard University Press, 1981).

25. Samuel Taylor Coleridge, *Biographia Literaria*, ed. J. Shawcross, 2 vols (Oxford: Clarendon Press, 1907) vol. i, p. 195.

26 Adam Smith, *The Theory of Moral Sentiments*, eds D. D. Raphael and A. L. Macfie (Indianapolis: Liberty Classics, 1976) p. 317.

27. See Mary J. Gregor, *Laws of Freedom: A Study of Kant's Method of Applying the Categorical Imperative in the Metaphysik des Sitten* (Oxford: Blackwell, 1963)

28. See 'On a Supposed Right to Lie because of Philanthropic Concerns', in Immanuel Kant, *Grounding for the Metaphysic of Morals*, trans. James W. Ellington (Indianapolis and Cambridge: Hackett, 1981) pp. 63–7.

29. Henry Home, Lord Kames, *Elements of Criticism*, 3 vols (Edinburgh: Kincaid, Bell, 1762) vol. p. 32.

30. John Mullan, *Sentiment and Sociability: The Language of Feeling in the Eighteenth Century* (New York and London: Oxford University Press, 1988) pp. 51–3.

31. Charles Taylor, *Sources of the Self* (Cambridge: Cambridge University Press, 1987) pp. 339–40.

32. Jochen Barkhausen, *Die Vernuft des Sentimentalismus* (Tübingen: Gunter Narr, 1983) p. 15. For Barkhausen the important common element is a utopian motive of social improvement. Another link is the notion of 'utility' in Hume and Smith.

33. 'Preface' to *An Introduction to the Principles of Morals and Legislation* (New York: Hafner/Macmillan, 1948) p. xxxii.

34. Chris Jones, *Radical Sensibility: Literature and Ideas in the 1790s* (London: Routledge, 1993). Wollstonecraft's conflict over sensibility is also central to J. G. Barker-Benfield, *The Culture of Sensibility: Sex and Society in Eighteenth-Century Britain* (Chicago and London: University of Chicago Press, 1992); Gary Kelly, *Revolutionary Feminism: the Mind and Career of Mary Wollstonecraft* (New York and London: Macmillan and St. Martin's Press, 1993); Syndy Macmillen Conger, *Mary Wollstonecraft and the Language of Sensibility* (London and Toronto: Associated University Presses, 1994).

35. William Godwin, *Memoirs of Wollstonecraft*, facsimile reprint (Oxford: Woodstock Books, 1993) p. 11.

36. Kelly, *Revolutionary Feminism*, pp. 91–3.

37. Mary Wollstonecraft, *A Vindication of the Rights of Woman*, ed. Miriam Brody (Harmondsworth, Penguin, 1992) p. 192.

38. Jean-Jacques Rousseau, *Les Confessions*, ed. J. Voisine (Paris: Garnier, 1964) p. 265; *The Confessions*, trans. J. M. Cohen (Harmondsworth: Penguin, 1954) pp. 219–20.

39. See Chapter 3, pp. 86–8.

Chapter 2   Feeling and/as Fiction: Illusion, Absorption and Emotional Quixotry

1. I discuss this episode in detail in my *The Sentiment of Reality: Truth of Feeling in the European Novel* (London: Unwin 1983) pp. 92–107.

2. Helena Percas de Ponseti, *Cervantes y su concepto del arte*, 2 vols (Madrid: Gredos, 1975) vol. ii, pp. 585–602.

3. Michael Fried, *Absorption and Theatricality: Painting and Beholder in the Age of Diderot* (Chicago and London: Chicago University Press, 1988).

4. 'Le fils naturel' and 'Entretiens sur Le fils naturel', in *Diderot: Oeuvres*, vol. iv, *Esthétique-Théâtre*, ed. Laurent Versini (Paris: Laffont,1996) esp. pp. 1136–7.

5. 'Éloge de Richardson', in Diderot: *Oeuvres*, vol. iv, p. 156.

6. Marian Hobson, *The Object of Art: the Theory of Illusion in Eighteenth-Century France* (Cambridge: Cambridge University Press, 1982) pp. 47–50, 299–300.

7. 'Paradoxe sur le comedien', in *Diderot: Oeuvres*, vol. iv, pp. 1367–426.

8. *La religieuse* and *Jacques le fataliste et son maître* were both published posthumously in 1796.

9. Denis de Rougement, *Passion and Society* (London, Faber, 1956); René Girard, *Deceit, Desire and the Novel* (Baltimore, MD: Johns Hopkins University Press, 1966).

10. Janice A. Radway, *Reading the Romance: Women, Patriarchy and Popular Literature* (Chapel Hill, NC and London: University of North Carolina Press, 1984) pp. 192–3.

11. The phrase occurs in *Nineteen Eighty-Four* (London: Secker & Warburg, 1949).

12. The literary emphasis of the present study could be paralleled by a consideration of the imaginative element in feeling at large, a recognition reflected in the development of psychotherapy. See Thomas J. McCarthy, *Relationships of Sympathy: the Writer and the Reader in British Romanticism* (London: Ashgate, 1997) pp. 92–3 and *passim*.

13. See especially *Love's Knowledge: Essays on Philosophy and Literature* (New York: Oxford University Press, 1990); *The Fragility of Goodness: Luck and Ethics in Greek Tragedy and Philosophy* (Cambridge: Cambridge University Press, 1986).

14. John Horton, 'Life, Literature and Ethical Theory: Martha Nussbaum on the Role of the Literary Imagination in Ethical Thought', in *Literature and the Political Imagination*, eds John Horton and Andrea T. Baumeister (London and New York: Routledge, 1996) p. 86.

15. Laurence Sterne, *The Life and Opinions of Tristram Shandy, Gentleman*, ed. James A. Work (New York: Bobbs-Merrill, 1940) pp. 416–26.

16. For a fuller discussion of this extended subnarrative see Michael Bell, 'How Primordial is Narrative?', in *Narrative in Culture*, ed. Cris Nash (London and New York: Routledge, 1992) pp. 180–87.

17. Henry Brooke, *The Fool of Quality*, ed. E. A. Baker (London: Routledge, 1906) p. 206.

Chapter 3   Friedrich Schiller and the Aestheticizing of Sentiment

1. Immanuel Kant, *Critique of Practical Reason*, trans. Lewis White Beck (New York: Macmillan, 1993) p. 75.

2. Friedrich Schiller *On the Aesthetic Education of Man in a Series of Letters*, Bilingual edition, ed. and trans. Elizabeth M. Wilkinson and L. A. Willoughby (Oxford: Oxford University Press, 1967) p. 1.

3. Immanuel Kant, *Critique of Judgement*, trans. J. H. Bernard (New York: Hafner, 1972) pp. 140–1.

4. Friedrich Schiller, 'Über Naiv und Sentimentalische Dichtung', *Sämtliche Werke*, ed. Gerhard Fricke and Herbert G. Göpfert, (Munich: Hauser, 1993)

vol. v, p. 695. Translated as *On the Naive and Sentimental in Literature* by Helen Watanabe-O'Kelly (Manchester: Carcanet, 1981) p. 22. Present translations my own.

5. Terry Eagleton, *The Ideology of the Aesthetic* (Oxford: Blackwell, 1990) p. 110.
6. Marc Redfield, *Phantom Formations: Aesthetic Ideology and the Bildungsroman* (Ithaca, NY: Cornell University Press, 1996).
7. Walter Benjamin, *Illuminationen* (Frankfurt am Main: Suhrkamp, 1955) pp. 174–6; *Illuminations*, trans. Harry Zohn (London: Cape, 1970) pp. 243–4.
8. See 'Narration as Action: "Die Bekenntnisse einer schönen Seele" and Angela Carter's *Nights at the Circus*', *German Life and Letters*, vol. 45, no. 1 (January 1992) 16–32.
9. Schiller to Goethe, 17 August 1795. *Goethe: Gedenkausgabe*, ed. Ernst Beutler (Zurich and Stuttgart: Artemis, 1950–64) vol. 20, p. 98.
10. R. H. Stephenson, *Goethe's Wisdom Literature: a Study in Aesthetic Transmutation* (Bern and Frankfurt am Main: Peter Lang, 1983) p. 254.
11. Letter to H. Meyer, 20 June 1796. Karl Viëtor, *Goethe*, vol. ii (Bern: Francke, 1949) p. 282.
12. Letter to Goethe, 7 September 1797. *Goethe: Gedenkausgabe*, vol. 20, pp. 416–18.

Chapter 4   Wordsworth: the Man of Feeling, Recollected Emotion and the 'Sentiment of Being'

1. John Beer, *Wordsworth and the Human Heart* (London: Macmillan, 1978) and *Wordsworth in Time* (London: Faber, 1979); James K. Chandler, *Wordsworth's Second Nature: a Study of the Poetry and Politics* (Chicago and London: University of Chicago Press, 1984); Geoffrey Hartman, *Wordsworth's Poetry 1787–1814* (New Haven, CT and London: Yale University Press, 1964), *Unmediated Vision: an Interpretation of Wordsworth, Hopkins, Rilke, and Valéry* (New York: Harcourt, Brace & World, 1966) and *The Unremarkable Wordsworth* (London: Methuen, 1987); Marjorie Levinson, *Wordsworth's Great Period Poems* (Cambridge: Cambridge University Press, 1986); Alan Liu, *Wordsworth: the Sense of History* (Stanford, CA: Stanford University Press, 1989); Jerome McGann, *The Romantic Ideology* (Chicago and London: University of Chicago Press, 1983); Jonathon Wordsworth, *The Music of Humanity* (London: Nelson, 1969).
2. Jonathon Bate, *Romantic Ecology: Wordsworth and the Environmental Tradition* (London: Routledge, 1991).
3. *The Prelude* (1850), Book iii, ll. 281–7. *Wordsworth's Prelude*, eds Ernest de Selincourt and Helen Darbyshire (Oxford: Oxford University Press, 1959) p. 87.
4. *Lyrical Ballads*, eds R. L. Brett and A. R. Jones (London and New York: Routledge, 1991) pp. 246, 266.
5. What 'distinguishes these Poems from the popular Poetry of the day ... is ... that the feeling therein developed gives importance to the action and situation, and not the action and situation to the feeling'. *Lyrical Ballads*, p. 248.
6. Letter to Richard Woodhouse, 27 October 1818. *The Letters of John Keats*, ed. H. E. Rollins (Cambridge, MA: Harvard University Press, 1958) vol. i, p. 387.

7. *The Complete Works of William Hazlitt*, ed. P. P. Howe, vol. viii (London and Toronto: Dent, 1931) p. 44. On Hazlitt's critical appreciation of Wordsworth, see Richard Bourke, *Romanticism and Political Modernity: Wordsworth, the Intellectual and Cultural Critique* (London: Harvester, 1993) pp. 66–7.
8. *The Complete Works of St John of the Cross*, trans. E. A. Peers (Wheathamsted: Clarke, 1978) vol. iii, p. 230.
9. See, for example, Jerome McGann, *The Poetics of Sensibility: a Revolution in Literary Style* (New York and London: Oxford University Press, 1996) and Chris Jones, *Radical Sensibility*.
10. *The Poetics of Sensibility*, pp. 90–2.
11. See Don H. Bialostosky, *Making Tales: The Poetics of Wordsworth's Narrative Experiments* (Chicago and London: University of Chicago Press, 1984); Mary Jacobus, *Tradition and Experiment in Wordsworth's Lyrical Ballads 1798* (Oxford: Clarendon Press, 1976); Stephen Maxfield Parrish, *The Art of the Lyrical Ballads* (Cambridge, MA: Harvard University Press, 1973).
12 Beer, *Wordsworth and the Human Heart*, p. 5.
13 *Excursion*, i, ll. 626–31. *The Poetical Works of William Wordsworth, The Excursion, The Recluse*, eds. E. de Selincourt and Helen Darbyshire (Oxford: Clarendon Press, 1949) p. 29.
14. 'The Ruined Cottage', ll. 12–18, in Jonathon Wordsworth, *The Music of Humanity*, p. 33.
15. W. B. Yeats, *Collected Poems* (London and New York: Macmillan, 1950) p. 339. I discuss the implication of this dramatic placing in *Literature, Modernism and Myth: Belief and Responsibility in the Twentieth Century* (Cambridge: Cambridge University Press, 1997) pp. 52–8.
16. Gerhart Sauder, *(Empfindsamkeit, vol. i, Vorausetzungen und Elemente* (Stuttgart: Metzler, 1974) p. 90.
17. David Ferry, *The Limits of Mortality: an Essay on Wordsworth's Major Poems* (Middletown, CT: Wesleyan University Press, 1959).
18. See '... Poetically Man Dwells ...', in *Poetry, Language, Thought*, trans. Albert Hofstadter (New York: Harper & Row, 1971) pp. 213–29.
19. See 'The Nature of Language', in *On the Way to Language*, trans. Peter D. Hertz (New York: Harper & Row, 1982) esp. pp. 89–90.
20. William A. Ullmer, 'Wordsworth, the One Life, and The Ruined Cottage', *Studies in Philology*, XCIII, no. 3(1996) pp. 305–31.
21. *Wordsworth in Time*, pp. 116, 191.
22. David Perkins, *Wordsworth and the Poetry of Sincerity* (Cambridge, MA: Harvard University Press, 1964) pp. 209–12.

Chapter 5   Victorian Sentimentality: the Dialectic of Sentiment and Truth *of* Feeling

1. Fred Kaplan, *Sacred Tears: Sentimentality in Victorian Literature* (Princeton, NJ: Princeton University Press, 1987).
2. Winfried Herget (ed.), *Sentimentality in Modern Literature and Popular Culture* (Tübingen: Gunter Narr, 1991).
3. Philip Fisher, *Hard Facts: Setting and Form in the American Novel* (New York and Oxford: Oxford University Press, 1985); Jane Tompkins, *Sensational Designs* (New York and Oxford: Oxford University Press, 1985).

4. Jane Austen, *Emma*, ed. R. W. Chapman (New York and London: Oxford University Press, 1923), vol. 1, ch. 18, p. 149.

5. Harriet Beecher Stowe, *Uncle Tom's Cabin*, ed. Jean Fagan Yellin (New York and Oxford: Oxford University Press, 1998) p. 94.

6. *A Key to Uncle Tom's Cabin* (London: Clarke, Beeton, 1853).

7. Elizabeth Ammons, 'Stowe's Dream of the Mother Saviour', in *New Essays on Uncle Tom's Cabin*, ed. Eric J. Sundquist (Cambridge: Cambridge University Press, 1986) pp. 155–95.

8. On this see H. N. Fairchild, *Protestantism and the Cult of Sentiment* (New York: Columbia University Press, 1938).

9. George Eliot's review of *Dred: A Tale of the Great Dismal Swamp*, in Elizabeth Ammons, (ed.) *Critical Essays on Harriet Beecher Stowe* (Boston: G. K. Hall, 1980).

10. 'Après une lecture', *Poésies Complètes*, ed. Maurice Allem (Paris: Gallimard, 1957) p. 423.

11. *Middlemarch*, ed. Gordon S. Haight (Boston: Houghton Mifflin, 1956) ch. 80, p. 578.

12. Wolfgang Herrlinger, *Sentimentalismus und Anti-Sentimentalismus: Studien zum Englischen Roman bis zur Mitte des 19. Jahrhunderts* (Tübingen: Niemeyer, 1987).

13. Charles Dickens, *The Posthumous Papers of the Pickwick Club*, ed. Bernard Darwin (London and New York: Oxford University Press, 1948) p. 421.

14. See Stephen Gill, *Wordsworth and the Victorians* (Oxford: Oxford University Press, 1998) pp. 145–69.

15. F. R. Leavis, *The Great Tradition: George Eliot, Henry James, Joseph Conrad* (London: Chatto & Windus, 1948) p. 78.

16. Whereas in *The Great Tradition* Dickens was dismissed except for *Hard Times*, in F. R. and Q. D. Leavis, *Dickens the Novelist* (London: Chatto & Windus, 1970) he was one of the supreme artists of the English novel. In Q. D. Leavis, *Fiction and the Reading Public* (1932), Dickens was evidence of the sentimental decline accompanying mass readership since the eighteenth century.

17. Leavis *Great Tradition*, p. 122.

18. David Carroll, 'The Unity of *Daniel Deronda*', *Essays in Criticism*, 9 (1959) pp. 369–80.

19. Deidre David, *Fictions of Resolution in Three Victorian Novels: North and South, Our Mutual Friend, Daniel Deronda* (London: Macmillan, 1981) pp. 147–72.

20. George Eliot, *Daniel Deronda*, ed. Graham Handley (New York and Oxford: Oxford University Press, 1988) pp. 307–8.

21. Banned from reading during his imprisonment, Dostoevsky managed to read *Oliver Twist* and *Dombey and Son* while in the sanatorium.

22. Elizabeth Gaskell, *North and South*, ed. Jenny Uglow (London: Dent, 1993) p. 37.

23. *Collected Works of John Stuart Mill*, vol. i, *Autobiography and Literary Essays*, eds John M. Robson and Jack Stillinger (London and Toronto: Routledge & Kegan Paul, University of Toronto, 1981) p. 147.

24. *Middlemarch*, ch. 15, pp. 108–12; Jean Jacques Rousseau, *Les Confessions*, ed. Jacques Voisine (Paris: Garnier, 1969) p. 415–17.

25. William Blake, 'The Marriage of Heaven and Hell', *Poetry and Prose of William Blake*, ed. Geoffrey Keynes (London: Nonesuch, 1927) p. 182.

26. 'Other poetry becomes trifling when we are walking through the Valley of the Shadow of Death. Wordsworth's alone retains its power ... Wordsworth is the

only poet who will bear reading in times of distress.' Leslie Stephen, *Hours in a Library*, in *Selected Writings in British Intellectual History*, ed. Noel Annan (Chicago and London: University of Chicago Press, 1979) pp. 202, 220–1.

27. Thomas Carlyle, 'Characteristics', in *Critical and Miscellaneous Essays*, 5 vols (London: Chapman & Hall, 1899) p. 24.

28. Although several of the authors make shrewd and legitimate criticisms of modern sentimentality in a variety of areas, a repressive condescension can be felt in *Faking It: the Sentimentalisation of Modern Society*, ed. Digby Anderson (London: Social Affairs Unit, 1998).

Chapter 6   Feeling as Illusion: Rousseau to Proust

1. Jean-Jacques Rousseau *Les Confessions*, ed. Jacques Voisine (Paris: Garnier) Bk. 9, pp. 509–28; *The Confessions*, trans. J. M. Cohen (Harmondsworth: Penguin, 1954) pp. 404–16.

2. Jean-Jacques Rousseau, *Les rêveries du promeneur solitaire*, ed. Henri Roddier (Paris: Garnier, 1960) p. 72; *The Reveries of the Solitary Walker*, trans. Peter France (Harmondsworth: Penguin, 1979) p. 90. Translations my own.

3. 'I wandered lonely as a cloud', *The Poetical Works of William Wordsworth*, eds E. de Selincourt and Helen Darbyshire, vol. ii (Oxford: Oxford University Press, 1952) p. 216.

4. Marcel Proust, *À la recherche du temps perdu*, ed. Pierre Clarac and André Ferré, vol. i, *Du coté de chez Swann* (Paris: Gallimard, 1954) p. 61; *Remembrance of Things Past*, trans. S. K. Scott Montcrieff, 2 vols (New York: Random House, 1934) vol. i, p. 46. Translations my own.

5. Melvin New, for example, pursues further interesting parallels between Proust and Sterne but finds no evidence of direct influence: 'Proust's Influence on Sterne: Remembrance of Things to Come', *Modern Language Notes*, vol. 103, no. 5 (1988), pp. 1031–55.

6. For a fuller discussion of this point see Michael Bell, 'Sterne and the Twentieth Century', in *Laurence Sterne in Modernism and Postmodernism* eds David Pierce and Peter de Voogd (Amsterdam and Atlanta, GA: Rodopi, 1996) pp. 43–8.

7. Lisa Appignanesi, *Femininity and the Creative Imagination: a Study of Henry James, Robert Musil and Marcel Proust* (London: Vision Press, 1973).

8. *Lectures and Notes on Shakespeare and Other English Poets*, ed. T. Ashe (London: Bell, 1908) p. 360.

9. *À la recherche du temps perdu*, vol. iii, *Le Temps retrouvé*, p. 870; *Remembrance of Things Past*, p. 994. Translations my own.

Chapter 7   Modernism and the Attack on Sentiment

1. James Joyce, *A Portrait of the Artist as a Young Man*, eds Chester G. Anderson and Richard Ellman (New York: Viking, 1964) pp. 215–25.

2. *Literary Essays of Ezra Pound*, ed. T. S. Eliot (New York: New Directions, 1968) p. 399.

3. T. S. Eliot *Selected Essays* (London: Faber, 1950) p. 21.

4. As when Tom Brangwen looks at his wife after the birth of their first child: *The Rainbow*, ed. Mark Kinkead-Weekes (Cambridge: Cambridge University Press, 1989) p. 77.

5. See *The Letters of D. H. Lawrence*, vol. ii, eds George J. Zytaruk and James Boulton (Cambridge: Cambridge University Press, 1981) pp. 137–8, 182–3.

6. '... ich las in Diderot's Jakob der Fatalist, als mir eine neue Möglichkeit aufging, den alten ZIFFEL-plan zu verwirklichen die Art Zweigespräche einzuflechten, hatte mir schon bei skivi gefallen ...' Bertolt Brecht, *Notebooks*, 1 October 1940, *Arbeitsjournal*, vol. i, 1938–42, ed. Werner Hecht (Frankfurt am Main: Suhrkamp, 1973) p. 181.

7. *Brecht on Theatre*, trans. John Willett (New York: Hill & Wang, 1966) p. 227.

8. Bertolt Brecht, *Die Dreigroschenoper* (Frankfurt: Suhrkamp, 1963) p. 87. *The Threepenny Opera*, in *Bertolt Brecht: Plays* (London: Methuen, 1961) vol. i, p. 153.

9. Alasdair MacIntyre, *After Virtue*, (London: Duckworth, 1981) pp. 109–20.

10 Friedrich Nietzsche, *Götzendämmering* (1889). 'In experiencing, one must not look back towards oneself, or every glance becomes an evil eye': *Twilight of the Idols*, trans. R. J. Hollingdale (Harmondsworth: Penguin, 1990) p. 82.

11. This motif occurs in *Die Fröhliche Wissenschaft (The Joyful Science)* 1882, and *Also Sprach Zarathustra (Thus Spake Zarathustra)* (1883–5).

12. *Die Geburt der Tragödy* (1872). *The Birth of Tragedy*, trans. Walter Kaufmann (New York: Random House, 1957) p. 52.

13. 'In a formula: his virtue is the *consequence* of his happiness ...': *Twilight of the Idols*, p. 59.

14. Charles Taylor, *The Ethics of Authenticity* (Cambridge, MA and London: Harvard University Press, 1989).

15. For example, see the comments on Sainte-Beuve and George Sand in *Twilight of the Idols*, pp. 79–81.

16. See on this Keith Ansell-Pearson who begins with an apt quotation from Karl Löwith: 'As a critic of the existing world, Nietzsche was to the nineteenth century what Rousseau had been to the eighteenth century. He is a Rousseau in reverse: a Rousseau, because of his equally penetrating criticism of European civilization, and in reverse, because his critical standards are the exact opposite of Rousseau's ideal of man.' *Nietzsche Contra Rousseau* (Cambridge: Cambridge University Press, 1991) p. 19.

Chapter 8   Henry James and D. H. Lawrence: 'Felt Life' and Truth *to* Feeling.

1. Leon Edel, *Henry James*, 2 vols (Harmondsworth: Penguin, 1977) vol. ii, p. 457.

2. Henry James, *The Golden Bowl*, 2 vols (New York: Scribners, 1909) vol. i, p. 187.

3. Henry James, Preface to *The Portrait of a Lady*, 2 vols (New York: Scribners, 1908) pp. ix–x.

4. *Hamlet*, I, ii, 65; III, iv, 180: Arden edition, ed. Harold Jenkins (New York and London: Methuen, 1982) pp. 183, 330. See also the lines from *The Tempest* quoted as an epigraph to this study.

5. *Macbeth*, I, v, 17: Arden edition, ed. Kenneth Muir (London: Methuen, 1997) p. 27.

6. Laurence Sterne, *A Sentimental Journey through France and Italy*, ed. Ian Jack (New York and London: Oxford University Press, 1968) p. 94.

7. Denis de Rougemont *Passion and Society*, trans. Montgomery Belgion, rev. edn (London: Faber, 1956); C. S. Lewis, *The Allegory of Love: a Study in Medieval Tradition* (London: Oxford University Press, 1936).

8. 'Les vraies passions sont égoistes', Stendhal, *Le rouge et le noir*, ed. P.-G. Castex (Paris: Garnier, 1989) p. 128; *Scarlet and Black*, trans. Margaret R. B. Shaw (Harmondsworth: Penguin, 1953) p. 149.

9. Henry James, *The Ambassadors* 2 vols (New York: Scribners, 1909) vol. i, pp. 216–18.

10. See *The Future of the Novel*, ed. Leon Edel (New York: Vintage, 1956) pp. 247–8.

11. *The Winter's Tale*, IV, iv, 97: Arden edition, ed. J. H. Pafford (London: Methuen, 1965) p. 94.

12. *The Complete Poems of D. H. Lawrence*, 2 vols, eds V. de Sola Pinto and Warren Roberts (New York: Viking, 1964) vol. i, p. 148; *Phoenix II: Uncollected, Unpublished and Other Prose Works of D. H. Lawrence*, eds Warren Roberts and Harry T. Moore (London: Heinemann, 1968) pp. 597–601.

13. Lawrence develops the significance of this phrase in *Fantasia of the Unconscious* (1923). See *Fantasia of the Unconscious and Psychoanalysis and the Unconscious* (London: Heinemann, 1926) pp. 121–6. The classic fictional treatment is in the 'Class-room' chapter of *Women in Love*, eds David Farmer, John Worthen and Lindeth Vasey (Cambridge: Cambridge University Press, 1987) pp. 40–5.

14. See *The Letters of D. H. Lawrence*, vol. i, p. 88; vol. ii, p. 90.

15. 'One realm we have never conquered: the pure present. One great mystery of time is terrra incognita to us: the instant.' 'Introduction' to American edition of *New Poems in Phoenix: The Posthumous Papers of D. H. Lawrence*, ed. Edward D. McDonald (London: Heinemann, 1936) p. 222.

16. *Phoenix*, p. 256. For Lawrence's critique of Wordsworth's anthropomorphic emotional idealizing see *PII*, pp. 447–8.

17. *William Wordsworth's Convention of Cintra*, Facsimile edition, introduced by Gordon Kent Thomas (Provo, UT: Brigham Young University Press, 1983) pp. 187–8.

18. This is a principal theme of Michael Bell, *D. H. Lawrence: Language and Being* (Cambridge: Cambridge University Press, 1992).

19. For an account of these productions, see Keith Sagar and Sylvia Sklar, 'Major Productions of Lawrence's Plays', *The D. H. Lawrence Handbook*, ed. Keith Sagar (Manchester: Manchester University Press, 1982) pp. 283–328.

20. *The Complete Plays of D. H. Lawrence* (New York: Viking, 1965) p. 208.

21. *Studies in Classic American Literature* (London: Heinemann, 1924) pp. 1–2.

22. For expanded comments on Bakhtin in relation to Lawrence, and on Lawrence's sense of the present, see Michael Bell, 'Lawrence and the Present', *D. H. Lawrence Studies* (Journal of the D. H. Lawrence Society of Korea), vol. 8 (July 1999), pp. 9–20.

23. *Letters*, ii, pp. 182–3.

24. Eliot offered this judgement in *After Strange Gods* (London: Faber, 1934). Although he subsequently withdrew the book from publication it represents his continuing view of Lawrence.

25. *Phoenix*, pp. 170–87.

26. See Roland Barthes' intellectual confection 'The Death of the Author', reprinted in David Lodge (ed.), *Modern Criticism and Theory: A Reader* (London and New York: Longman, 1988) pp. 167–72.

27. Edward W. Said, *Orientalism*, new edn (London: Penguin, 1995).
28. For an expanded discussion of this point see Michael Bell, *Literature, Modernism and Myth: Belief and Responsibility in the Twentieth Century* (Cambridge: Cambridge University Press, 1997) pp. 148–58.

Conclusion: Literature, Criticism and the Culture of Feeling

1. See note 14 to Chapter 2.
2. See note 9 to Chapter 7.

Select Bibliography

Ammons, Elizabeth, 'Stowe's Dream of the Mother Saviour', in *New Essays on Uncle Tom's Cabin*, ed. Eric J. Sundquist (Cambridge: Cambridge University Press, 1986) pp. 155–95.

Anderson, Digby (ed.), *Faking it: the Sentimentalisation of Modern Society* (London: Social Affairs Unit, 1998).

Ansell-Pearson, Keith, *Nietzsche Contra Rousseau* (Cambridge: Cambridge University Press, 1991).

Appignanesi, Lisa, *Femininity and the Creative Imagination: a Study of Henry James, Robert Musil and Marcel Proust* (London: Vision Press, 1973).

Armstrong, Nancy, *Desire and Domestic Fiction: a Political History of the Novel* (New York and Oxford: Oxford University Press, 1987).

Atkinson, Geoffroy, *The Sentimental Revolution: French Writers of 1690–1740* (Seattle and London: University of Washington Press, 1965).

Augustine, *The Confessions*, trans. Henry Chadwick (Oxford and New York: Oxford University Press, 1991).

Austen, Jane, *Emma*, ed. R. W. Chapman (New York and London: Oxford University Press, 1923).

Babbitt, Irving, *Rousseau and Romanticism* (Boston and New York: Houghton Mifflin, 1919).

Barker-Benfield, G. J., *The Culture of Sensibility* (Chicago and London: University of Chicago Press, 1993).

Barkhausen, Jochen, *Die Vernunft des Sentimentalismus* (Tübingen: Gunter Narr, 1983).

Barthes, Roland, 'The Death of the Author', reprinted in David Lodge (ed.), *Modern Criticism and Theory: A Reader* (London and New York: Longman, 1988) pp. 167–72.

Bate, Jonathon, *Romantic Ecology: Wordsworth and the Environmental Tradition* (London: Routledge, 1991).

Beer, John, *Wordsworth and the Human Heart* (London: Macmillan, 1978).

—— *Wordsworth in Time* (London, Faber, 1979).

Bell, Michael, *D. H. Lawrence: Language and Being* (Cambridge: Cambridge University Press, 1992).

—— 'How Primordial is Narrative?', in *Narrative in Culture,* ed. Cris Nash (London and New York: Routledge, 1992) pp. 172–98.

—— 'Lawrence and the Present', *D. H. Lawrence Studies* (Journal of the D. H. Lawrence Society of Korea), vol. 8 (July 1999) pp. 9–20.

—— *Literature, Modernism and Myth: Belief and Responsibility in the Twentieth Century* (Cambridge: Cambridge University Press, 1997).

—— 'Narrative as Action: "Die Bekenntnisse einer Schönen Seele" and Angela Carter's *Nights at the Circus*', *German Life and Letters,* vol. 45, no. 1 (January 1992) 16–32.

—— *The Sentiment of Reality: Truth of Feeling in the European Novel* (London: Unwin, 1983).

—— 'Sterne and the Twentieth Century', in *Laurence Sterne in Modernism and Postmodernism*, eds David Pierce and Peter de Voogd (Amsterdam and Atlanta, GA: Rodopi, 1996).

Benjamin, Walter, *Illuminationen* (Frankfurt am Main: Suhrkamp, 1955).

—— *Illuminations* trans. Harry Zohn (London: Cape, 1970).

Bentham, Jeremy, *An Introduction to the Principles of Morals and Legislation* (New York: Hafner Macmillan, 1948).

—— *Theory of Fictions*, ed. C. K. Ogden (London: Routledge & Kegan Paul, 1932).

Bialotosky, Don H., *Making Tales: the Poetics of Wordsworth's Narrative Experiments* (Chicago and London: University of Chicago Press, 1984).

Blake, William, *Poetry and Prose*, ed. Geoffey Keynes (London: Nonesuch, 1927).

Bourke, Richard, *Romanticism and Political Modernity: Wordsworth, the Intellectual and Cultural Critique* (London: Harvester, 1993).

Brecht, Bertolt, *Brecht on Theatre*, trans. John Willett (New York: Hill & Wang, 1966).

—— *Die Dreigroschenoper* (Frankfurt am Main: Suhrkamp, 1963).

—— *Plays* (London: Methuen, 1961).

Brissenden, A. H., *Virtue in Distress: Studies in the Novel of Sentiment from Richardson to Sade* (London: Macmillan, 1974).

Brooke, Henry, *The Fool of Quality,* ed. Ernest A. Baker, (London: Routledge, 1906).

Carlyle, Thomas, *Critical and Miscellaneous Essays* (London: Chapman & Hall, 1999).

Carroll, David, 'The Unity of Daniel Deronda', *Essays in Criticism*, 9 (1959) 396–80.

Chandler, James K., *Wordsworth's Second Nature: a Study of the Poetry and the Politics* (Chicago and London: University of Chicago Press, 1984).

Cixous, Hélène, 'Le rire de la Méduse', *L'Arc* (1975), 39–45; revised as 'The Laugh of the Medusa', *Signs* (Summer 1976).

Clarke, Suzanne, *Sentimental Modernism: Women Writers and the Revolution of the Word* (Bloomington: University of Indiana Press, 1993).

Cleland, John, *Fanny Hill, or Memoirs of a Woman of Pleasure,* ed. Peter Wagner (Harmondsworth: Penguin, 1995).

Coleridge, Samuel Taylor, *Biographia Literaria*, ed. J. Shawcross (Oxford: Clarendon Press, 1907).

—— *Lectures and Notes on Shakespeare and Other English Poets*, ed. T. Ashe (London: Bell, 1908).

Conger, Sindy M., *Mary Wollstonecraft and the Language of Sensibility* (Cranbury, NJ and London: Associated. University Presses, 1994).

Damasio, Antonio R., *Descartes' Error: Emotion, Reason and the Human Brain* (London: Macmillan, 1966).

David, Deirdre, *Fictions of Resolution in Three Victorian Novels: North and South, Our Mutual Friend, Daniel Deronda* (London: Macmillan, 1981).

de Rougement, Denis, *Passion and Society,* trans. Montgomery Belgion, rev. edn (London: Faber, 1956).

Derrida, Jacques, *De la grammatologie* (Paris: Editions de Minuit, 1967).

Dickens, Charles, *The Posthumous Papers of the Pickwick Club*, ed. Bernard Darwin (London and New York: Oxford University Press, 1948).

Diderot, Denis, *Oeuvres*, vol. iv, *Esthétique-Théâtre*, ed. Laurent Versini (Paris: Laffont, 1996).

Eagleton, Terry, *The Ideology of the Aesthetic* (Oxford: Blackwell, 1990).

Edel, Leon, *Henry James* (Harmondsworth: Penguin, 1977).

Edelman, Gerald, *Bright Air, Brilliant Fire: On the Matter of the Mind* (London: Penguin, 1994).

Eliot, George, *Middlemarch*, ed. Gordon S. Haight (Boston: Houghton Mifflin, 1956).

—— *Daniel Deronda*, ed. Graham Handley (New York and Oxford: Oxford University Press, 1988).

Eliot, T. S., *Selected Essays* (London: Faber, 1950).

—— *After Strange Gods* (London: Faber, 1934).

—— On Poetry and Poets (New York: Farrar, Straus & Giroux, 1943).

Engells, James, *The Creative Imagination: Enlightenment to Romanticism* (Cambridge, MA and London: Harvard University Press, 1981).

Erämetsä, Erik, *A Study of the Word 'Sentimental' and Other Linguistic Characteristics of Eighteenth-Century Sentimentalism in England* (Helsinki, Suomalainen Tiedeakatemia, 1951).

Fairchild, H. N., *Religious Trends in English Poetry*, vol. 1, *1700–1740 Protestantism and the Cult of Sentiment* (New York: Columbia University Press, 1938).

Ferry, David, *The Limits of Mortality: An Essay on Wordsworth's Major Poems* (Middletown, CT: Wesleyan University Press, 1959).

Fertig, Ludwig, *Johann Wolfgang von Goethe – der Mentor* (Darmstadt: Wissenschaftliche Buchgesellschaft, 1991).

Fisher, Philip, *Hard Facts: Setting and Form in the American Novel* (New York and Oxford: Oxford University Press, 1985).

Foxon, David, 'Libertine Literature in England 1660–1745', *The Book Collector* (Spring, Summer, Autumn, Winter, 1963).

Fried, Michael, *Absorption and Theatricality. Painting and Beholder in the Age of Diderot* (Chicago and London: Chicago University Press, 1988).

Gaskell, Elizabeth, *North and South*, ed. Jenny Uglow (London: Dent, 1993).

Gill, Stephen, *Wordsworth and the Victorians* (Oxford: Oxford University Press, 1998).

Gilot, Michel and Jean Sgard (eds), *Le vocabulaire du sentiment dans l'oeuvre de Jean-Jacques Rousseau* (Geneva and Paris: Slaktine, 1980).

Girard, René, *Deceit, Desire and Novel* (Baltimore: Johns Hopkins University Press, 1966).

Godwin, William, *Memoirs of Wollstonecraft*, facsimile (Oxford: Woodstock Books, 1993).

Goethe, Johann Wolfgang von, *Gedenkausgabe*, ed. Ernst Beutler (Zurich and Stuttgart: Artemis, 1950–64).

Hagstrum, Jean, *Sex and Sensibility: Ideal and Erotic Love from Milton to Mozart* (Chicago and London: Chicago University Press, 1980).

Hartman, Geoffrey, *Unmediated Vision: an Interpretation of Wordsworth, Hopkins, Rilke, and Valéry* (New York: Harcourt Brace & World, 1966).

—— *The Unremarkable Wordsworth* (London: Methuen, 1987).

—— *Wordsworth's Poetry 1787–1814* (New Haven, CT and London: Yale University Press, 1964).

Hazlitt, William, *Complete Works*, ed. P. P. Howe (London and Toronto: Dent, 1931).

Hegel, G. W. F., *The Phenomenology of Mind*, trans J. B. Baillie (London and New York: Allen & Unwin/ Humanities Press, 1966).

Heidegger, Martin, *On the Way to Language*, trans. Peter D. Hertz (New York: Harper & Row, 1982).

—— *Poetry, Language, Thought*, trans. Albert Hofstadter (New York: Harper & Row, 1959).

Herget, Winfried, (ed.), *Sentimentality in Modern Literature and Popular Culture* (Tübingen: Gunter Narr, 1991).

Herrlinger, Wolfgang, *Sentimentalismus und Anti-Sentimentalismus: Studien zum Englischen Roman bis zur Mitte des 19. Jahrhunderts* (Tübingen: Niemeyer, 1987).

Hobson, Marian, *The Object of Art: the Theory of Illusion in Eighteenth-Century France* (Cambridge: Cambridge University Press, 1982).

Home, Henry, Lord Kames, *Elements of Criticism*, 3 vols (Edinburgh: Kincaid, Bell, 1762).

Horton, John and Andrea T. Baumeister (eds), *Literature and the Political Imagination* (London and New York: Routledge, 1996).

Hume, David, *A Treatise of Human Nature*, ed. L. A. Selby-Bigge, rev. P. H. Nidditch (Oxford: Oxford University Press, 1978).

Hunt, Lynne, *The Invention of Pornography* (New York: Zone Books, 1993).

Hutcheson, Francis, *An Enquiry into the Original of our Ideas of Beauty and Virtue* (1725).

Jacobus, Mary, *Tradition and Experiment in Wordsworth's Lyrical Ballads 1798* (Oxford: Clarendon Press, 1976).

James, Henry, *The Ambassadors* (New York: Scribners, 1909).

—— *The Future of the Novel*, ed. Leon Edel (New York: Vintage, 1956).

—— *The Golden Bowl* (New York: Scribners, 1909).

—— *The Spoils of Poynton, A London Life, The Chaperone* (New York: Scribners, 1908).

Johnson, Claudia L., *Equivocal Beings: Politics, Gender and Sentimentality in the 1790s: Wollstonecraft, Radcliffe, Burney, Austen* (London and Chicago: University of Chicago Press, 1995).

Jones, Chris, *Radical Sensibility: Literature and Ideas in the 1790s* (London: Routledge, 1993).

Joyce, James, *A Portrait of the Artist as a Young Man*, eds Chester G. Anderson and Richard Ellman (New York: Viking, 1964).

Kant, Immanuel, *Critique of Judgement*, trans. J. H. Bernard (New York: Hafner, 1972).

—— *Grounding for the Metaphysics of Morals, On a Supposed Right to Lie Because of Philanthropic Concerns*, trans. James W. Ellington (Indianapolis and Cambridge: Hackett, 1981).

Kaplan, Fred, *Sacred Tears: Sentimentality in Victorian Literature* (Princeton, NJ: Princeton University Press, 1987).

Keats, John, *Letters*, ed. H. E. Rollins (Cambridge, MA: Harvard University Press, 1958).

Kelly, Gary, *Revolutionary Feminism: the Mind and Career of Mary Wollstonecraft* (New York and London: Macmillan and St. Martin's Press, 1993).

Keymer, Tom, *Richardson's Clarissa and the Eighteenth-Century Reader* (Cambridge: Cambridge University Press, 1992).

Lawrence, David Herbert, *Fantasia of the Unconscious and Psychoanalysis and the Unconscious* (London: Heinemann, 1961).

—— *The Letters of D. H. Lawrence*, vol. i, ed. James T. Boulton (Cambridge: Cambridge University Press, 1979).

—— *The Letters of D. H. Lawrence*, vol. ii, eds. George Zytaruk and James T. Boulton (Cambridge: Cambridge University Press, 1981).

—— *Phoenix: The Posthumous Papers of D. H. Lawrence,* ed. Edward D. McDonald (London: Heinemann, 1936).

—— *Phoenix II: Uncollected, Unpublished and Other Prose Works of D. H. Lawrence,* ed. Warren Roberts and Harry T. Moore (London: Heinemann, 1968).

—— *Studies in Classic American Literature* (London: Heinemann, 1924).

—— *Study of Thomas Hardy and Other Essays,* ed. Bruce Steele (Cambridge: Cambridge University Press, 1985).

—— *The Complete Plays of D. H. Lawrence* (New York: Viking, 1966).

—— *The Complete Poems of D. H. Lawrence,* eds Vivian de Sola Pinto and Warren Roberts (New York: Viking, 1964).

—— *The Rainbow,* ed. Mark Kinkead-Weekes (Cambridge: Cambridge University Press, 1989).

—— *Women in Love,* ed. David Farmer, John Worthen and Lindeth Vasey (Cambridge: Cambridge University Press, 1987).

Leavis, F. R., *The Great Tradition: George Eliot, Henry James, Joseph Conrad* (London: Chatto & Windus, 1948).

Leavis, F. R. and Leavis, Q. D., *Dickens the Novelist* (London: Chatto & Windus, 1970).

Levinson, Marjorie, *Wordsworth's Great Period Poems* (Cambridge: Cambridge University Press, 1986).

Lewis, C. S., *The Allegory of Love: A Study in Medieval Tradition* (London: Oxford University Press, 1936).

Liu, Alan, *Wordsworth: the Sense of History* (Stanford, CA: Stanford, University Press, 1989).

Lockeridge, Lawrence, *The Ethics of Romanticism* (Cambridge: Cambridge University Press, 1989).

McCarthy, Thomas J., *Relationships of Sympathy: the Writer and Reader in British Romanticism* (London: Ashgate, 1997).

McGann, Jerome, *The Poetics of Sensibility: a Revolution in Literary Style* (New York and London: Oxford University Press, 1996).

—— *The Romantic Ideology* (Chicago and London: Chicago University Press, 1983).

MacIntyre, Alasdair, *After Virtue* (London: Duckworth, 1981).

Marshall, David, *The Surprising Effects of Sympathy: Marivaux, Diderot, Rousseau and Mary Shelley* (Chicago and London: University of Chicago Press, 1988).

Mill, John Stuart, *Collected Works,* vol. i, *Autobiography and Literary Essays,* ed. John M. Robson and Jack Stillinger (London and Toronto: Routledge & Kegan Paul, 1981).

Morrow, G. R., 'The Significance of the Doctrine of Sympathy in Hume and Adam Smith', *Philosophical Review, vol.* 32 (1923), pp. 60–78.

Mullan, John, *Sentiment and Sociability. The Language of Feeling in the Eighteenth Century* (New York and London: Oxford University Press, 1988).

Musset, Alfred de, *Poésies Complètes,* ed. Maurice Allem (Paris: Gallimard, 1957).

Nashe, Thomas, *The Unfortunate Traveller,* ed. J. B. Steane (Harmondsworth: Penguin, 1972).

New, Melvin, 'Proust's Influence on Sterne: Remembrance of Things to Come', *Modern Language Notes,* vol. 103, no. 5(1988), pp. 1031–55.

Nietzsche, Friedrich, *The Birth of Tragedy,* trans. Walter Kaufman (New York: Random House, 1957).

—— *Twilight of the Idols,* trans. R. J. Hollingdale (Harmondsworth: Penguin, 1990).

Nussbaum, Martha, *The Fragility of Goodness: Luck and Ethics in Greek Tragedy and Philosophy* (Cambridge: Cambridge University Press, 1986).
—— *Love's Knowledge: Essays on Philosophy and Literature* (New York: Oxford University Press, 1990).
Nuttall, A. D., *A Common Sky: Philosophy and the Literary Imagination* (London: Chatto & Windus, 1974).
Orwell, George, *Nineteen-Eighty Four* (London: Secker & Warburg, 1949).
Parrish, Stephen Maxfield, *The Art of the Lyrical Ballads* (Cambridge, MA: Harvard University Press, 1973).
Percas de Ponseti, Helena, *Cervantes y su concepto del arte* (Madrid: Gredos, 1975).
Perkins, David, *Wordsworth and the Poetry of Sincerity* (Cambridge, MA: Harvard University Press, 1964).
Polanyi, Michael, *The Tacit Dimension* (New York: Doubleday, 1966).
Pound, Ezra, *Literary Essays*, ed. T. S. Eliot (New York: New Directions, 1968).
Proust, Marcel, *À la recherche du temps perdu*, eds Pierre Clarac and André Ferré (Paris: Gallimard, 1954).
Radway, Janice, *Reading the Romance: Women, Patriarchy and Popular Literature* (Chapel Hill and London: University of North Carolina Press, 1991).
Redfield, Marc, *Phantom Formations: Aesthetic Ideology and the Bildungsroman* (Ithaca, NY: Cornell University Press, 1996).
Rogers, Winfield H., 'The Reaction against Melodramatic Sentimentality in the English Novel, 1796–1830', *PMLA*, vol. XLIX (1934), pp. 98–122.
Rousseau, Jean-Jacques, *Émile*, ed. Michel Launay (Paris: Garnier-Flammarion, 1966).
—— *Les Confessions*, ed. Jacques Voisine (Paris: Garnier, 1964).
—— *Les Rêveries du promeneur solitaire* ed. Henri Roddier (Paris: Garnier, 1969).
Sagar, Keith, (ed.), *The D. H. Lawrence Handbook* (Manchester: University of Manchester Press, 1982).
Said, Edward W., *Orientalism*, new edn (London: Penguin, 1995).
St John of the Cross, *Complete Works*, trans. E. A. Peer (Wheathamstead: Clarke, 1978).
Sauder, Gerhart, *Empfindsamkeit*, vol. i, *Voraussetzungen und Elemente* (Stuttgart: Metzler, 1974).
Schiller, Friedrich, *On the Aesthetic Education of Man in a Series of Letters*, trans. Elizabeth M. Wilkinson and L. A. Willoughby (Oxford: Oxford University Press, 1967).
—— *On the Naive and Sentimental in Literature*, trans. Helen Watanabe-O'Kelly (Manchester, Carcanet, 1981).
—— *Sämmtliche Werke*, eds Gerhard Fricke and Herbert G. Göpfert (Munich: Hauser, 1993).
Schlegel, Dorothy B., *Shaftesbury and the French Deists* (Chapel Hill and London: University of North Carolina Press, 1956).
Shaftesbury, Anthony Ashley Cooper, Earl of, *Characteristics of Men, Manners, Opinions and Times*, ed. John M. Robertson (New York: Bobbs-Merrill, 1964).
Shakespeare, William, *Hamlet*, ed. Harold Jenkins (London and New York: Methuen, 1982).
—— *Macbeth*, ed. Kenneth Muir (London: Methuen, 1997).
—— *A Winter's Tale*, ed. J. H. Pafford (London: Methuen, 1965).
Smith, Adam, *The Theory of Moral Sentiments*, eds D. D. Raphael and A. L. MacFie (Indianapolis: Liberty Classics, 1981).

Sousa, Ronald de, *The Rationality of Emotion* (Boston: MIT Press, 1987).

Spectator, The, ed. Donald F. Bond (London: Oxford University Press, 1965).

Starobinski, Jean, *Jean-Jacques Rousseau: Transparency and Obstruction*, trans. Arthur Goldhammer (Chicago and London: University of Chicago Press, 1988).

Starr, G. A., *Sentimental Novels of the Late Eighteenth-Century* (New York: Columbia University Press, 1994).

Stendhal, *Le Rouge et le Noir*, ed. P.-G. Castex (Paris: Garnier, 1989).

Stephen, Leslie, *Selected Writings in British Intellectual History*, ed. Noel Annan (Chicago and London: University of Chicago Press, 1979).

Stephenson, R. H., *Goethe's Wisdom Literature: A Study in Aesthetic Transmutation* (Berne and Frankfurt am Main: Peter Lang, 1983).

Sterne, Laurence, *The Life and Opinions of Tristram Shandy, Gentleman*, ed. James A. Work (New York: Bobbs Merrill, 1940).

—— *A Sentimental Journey through France and Italy*, ed. Ian Jack (New York and London: Oxford University Press, 1968).

Stone, Lawrence, *The Family, Sex and Marriage in England 1500 to 1800* (London: Weidenfeld & Nicolson, 1977).

Stowe, Harriet Beecher, *A Key to Uncle Tom's Cabin* (London: Clarke, Beeton, 1853).

—— *Uncle Tom's Cabin*, ed. Jean Fagan Yellin (New York and Oxford: Oxford University Press, 1998).

Sundquist, Eric J., *New Essays on Uncle Tom's Cabin* (Cambridge: Cambridge University Press, 1938).

Szondi, Peter, '*Tableau* and *coup de théâtre*: on the social psychology of Diderot's bourgois tragedy', *New Literary History*, vol. 11 (1980), pp. 323–43.

Taylor, Charles, *The Ethics of Authenticity* Cambridge MA and London: Harvard University Press, 1989).

—— *Sources of the Self* (Cambridge: Cambridge University Press, 1987).

Todd, Janet, *Sensibility: an Introduction* (London: Methuen, 1986).

Tompkins, Jane, *Sensational Designs* (New York and London: Oxford University Press, 1985).

Tompkins, J. M. S., *The Popular Novel in England 1770–1800* (London: Constable, 1932).

Trilling, Lionel, *Sincerity and Authenticity* (London and New York: Oxford University Press, 1972).

Ullmer, William A., 'Wordsworth, the One Life, and The Ruined Cottage', *Studies in Philology*, vol. XCIII, no. 3 (1996), pp. 305–31.

Van Sant, Ann Jessie, *Eighteenth-Century Sensibility and the Novel* (Cambridge: Cambridge University Press, 1993).

Viëtor, Karl, *Goethe* (Bern: Francke, 1949).

Walton, Kendall L., *Mimesis and Make-Believe: On the Foundations of the Representational Arts* (Cambridge, MA and London: Harvard University Press, 1990).

Wordsworth, Jonathon, *The Music of Humanity* (London: Nelson, 1969).

Wordsworth, William, *Concerning the Convention of Cintra*, facsimile edition, introduced by Gordon Kent Thomas (Provo, UT: Brigham Young University Press, 1992).

—— *The Poetical Works of William Wordsworth*, eds E. de Selincourt and Helen Darbyshire, vol. ii (Oxford: Oxford University Press, 1952).

—— *The Poetical Works of William Wordsworth, The Excursion and the Recluse*, eds E. de Selincourt and Helen Darbyshire (Oxford: Clarendon Press, 1949).

—— *Wordsworth's Prelude,* eds E. de Selincourt and Helen Darbyshire (Oxford: Oxford University Press, 1959).

Wordsworth, William and Samuel Taylor Coleridge, *Lyrical Ballads*, eds R. L. Brett and A. R. Jones (London and New York: Routledge, 1991).

Yeats, William Butler, *Collected Poems* (London and New York: Macmillan, 1950).

Index

Absorption, 59–64, 79
Addison, Joseph, 17, 31, 37–9, 41, 48, 64, 66
Aesthetic, 29–30, 70–4, 76–91, 96–8, 136, 159, 167, 185–7, 196
Allcott, Louisa May, 137
Ammons, Elizabeth, 124
Appignanesi, Lisa, 154, 193
Aristotle, 166, 206–7
Armstrong, Nancy, 25
Arnold, Matthew, 115
Atkinson, Geoffroy, 18
Augustine, 6–9, 20, 28, 96, 145, 152
Austen, Jane, 119, 139–41, 185
Authenticity, 88–9, 166, 168–9, 173, 191

Babbit, Irving, 3
Barker-Benfield, J. G., 4
Barkhausen, Jochen, 3, 50
Barrow, Isaac, 20.
Bahktin, Mikhail, 196
Bate, Jonathon, 93–4
Baumgarten, Alexander, 30
Beer, John, 92, 99, 111
Bell, Michael, 4
Benjamin, Walter, 83–4
Bentham, Jeremy, 51, 114, 142–4
Bible, 75–6, 88–9, 125–6
Blake, William, 144
Boleyn, Ann, 38, 48
Brecht, Bertolt, 160, 162–5, 193
Brissenden, R. F., 4
Brontë, Charlotte, 140, 188–9
Brontë, Emily, 140, 188–9
Brooke, Henry, 67–8, 70–1
Burke, Edmund, 53–4, 93
Burns, Robert, 188
Byron, Lord George, 145–6

Carlyle, Thomas, 136, 142, 146–8
Carroll, David, 134
Cervantes, Miguel de, 58–9, 61, 67, 84, 95, 125

Chandler, James, 92–3
Chaucer, Geoffrey, 92, 175
Christ, Jesus, 7, 76, 125–6
Christianity, 2, 6–8, 17, 75–6, 86, 124–6, 171
Cixous, Hélène, 26
Clarke, Suzanne, 5
Cleland, John, 13–6
Coleridge, Samuel Taylor, 36–7, 92, 110, 156
Conger, Syndy Macmillen, 4
Conrad, Joseph, 185
Constant, Benjamin, 45

Dahlberg, Edward, 190
Dante, 11, 58
Darwin, Charles, 175, 184
David, Deidre, 135–7
Davie, Donald, 115
Defoe, Daniel, 14
Deism, 16, 18, 39, 112
Della Cruscans, 99
Derrida, Jacques, 18
Descartes, René, 107, 113
Dickens, Charles, 23, 118, 126–34, 136–8, 140, 142, 145–6, 159, 182
Diderot, Denis, 28, 48, 58–62, 66, 68, 72, 99–100, 159, 162
Dos Passos, John, 190
Dostoevsky, Feodor, 106, 132, 138–9, 187
Douglass, Frederick, 124

Eagleton, Terry, 77, 82–3
Eliot, George, 126–8, 133–43, 148, 159, 182, 197
Eliot, T. S., 11, 13, 22, 91, 134, 162, 198
Epictetus, 37

Ferry, David, 109
Fiction, 5–9, 13, 15–16, 25–6, 28–9, 35, 37–9, 41, 44, 47–8, 51, 53, 56–66, 68, 70–2, 84, 95, 99, 102, 114,

Fiction, (*continued*)
  121–3, 127, 130, 149–53, 158–9,
  184–5, 206
Fielding, Henry, 17, 19–20, 23–4, 26,
  31, 87, 124, 127, 132, 188
Fielding, Sarah, 22–3, 25, 124
Fisher, Philip, 5, 119
Flaubert, Gustave, 63, 153, 159, 161
Foxon, David, 13
French Revolution, 4, 52, 83, 116
Freud, Sigmund, 104, 148
Fried, Michael, 59

Galsworthy, John, 201–3
Garnett, Edward, 162, 197
Gaskell, Elizabeth, 140–1
Gender, 4, 13, 24–8, 52–6, 64, 87–8,
  154, 193
George III, 47
Gandhi, Mahatma, 125
Gill, Eric, 198
Gill, Peter, 193
Girard, René, 62
Godwin, William, 52–3, 56, 88
Goethe, Johann Wolfgang von, 25, 53,
  58, 67–8, 80, 87–91, 110, 112, 119,
  146–7, 155, 188
Gourmont, Remy de, 11
Grass, Günter, 164,
Greuze, Jean-Baptiste, 59
Grove, Henry, 31–2

Hagstrum, Jean, 18, 175–6
Hardy, Thomas, 141, 197
Hartman, Geoffrey, 92
Hawthorne, Nathaniel, 119
Hazlitt, William, 97
Hegel, G. W. F., 78, 88
Heidegger, Martin, 109–10, 115, 207
Hemingway, Ernest, 190–2
Henry VIII, 38
Herder, J. G., 78, 89
Herget, Winfried, 119
Herrlinger, Wolfgang, 5, 127
Hölderlin, Friedrich, 109
Hobbes, Thomas, 16, 31
Hobson, Marian, 61–3
Homer, 67, 79, 161
Horton, John, 65, 72, 206

Hume, David, 1, 18, 30, 39–43, 46, 69,
  144
Hutcheson, Francis, 29–30, 39, 43, 75,
  172

Illusion, 57–9, 61–3, 76 96, 115, 150–9,
  162, 203
Imagination, 5–7, 15–16, 18–19, 28–9,
  33–9, 40–2, 47–8, 54, 56–7, 65, 94,
  152, 206
Imlay, Gilbert, 52
Impersonality, 104, 108, 161–2
Irving, Henry, 61

James, Henry, 12–13, 77, 133, 154,
  170–82, 187, 189, 193, 197
Johnson, Claudia, 25
Johnson, Samuel, 20, 22, 94
Jones, Chris, 4, 52
Joyce, James, 155, 160–2, 177

Kafka, Franz, 132
Kames, Lord, Henry Home, 47–9, 62,
  84, 122–3
Kant, Immanuel, 30, 33–4, 45–6, 7–8,
  80–1, 86–7, 132, 184, 201
Kaplan, Fred, 4, 119
Keats, John, 97, 102
Kelly, Gary, 54
King, Martin Luther, 125
Klopstock, F. G., 80

Lafayette, Madame de, 63, 150.
La Place, Pierre Antoine de, 62
Lawrence, D. H., 141, 162, 170–1,
  186–205
Lawrence, T. E., 203
Leavis, F. R., 115, 133–4, 136, 182–3
Levinson, Marjorie, 92
Lewis, C. S., 175
Liu, Alan, 92,
Locke, John, 14–16, 28, 35–7, 51, 72,
  113
Lockeridge, Laurence, 29

Macaulay, Lord, Thomas Babington,
  201
MacIntyre, Alasdair, 3, 6, 166, 206–7
Mackenzie, Henry, 25

Macpherson, James, 58
Magnus, Maurice, 189,
Mandeville, Bernard, 16
Marmontel, Jean-François, 145
McGann, Jerome, 4, 92, 99
Meredith, George, 142
Mill, James, 144–5
Mill, John Stuart, 142–6
Milton, John, 92, 94, 103, 175–6
Moore, Edward, 99–100
Moral sense, 29–30, 34, 39–41, 43, 172, 178
Mullan, John, 4, 49
Musset, Alfred de, 126
Myth, 9, 25, 28, 51, 55, 62, 66, 84, 86, 92–5, 116, 132, 140, 150, 153, 159, 175–6

Nashe, Thomas, 12–13, 175, 221
Newton, Isaac, 103
Nietzsche, Friedrich, 30, 166–70, 189, 197–8, 206–7
Nussbaum, Martha, 65, 206
Nuttall, Anthony, D., 3, 69–73, 77, 103, 191

Olivier, Laurence, 61
Orwell, George, 64

Paine, Thomas, 52
Pascal, Blaise, 138
Pater, Walter, 136
Perkins, David, 115
Pickthall, Reginald, 203–4
Polanyi, Michael, 2
Ponseti, Helena Percas de, 58
Pornography, 13–16, 200
Pound, Ezra, 161
Proust, Marcel, 48, 63, 90, 105, 150, 153–9, 177

Radway, Janice, 5, 64, 158
Reading, 5–9, 16, 20, 62–6, 125–6, 128, 134–5, 145, 153, 155–9, 202, 205–6
Redfield, Marc, 83
Richardson, Samuel, 13–14, 16, 19, 23–5, 28, 39, 47, 55–6, 62–3, 65–6, 69–70, 99–100, 121, 135, 188
Rochester, Earl of, John Wilmot, 14

Romanticism, 3, 79, 98, 110, 115, 153, 187
Rougement, Denis de, 62, 175
Rousseau, Jean-Jacques, 18, 26–8, 31, 33, 49, 52, 54–6, 63, 76, 84–6, 89, 96, 100, 104, 107, 109, 113, 119, 121, 143–5, 150–2, 156–9, 167–8, 188
Ruskin, John, 153

Said, Edward, 203–4
Saint-Pierre, Bernardin de, 107
Sand, George, 155–8
Sartre, Jean-Paul, 63, 191
Sauder, Gerhart, 29, 107
Schelling, F, W., 110
Schiller, Friedrich, 56, 74–91, 95–8, 100, 105, 109–10, 113, 117, 135–6, 138, 146–7, 150, 164, 167, 187–8, 196
Schopenhauer, Arthur, 167
Senancour, Etienne Jean-Baptiste Ignace Pivert de, 63, 152
Sensibility, 4, 11, 13, 15–16, 18, 25, 31, 34, 41, 49, 51–6, 59, 69, 72, 78–81, 85–6, 89, 94, 98–100, 106, 116, 118, 121, 126–7, 134, 138, 142, 144, 146–8, 154, 157, 172, 175, 187
Sentiment, 2–5, 9, 11–12, 16–19, 26, 28–9, 31, 34–5, 37–8, 40, 47–8, 50–1, 54–5, 57, 61, 65, 67–9, 71–2, 74, 78–9, 81, 84, 86, 89, 93, 95–6, 98–101, 103, 105, 111, 113, 118–21, 124, 126–37, 139–43, 145–51, 153, 155, 159–61, 164–5, 167–76, 174, 180, 182, 186–8, 190–1, 200, 206
   as principle or feeling, 18–25, 27–9, 46, 49, 54–6, 75–6, 86, 88, 91, 93, 112–13, 116, 119, 128, 139, 145, 166
   as trope, 128–33
   as symptom, 128, 133–9, 141, 161
Sentimentalism, 2–5, 11, 16–19, 23–4, 26, 31–7, 39, 48, 50, 57, 64–5, 72, 75, 77–80, 86, 88, 90, 92, 95, 98, 100–3, 108–9, 112, 116–17, 119, 127–8, 134–5, 139, 146, 158–9, 162, 165, 174, 186–91, 201–2, 204, 207

Sentimentality, 2–5, 35, 86, 91, 98, 117–19, 132–9, 147–9, 155, 158–9, 160–2, 164–5, 169, 186–91, 195, 202, 206

Sévigné, Madame de, 153

Shaftesbury, Third Earl of, Anthony Ashley Cooper, 16–18, 24, 29–33, 35, 47, 71–3, 75, 77, 112, 127, 150, 164, 167, 172, 187–8, 196

Shakespeare, William, 38, 61–2, 82, 106, 131, 156–7, 161, 173–5, 186

Shelley, Percy Bysshe, 188

Sincerity, 3, 91, 106, 128, 142, 144, 166, 168–9, 178–80, 196, 202

Smith, Adam, 43–50, 55, 75

Smollett, Tobias, 127

Spectator, 17, 31–9, 47–8, 66, 76

Spenser, Edmund, 92, 94, 103, 175

Stanhope, Lady Esther, 203

Steele, Richard, 17, 38–9

Stendhal, 63, 152–3, 176

Stephen, Leslie, 145

Stephenson, R. H., 88

Sterne, Laurence, 19, 49, 62, 65, 67–73, 77, 84, 90, 99, 101, 106, 127, 130, 135, 154, 156, 174–6, 180–1, 188–9

St John of the Cross, 98

Stone, Lawrence, 11

Stowe, Harriet Beecher, 120–6, 132, 136, 165

Strachey, Lytton, 136

Strindberg, August, 193

Swift, Jonathan, 188

Swinburne, Algernon, 189

Sympathy, 7, 17, 39–49, 53, 67, 70, 72, 97, 100, 106–7, 111, 118, 121, 201

Taylor, Charles, 2, 50, 168

Theatre, 47–8, 59–61, 79, 130, 161–5

Tressell, Robert, 65

Todd, Janet, 4, 25, 124

Tolstoy, Count Leo, 97, 106, 138, 194

Tompkins, Jane, 5, 119

Trilling, Lionel, 3, 166, 168–9, 191

Trollope, Anthony, 184

Ullmer, William A., 111

Utilitarianism, 50–1, 142–4, 148

Verga, Giovanni, 199

Viëtor, Karl, 89

Voltaire, 22–3

Walton, Kendall L., 5

Washington, Madison, 124

Watts, Isaac, 17

Wesley, John, 17

Whichcote, Benjamin, 17

Wilde, Oscar, 118, 189

Wittgenstein, Ludwig, 2, 17, 30

Wollstonecraft, Mary, 4, 52–6, 88, 116, 120

Wordsworth, Dorothy, 116

Wordsworth, Jonathon, 92, 107

Wordsworth, William, 51, 91–117, 120, 133, 143, 145, 151–3, 188, 191–2, 200, 204–5

Yeats, William Butler, 104